Recent Titles in
Contributions in Legal Studies

The Death Penalty and Racial Bias: Overturning Supreme Court Assumptions
Gregory D. Russell

The Rehnquist Court: In Pursuit of Judicial Conservatism
Stanley H. Friedelbaum

Parallel Importation in U.S. Trademark Law
Timothy H. Hiebert

John Marshall's Law: Interpretation, Ideology, and Interest
Thomas C. Shevory

Group Defamation and Freedom of Speech: The Relationship Between Language and Violence
Monroe H. Freedman and Eric M. Freedman, editors

Innovation, Reaction, and Atrophy: The Impact of Judicial-Selection Method on Policy in State Supreme Courts
Daniel R. Pinello

Controversy, Courts, and Community: The Rhetoric of Judge Miles Welton Lord
Verna C. Corgan

Constitutional Politics in the States: Contemporary Controversies and Historical Patterns
G. Alan Tarr, editor

Law and the Great Plains: Essays on the Legal History of the Heartland
John R. Wunder, editor

Judicial Entrepreneurship: The Role of the Judge in the Marketplace of Ideas
Wayne V. McIntosh and Cynthia L. Cates

Solving the Puzzle of Interest Group Litigation
Andrew Jay Koshner

Presidential Defiance of "Unconstitutional" Laws: Reviving the Royal Prerogative
Christopher N. May

Promises on Prior Obligations at Common Law

Kevin M. Teeven

Contributions in Legal Studies, Number 85

GREENWOOD PRESS
Westport, Connecticut • London

Library of Congress Cataloging-in-Publication Data

Teeven, Kevin M.
Promises on prior obligations at common law / Kevin M. Teeven.
p. cm.—(Contributions in legal studies, ISSN 0147–1074 ; no. 85)
Includes bibliographical references and index.
ISBN 0–313–30652–4 (alk. paper)
1. Consideration (Law)—United States. 2. Promise (Law)—United States. 3. Obligations (Law)—United States. I. Title. II. Series.
KF807.2.T44 1998
346.7302—dc21 97–53289

British Library Cataloguing in Publication Data is available.

Library of Congress Catalog Card Number: 97–53289
ISBN: 0–313–30652–4
ISSN: 0147–1074

First published in 1998

Greenwood Press, 88 Post Road West, Westport, CT 06881
An imprint of Greenwood Publishing Group, Inc.

Printed in the United States of America

The paper used in this book complies with the Permanent Paper Standard issued by the National Information Standards Organization (Z39.48–1984).

10 9 8 7 6 5 4 3 2 1

To the memory of my father

Contents

Preface

This monograph presents an analysis of the evolution and reform of the legal principles applicable to promises on prior obligations from their inception in sixteenth century England to the American present. The field of prior obligations consists of the two most maligned corollaries to common law contract's doctrine of consideration: the preexisting duty rule and the past consideration rule. The rules for promises looking to the past arose during the decades immediately following the emergence of the pivotal contract test of consideration; and, in time, the legal argumentation surrounding promises on prior obligations helped flesh out the full meaning of the doctrine of consideration itself.

The present study concerns the historical development of legal thought related to the issue of enforcement of promises grounded in the past. Lawyers writing about the historical development of law are interested in how lawyers and judges rationalized doctrinal modifications, over time, within the confines of the intellectual system of the common law. It is unsatisfactory to the lawyerly mind for a commentator to assume the very matters which lawyers studying the legal history of their discipline investigate and analyze. Although it is unfathomable that a Holdsworth-like study will ever be written for the whole of the American common law, the past decade or so has evidenced some renewed interest in legal analysis of the doctrinal development of American common law contract. The legal history of the origins and development of English common law contract doctrine has been extensively canvassed by Maitland, Ames and Fifoot and more recently by Milsom, Simpson and Baker among others, but a parallel project providing a detailed, lawyerly analysis of the translation of English doctrine into American contract law has yet to be fully articulated. While my 1990 monograph on the history of common law contract took a global look at the overall evolutionary process, the present more limited study attempts, in some small way, to pursue that project of studying the transmutation of English doctrine into the American common law of contract, as necessitated by the evolving American environment. If, as an aftermath of the present elaboration of doctrinal developments and their reforms, others are desirous of explaining this elaboration of doctrine from the perspective of allied disciplines or their political ideals (sometimes articulated as contract theories), so much the better.

The focus here is principally on the common law rationalization of those reforms which have partially removed the bar to enforcement of promises on prior obligations. The impetus for liberalization of the exclusive contract bargain test came from the growing unease both with the dashing of legitimate consensual expectations and with the perceived unfairness to naive, ill-informed and otherwise disadvantaged parties. Caselaw found in the early history of the common law of contract took some cognizance of these factors, but much was swept aside during the formalism of the nineteenth century around the time of the emergence of the exclusive bargain consideration theory. The broad scope of modern promissory transactions would prove too complex, however, for a single theory of contract liability. Eventually, fused American courts of law and equity began to permit enforcement of promises on prior obligations on the periphery of bargain on the bases of fairness, consent and efficiency. This study shows how American courts adapted English precedent to republican notions of equity and equality.

The modern expansion of *contractual* liability to include promises grounded in the past encompasses some of the most important reforms of the consideration contract since the genesis of that construct. Indeed, the major field of growth in promissory transactions over the past century has been the common law absorption of equity-based liability on quasi-gratuitous promises near the outer boundaries of reciprocal exchanges. As a consequence of these developments, contractual liability can no longer be defined solely in terms of bargain consideration since contract law now includes a broader range of promissory liability. These reforms have significantly quieted the movement for abolition of the doctrine of consideration itself. And, in respect to those aspects of traditional prior obligations rules not completely erased, the present study suggests ideas for further common law reform which can be drawn from accommodating notions buried in the centuries of caselaw and from more recent solutions fashioned in some jurisdictions.

A word is in order regarding my previous work in this area and my appreciation for the support others have given me on this project. Some portions of Part I appeared in a substantially different form in volume 47 of the University of Alabama Law Review in 1996. Also, I want to express my gratitude to Sharon Rochester for her exemplary and patient efforts on the word processor through a number of drafts of this manuscript. And, without intending to exclude the many individuals who have been supportive during this period, I want to express my appreciation to Gordon Fleet and Charles Stoner for their kind support and in particular to Khaw Lake Tee for her encouragement and for the inspiration provided by her commitment to legal scholarship. Appreciation is also extended to the University of Sydney School of Law and Bradley University.

Promises on Prior Obligations at Common Law

Chapter 1

Introduction: Prior Obligations

The past consideration rule and the preexisting duty rule encompass the most heavily criticized cases of judicial refusal to enforce promises due to failure to comply with the common law doctrine of consideration. Modern expressions of these two rules, formulated during the formative period of the doctrine of consideration, deny enforcement of the greatest percentage of promises barred today on account of lack of consideration. The complete removal of these two obstacles to enforcement of voluntary consent would respond to most of the principal reasons given for abolition of this incredibly resilient doctrine. The present study comprises a doctrinal study of the development, reform and persistence of these two prior obligations rules. These reforms include some of the most significant examples of the modern erosion of the doctrine of bargain consideration; they cover a majority of the sections of the Restatement Second of Contracts wherein modern promises are binding in the absence of consideration. Indeed, the enforcement of informal promises arising in non-bargain circumstances, in order to realize reasonable expectations, represents the principal area of growth in modern contract law.

It is perhaps appropriate to begin with factual examples of the potential application of each rule. One, if a roofing company roofs the wrong schoolhouse over the summer when no one is around, and the school board of the school roofed subsequently promises to pay for the benefit received, does the past consideration rule bar enforcement of the subsequent promise? Two, if an excavation company informs a landowner that it can't finish a project at the originally agreed-upon price due to the unanticipated discovery of granite in the soil, and the landowner subsequently agrees to pay more, does the preexisting duty rule bar enforcement of the subsequent promise?

Promises falling within the boundaries of both the preexisting duty rule and the past consideration rule share the common elements of a promise made in recognition of a prior moral or legal duty. The distinction between the two rules resides in there being an existing legal duty when a promise falling under the preexisting duty rule is made, but no legal duty exists when a subsequent promise governed by the past consideration rule is made. Under the traditional application of each of these prior obligation rules, the lack of a bargained-for exchange precluded contractual enforcement of the above two examples of subsequent promises. The logic was that promises that satisfy the consideration construct look to a future bargained-for exchange while such subsequent promises attempt to reconcile the past. Opponents of the doctrine of consideration have criticized the historical assumption that promises grounded in the past should be subject to the same contract doctrine applied to bargained-for promises that look to the future. The attempted resolution of this disagreement has had to be rationalized over time within the confines of doctrinal demands.

The doctrine of consideration emerged by the mid-sixteenth century, several decades after the appearance of the modern contractual action of assumpsit, and it evolved into a doctrine formalizing the parameters of assumpsit. Assumpsit had originally appeared as a flexible hardship action to fill gaps in the law and to cure deficiencies in the predominant contractual obligations action of debt. The action of debt was not an action on a promise but rather was a proprietary action for reciprocal return of the *quid pro quo*; whereas the more recent upstart assumpsit was designed to enforce informal consensual promises for the nonfeasance of failing to perform. During this early period of flux, examples can be found in the caselaw of plaintiffs successfully employing assumpsit to enforce promises on prior obligations; however, this door was shut as the symbiotic relationship between the actions of debt and assumpsit eventually stimulated courts to translate the strict bargain demands of debt into assumpsit. The bar on prior obligations, effectuated by debt's reciprocal *quid pro quo*, became a part of the elaboration of the meaning of consideration; thus, as the consideration test became inextricably interwoven with assumpsit, contractual actions on promises grounded in the past were broadly stymied.

The principal justification for denial of promissory liability grounded in the past was that the only promises worthy of enforcement were those that fulfilled bargain's reciprocity demands; this provided a predictable test for determining when a promise became binding. In gauging whether a bargain existed, common law courts imposed a rule based on time; for a bargain to arise, the consideration had to follow the defendant's promise. (Some modern statutory reforms of the two prior obligation rules have therefore attempted to jettison both rules by simply declaring that a promise is enforceable if the only reason for opposition to enforcement is based on *when* the promise was made.)

Despite the fact that not all binding promises found in the centuries of caselaw fit the bargain paradigm, the monistic urge to isolate a single test based on a predictable point in time when liability arose ultimately prevailed. The advent of treatise writers, cited as authority by judges starting in the latter part of the eighteenth century, furthered this drift toward monism. Treatise writers have a bent for organizing and distilling scattered justifications for actionability into a single black letter positivist principle. Blackstone's civilian-inspired methodology, employed in crafting his lectures and later opus, provided the model for later commentators on the common law. The writings of caselaw annotators and of such American treatise writers as Kent, Williston and, in particular, Holmes successfully promoted the notion that the single predictable test for actionability in contract should be the market test of bargained-for consideration. Holmes held the only partially correct view that consideration's genesis was in debt's *quid pro quo*, and that belief influenced him to overemphasize the reciprocal aspects of consideration's meaning. The focused academic debate in the United States during the nineteenth century over whether promises on prior obligations could be enforced in the absence of a bargain contributed to the generalization that *no* promise would be deemed supported by consideration if it failed to comply with a strict bargain test. This reductionist generalization of benefit and detriment consideration into solely bargain consideration, for promises both prospective and retrospective, denied some types of promises formerly enforceable. Prior to the academic writers, common law courts could more easily enforce a promise on the periphery of bargain, but the widely circulated texts promoting general, predictable rules diminished the former judicial flexibility of providing diverse solutions and of burying occasional hardship relief in the jumbled caselaw.

The predictability factor lodged in bargain consideration of knowing exactly when a party would be bound was attractive to business traders, as well as to owners of vested property rights generally. Positivist adherence to the leading preexisting duty decision *Pinnel's Case* (1602) and to the influential Reporters' Note to the past consideration case *Wennall v. Adney* (1802) promoted the goal of predictability based on bargain. The predictability of the bargain test permitted entrepreneurial maneuverability, without fear of liability, short of the point in time when a bargain was struck. Thus, the vested property rights held by a party, either in a material benefit voluntarily bestowed to him or in an existing contract, could not be lost by a loose subsequent promise by that party either expressing gratitude for the benefit voluntarily conferred or cajoling completion of an existing contract's performance.

Contract principles based on predictability and vested property rights may have made sense during a more static preindustrial trading economy; such a proprietary view of contract law was still being anachronistically portrayed by Blackstone in the late 1760s. But these Lockean proprietary notions were called into question as modern mercantile and equitable concerns were raised for accommodation of increasingly volatile and unpredictable industrial circumstances. The strict application of the doctrine of consideration set the parties' positions in concrete, thwarting enforcement of subsequent promises made to adapt to changed circumstances and thus dashed the parties' adjusted expectations. The whole of modern life became too complex for such dogmatism. The bargain consideration principle ignores the difficulty of predicting unfolding values like an unexpected receipt of a material benefit or unanticipated circumstances arising during contract performance. Under either of these unanticipated events, the parties may find value in modifying their relationship through a subsequent promise. Without reform of the bargain demands applied to promises based on prior moral and legal obligations, there would continue to be a bar on the realization of legitimate expectations that the terms of a subsequent promise would apply to the unanticipated events of either receipt of an unsolicited benefit or a change in facts surrounding an existing contract. Economic efficiency mandated flexible means of adjustment to unforeseen modern circumstances in order to facilitate preservation of the productive potential of an ongoing relationship. An awareness emerged that flexible rules facilitating realization of fairness and reasonable expectations could actually aid in adjusting to the unpredictability of an industrial economy.

Empirical legal realists proposed malleable contract rules to accommodate the expectations reflected in consensual adjustments made in the context of a changed environment. In fashioning reforms, legal realists were generally opposed to the disingenuous use of fictions to overcome dated doctrine. The convoluted use of fictions to realize consent and fairness was rife in this field, e.g., the fiction of rescission to avoid the preexisting duty rule and the fiction of the implied previous request to circumvent the past consideration rule. Sometimes, American judges accomplished change by simply misapplying precedents. Realists abhorred doctrinal unresponsiveness to observable contractors' behavior intent on modifying their relationship. These law reformers shared a distrust of uncritical judicial obeisance to rules designed to emphasize the predictability of bargain obligations to the exclusion of consensual adjustments rearranging affairs pursuant to altered circumstances. They subscribed to the view that traditional dogma regarding promises on prior obligations should be tempered by flexible rules confirming parties' settlement of their affairs as they now exist. Moreover, reformers argued that those potential predictability problems engendered by exceptions to the preexisting duty rule and the past consideration rule were no greater than those created by static rules in a dynamic economic context, and, at any rate, they had to be tolerated to accommodate overarching concerns for fairness. In any event, predictability is not significantly compromised by modern enforcement of adjustments of the parties' relationship since liability is not implied-in-law but is predicated on consent; therefore a party is forewarned that, under certain circumstances, he or she should reasonably expect to be bound if a promise is extended.

The modern emphasis on realization of reasonable expectations aroused in a promisee was an impulse recognized before the turn of the twentieth century by writers as diverse as Pound, Williston, Pollock and Weber, among others. While judges and lawyers focused on formal doctrine, contracting parties' expectations were oriented toward the economic meaning of their relationship. The unpredictability of accelerating economic fluctuations ultimately prompted courts to take into account parties' consensual adjustments of expectations made after the occurrence of the unanticipated circumstances of receipt of an unsolicited benefit or a shift in the values of a preexisting contract brought on by a factual surprise.

The influence of the European consensual (or will) theory, later bolstered by Pragmatists' preference for the community value of freedom of choice and morality, lent support for recognition of parties' adjustment of their shared expectations. The consensual theory fell on fertile soil in the United States in the wake of the revolutionary act of the young Republic having willed to be self-governing. References to European contract law, and to the consensual theory in particular, are replete in early nineteenth century American caselaw reports and in the writings of James Kent and Joseph Story. The influence of civilian consensual ideas accelerated after the mid-nineteenth century abolition of the ancient forms of action and the fusion of law and equity; courts fell upon consent as a fair means of supplying structure lost by the end of the contract forms. As American courts began to focus more on consent, an increasing number of judges began rationalizing away the incompatibility between consent and bargain in the context of consensual adjustments of prior relations.

A consensual promise looking to the past would not be judicially enforceable, however, simply because it was made. Since the machinery of the judicial system is reserved for administrable promises falling within definable boundaries, critics of proposed reforms questioned the administrability of promissory liability outside the bargain construct. Proponents of reform argued that the existence of a good reason or *causa* for making a subsequent consensual promise would provide the parameters necessary to justify making exceptions to the strict timing elements of a bargained-for exchange; they also pointed out that the relative tightness of proposed reformed rules retained desired predictability. Throughout the history of the common law of contract, promises have only been enforced under circumstances thought to evidence a good reason, such as ritual formality, reliance, receipt of *quid pro quo,* bargain, *causa,* a legitimate business reason or some other expression evidencing consideration. The logic employed in those successful reforms of the prior obligation rules has included such notions buried in the history of assumpsit and its attendant doctrine of consideration. A close scrutiny of the history of contract decisions shows that, notwithstanding the denials of formalists, promises on the periphery of bargain were enforced from time to time when an accepted good reason or motive existed. Although a true bargain might not exist, modern courts often rationalize certain promises binding according to factors relevant to bargain, since promises on prior obligations involve an exchange of sorts, even though these promises round off the past rather than plan for the future. Flexibility has been necessary in isolating the good reason for making the subsequent promise since it might not be patent due to the transaction being a part of more extensive relations between the parties.

While civilian jurisdictions enforced promises on prior obligations when a form of *causa* other than bargain existed, an atavistic rejection of Mansfield's civilian-inspired suggestions by common law formalists during the second quarter of the nineteenth century suppressed these continental ideas. Strict application of the preexisting duty rule reinforced the view that once a deal is struck, each party must bear the risk of negative developments, short of impossibility. And the past consideration rule reinforced the notion that one should not intrude in another's business, except as a good neighbor, and if one did so, he shouldn't expect compensation for any unsolicited benefit conferred to the other, for the common law reflects a higher degree of individualism than that found in Roman or civil law. While doctrinaire judicial application of these two common law rules in the nineteenth century precluded a broad civilian solution, modern Mansfieldian reforms enacted and encouraged by the drafters of the Uniform Commercial Code and of the Restatement Second of Contracts are fundamentally civilian in coupling consent with a good reason as the bases for enforcement of promises on prior obligations. These reforms hark back to notions of *causa* buried in the origins of the doctrine of consideration.

One good reason modern courts have come to recognize as a justification for enforcement of promises outside the bargain construct is a consensual adjustment made to an imperfect exchange in order to realize changed expectations regarding exchange values. Application of the past consideration rule prohibition on enforcement is now often refused in the courts when the absence of a moral expectation of a gift suggests a form of unjust enrichment. The preexisting duty rule has likewise often been rejected when an unexpected change in circumstances necessitated renegotiation to correct the past. Significance has been attached to a consensual adjustment made in recognition of either an unfair exchange or an uncompensated restitutionary interest brought to light by the present knowledge of the facts.

The good reason or *causa* found in consensual adjustment of parties' relations had to be fair and equitable before a chancellor would be convinced, in conscience, that a case should fall under an exception to the preexisting duty rule or the past consideration rule. In some instances where *causa* for a subsequent promise was found, some nineteenth century courts began to recognize that it could be unfair to refuse enforcement of certain promises even though made in seemingly quasi-gratuitous contexts, such as a promise to grant a concession to a preexisting contract or a promise to pay for an unofficious benefit bestowed. In some of these cases, the plaintiff, who frequently tended to be less well versed in business than the defendant, either provided a benefit without first bargaining for an expected recompense or entered into a contract while lacking the expertise to adequately predict the outcome of circumstances still on the horizon. Inadequate exchange values may have been caused by inadequate predictive information or naivete, which loss would naturally go uncompensated in the absence of a subsequent promise. However, once a subsequent promise of adjustment or reimbursement was made, enforcement of the instigating subsequent promise could realize raised reasonable expectations and thereby provide a just result. The defendant's subsequent promise could be found in equity to constitute a consensual recognition that an injustice would occur in the absence of an adjustment, and renunciation of such a promise to adjust the past could be deemed an abuse of confidence reposed in the promisor. Indeed, the very existence of a voluntary promise provided a valuable indicator of fairness.

Corbin declared that a judicial finding of consideration to support a consensual promise on a prior obligation indicated that the change in performance expectations was fair and reasonable; he encouraged modern judges of law and equity to grant such relief. Support for a finding of fairness might include a showing of an equitable consideration like reliance, receipt of benefit or some other form of raised expectations. (Virtually all of the Restatement Second of Contracts sections devoted to binding contract modifications and to binding promises on moral obligations involve ingredients of either the reliance or the restitutionary interest.) The mid-nineteenth century fusion of courts of law and equity generated the possibility of converting the sporadic equitable relief granted on these varied grounds into common law black letter doctrine.

Once a separate court of equity was unavailable to soften the asperities generated by the tendency toward the mechanical application of common law contract principles, the possibility arose that such hardship relief could be more regularized by a fused court as a part of the common law. The absence of the ameliorating influence of chancery and the end of the structure provided by the forms of action flushed common law judges out from behind abstract contract doctrine to consider these policy matters. The common law mind began to corral scattered caselaw notions supporting enforcement of promises on prior obligations into the general principles preferred by contract planners and treatise writers. Twentieth century legal realists followed Corbin's urging to refine contract law by grouping cases into narrower factual categories. Hence new sub-rules of contract enforcement were proposed both for contract modifications, often connected to facts falling short of true impossibility, and for promises to pay for receipt of unsolicited benefits that didn't qualify under an action for restitution. To the degree that common law judges felt discomfort with this new equitable role, legislators and restaters of the law filled the void by intruding upon common law contract.

The infusion of equity's notions of morality and policy in modern American contract law doctrine is an expression of welfare state thought not always supportive of market ideas. In contrast, the nineteenth century individualistic market view was that entrepreneurs should be given wide maneuvering room in determining whether to conform to a promise. Damages rules reinforced this nineteenth century view by limiting the opportunity for the victim of a breach to recover for his resultant loss; however, before the turn of the twentieth century, emerging community notions of morality and fair play suggested that the victim of a broken promise should be adequately compensated. Majority American support for predictable, but inflexible, English common law doctrine had begun to ebb in light of inequities generated by the industrial age. Such equitable tendencies reflected the reform-minded influence engendered around the turn of the twentieth century by pragmatist adherents of the Progressive movement and by social scientists preaching the Social Gospel; the process has been carried forward during this century as Fuller and Dworkin, among others, espoused the use of reason and experience to resolve such moral dilemmas presented by modern human affairs.

Morality, good faith and consent, rather than market ideas, are the grounds for enforcement of non-bargained-for promises which in fairness look to past circumstances of changed facts or of concern for the restitutionary interest. The moral obligation factor is perhaps more apparent in restitutionary promises, but it can also be found as an alternative basis for relief to the unanticipated circumstances exception to the preexisting duty rule; for example, when an employer promises an employee a bonus for past work on account of an unanticipated extraordinary effort required, courts have rationalized the promise binding under either the moral obligation principle or, in the alternative, the unanticipated circumstances exception to the preexisting duty rule. Nevertheless, contract law restaters have strained to emphasize that the moral obligation principle is inapplicable to modifications of existing contract duties.

Enforcement of a promise subsequent to unanticipated events follows from the Mansfieldian natural law–based view that an honest man ought to honor a promise either to pay for an unofficious benefit received or to pay more for the completion of an unexpectedly difficult contract performance which was induced by a modification promise. Contrary to the ultimate rejection of these ideas in English law, Mansfield's moral obligation principle (and his complementary restitutionary action of quasi-contract) received a more positive reception in the United States. The American reception was encouraged by a republican reaction against those formal precedents which appeared inconsistent with the preferred natural law view that law and morality were intertwined. Additionally, American jurisprudence enjoyed the opportunity for experimentation afforded by the multiplicity of jurisdictions, wherein reform-minded state judges could carve out minority positions in support of equitable exceptions to the formalist prior obligation rules; in contrast, these formal rules were enforced more consistently and rigorously in the unitary jurisdictional setting covering England and Wales. In the ongoing process of adapting English doctrine to the evolving American environment, the gulf between the two common law systems continues to widen. And yet, the old precedents cannot be ignored since they remain the common law system's frame of reference and the point of departure for reforms today.

American experimentation with equitable exceptions to the preexisting duty rule and the past consideration rule did, however, require taking into account the potential risks of coercion, officiousness and naked opportunism, which risks the traditional strict application of the doctrine of bargain consideration had broadly prevented. Rather than judges flatly rejecting consensual accommodations made in light of the past, for fear of such abusive behavior, the emergence of new policing mechanisms and of a more sophisticated system of trial by jury helped assuage judicial concern about loss of the protective function performed by the doctrine of consideration. The development of the policing mechanisms of economic duress, good faith and unconscionability supplied needed protection against abuse and thereby made it easier for courts to make exceptions to the specific demands of bargain consideration. Furthermore, the circumstances themselves helped suggest whether the promise was voluntary, as when a good business reason existed for the promise or there was a lack of officiousness or gratuitous intent, and the care, forethought and formality taken in extending a subsequent promise were also indicators of voluntariness.

One good reason found for enforcement was the existence of the formality of a written promise on a prior obligation, which helped fulfill the traditional form functions of evidence, caution and channeling performed by the doctrine of consideration. Formality evidences the deliberation and seriousness of the promisor and may be relevant to show the absence of imposition. Studies of caselaw point out that once *causa* and written consent have been established, little judicial concern seems to be exhibited for establishing the presence of consideration; by this omission, such court decisions are unconsciously adopting Mansfield's forthright proposal that a written contract should be an alternative to consideration. Had trial by jury, and its attendant rules of evidence, been better developed when the action of assumpsit emerged, perhaps Mansfield's idea could have prevailed, but consideration was too well ensconced when Chief Justice Mansfield presided two centuries later. Nevertheless, a smattering of state legislatures have attempted to codify Mansfield's idea, at least so far as written promises on prior obligations are concerned. Such statutory solutions treat written promises grounded in the past as the rough equivalent of the ancient sealed covenant.

Thus the scattered hardship relief found in the last five centuries of caselaw, which enforced promises on prior obligations in the absence of consideration, were crystallized into enunciated common law and statutory principles in this century as a means of regularizing the equitable relief available. This process accomplished an abandonment of the absurdity of manipulating Holmesian bargain consideration principles in order to overcome the unfairness generated by rigid applications of the preexisting duty rule and the past consideration rule. These are not amorphous reforms opening all promises to enforcement, as Mansfield's detractors had forewarned, but rather they predictably bind promisors to consensual undertakings falling within stated boundaries where consent, reason and equity justify enforcement. The modern enforcement of certain promises, made either on prior moral obligations or to modify existing legal obligations, constitutes an acknowledgment that the bargain construct fails to encompass all promises the community finds worthy of contract enforcement. The reforms recognize equitable notions on the periphery of bargaining which can act as bases for relief. Amendments to the law of prior obligations cures some of the most castigated aspects of the doctrine of bargain consideration. Except in the minority of instances where statutes or caselaw have jettisoned the old law of prior obligations, however, the reforms do not fully annihilate traditional doctrine. Perhaps the greatest legislative energy expended to reform basic contract doctrine has focused on attempting to modify, if not ablolish, these two rules. Due to the entrenched position of bargain consideration, it is unrealistic to expect promises on prior obligations to be as widely enforceable as in civil law; still, the reforms of prior obligations rules bring the common law more in concert with civil law, the law of nations and the globalization of commercial transactions. Notwithstanding the reforms obtained and those encouraged, modern judges still instinctively apply principles of the common law of contract with one eye on their history. As a consequence, the logic for expansion of the categories of actionable promises grounded in the past will continue to emanate from ameliorating ideas found buried in doctrine enunciated in past caselaw.

Part I

Preexisting Duty Rule and Its Reform

Chapter 2

Emergence of Preexisting Duty Rule

The stubborn persistence of the much-criticized preexisting duty rule over the centuries evidences the impregnability of common law contract's core doctrinal fortress of consideration. This bar to enforcement of contractors' modified consent remains one of the most heavily litigated consideration-related issues heard in the appellate courts today. The rule appeared during the early stages of the development of the modern contract action of assumpsit and its companion doctrine of consideration; it became so closely identified with the test of contract liability that common law courts have appeared stymied from broadly loosening its grip, despite widespread condemnation of its denial of consensual adjustments of contractual relations made to accommodate the uncertainty of the unfolding future. The legal history of the judicial responses to the doctrinal, equitable and mercantile critiques of the rule elucidates why only certain suggested reforms were acceptable. The developmental process of reform sheds light on the rule's implications today, the extent of its survival and the possible means of avoiding the rule's bite. The evolution of the application of the preexisting rule provides insight into the problems the rule continues to present in a fluid economy and why further reform is required if contract law is to realistically accommodate the integration of fair consensual modifications necessitated by what transpires during the life of the contract.

The preexisting duty rule states that a subsequent promise to perform, or the performance of, an existing legal duty is not consideration for that subsequent promise. Thus, when a creditor agrees to accept less at the due date or a contractor is promised more to complete a project, these promises are not binding. The rule encompasses modifications, accords and discharges of preexisting contract duties. Since the accord rule was generalized to apply to a wide variety of preexisting duty situations,[1] this study will begin by focusing on the development of the rule established for an accord, a type of contract modification which results in discharge of the debtor's contractual obligation once satisfied.

ORIGINS OF RULE: *PINNEL'S CASE*

The genesis of the accord rule in assumpsit was in the older competing action of debt.[2] In a 1495 debt action, Brian, C. J. stated the accord rule that payment of a lesser sum in full satisfaction does not discharge the original obligation:

> This action is brought for £20, and the concord is that he shall pay only £10, which appears to be no satisfaction for the £20; for payment of £10 cannot be payment of £20. But if it were a horse, which horse is paid according to the concord, that is a good satisfaction; for it does not appear whether the horse is worth more or less than the sum in demand.[3]

To Brian it was simply that the part payment of £10 clearly cannot equal the whole of 20. Although this was not then a unanimous view,[4] it was accepted as the law in the sixteenth century.[5]

The surprisingly influential rule in *Pinnel's Case* (1602)[6] was simply a reiteration of this accepted debt rule and in fact was merely dictum since the case was resolved on a pleading point. The rationale for the rule that part payment did not discharge the liquidated[7] debt was that a debt action was based on a proprietary duty, and not on a promise, and part performance would not discharge that duty.[8] Liability in debt rested on the transaction and not on any promise; the debtor was charged because he received the property rights in money or goods, and that charge had to be discharged by a full reciprocal return, through payment.[9] However, if the accord required the debtor to do something other than pay a lesser sum, as provide a novelty, it was enforceable, as stated in what case reporter Coke claimed was a *per curiam* opinion:

> For it shall be intended that a horse, hawk or robe, etc. might be more beneficial to the plaintiff than the money in respect of some circumstances, or otherwise the plaintiff would not have accepted of it in satisfaction. But when the whole sum is due, by no intendment the acceptance of parcel can be a satisfaction to the plaintiff.[10]

In *Pinnel* the alleged novelty was paying early. Anderson, C. J. thought "strongly that it was a good plea . . . because perhaps it was more beneficial to him to have £5 when it was paid than £8 on the day."[11]

As long as debt's accord rule was confined to debt actions, where consideration was not required, it was perceived to be a rule inherent in the nature of debt, but, as assumpsit began to edge debt *sur contract* out, there was an attempt to translate the debt rule into consideration-bound assumpsit. *Richards v. Bartlett* (1584)[12] was the first assumpsit case relating debt's accord rule to the requirement of consideration. The defendant pleaded the existence of an accord agreement for the plaintiff to accept only three shillings on each pound due. The court rejected the defense, converting the logic of duty in debt into that of benefit and detriment in assumpsit by stating: "[f]or no new profit but damage comes to the plaintiff by this new agreement, and the defendant is not put to any labour or charge by it."[13] It seemed natural to the court to translate debt's proprietary duties into assumpsit as assumpsit began to supplant debt *sur contract's* long standing position as the central action on informal contracts.

Many critics inveighed against the consideration requirement in accords over the centuries; some disagreement even existed among critics over why consideration was ever required.[14] Some argued that had debt's proprietary duty logic not been inappropriately infused into the reasoning in early assumpsit cases, it would have been logical to say that since assumpsit was promissory-based, then a later promise agreeing to an accord should likewise be enforceable.[15] This was basically the approach in civil law. A compelling criticism challenges why the consideration requirement, relevant to the formation and enforcement of a contract, is relevant to the discharge of a contract[16] in that an accord does not create a new claim but only acts as a bar to enforcement of the original claim. Nonetheless, the sixteenth century view was that, although the plaintiff may have obviously been content to accept the lesser sum, the court required the defendant to also prove a bargain, and, under the influence of debt precedents grounded in reciprocity and property, the payment of a lesser amount did not qualify.[17]

A divergent contemporaneous view did exist, however, which treated cash-in-hand to the creditor as sufficient consideration for the creditor's concessionary promise.[18] If this contrarian view had prevailed and the bird-in-hand had qualified under benefit consideration, then the consensual action of assumpsit could have properly fulfilled its role of facilitating recovery on a promise, as opposed to debt's role of assuring reciprocal return of property. Language in *Pinnel's Case* seemed supportive of that approach: "[it] might be more beneficial to the plaintiff . . . or otherwise the plaintiff would not have accepted it in satisfaction."[19] This logic could not outweigh the influence on assumpsit of the older and better entrenched alternative action on informal promises of debt *sur contract*; and, as a consequence, fresh consideration became essential in place of debt's novelty for the defendant to avoid liability on an original, undisputed[20] proprietary claim. The substantial influence of the redoubtable case reporter Coke in promoting *Pinnel's Case* as a leading case should not be ignored; he seemed to infer in his report that prior judicial differences on the subject had now been "resolved by the whole court." Coke omitted referring to the existence of the alternative view of Anderson, C. J. that there appeared present a benefit in being paid early.

Assuming consideration existed in the form of a novelty or the like, was the creditor bound by an executory accord? In debt actions, it was inevitable that an executory accord would be ineffectual because of the need for actual receipt of the benefit (*quid pro quo*); hence there had to be an accord *and* satisfaction.[21] Although the early assumpsit case of *Richards v. Bartlett* had also been inclined toward debt's accord and satisfaction rule in dictum,[22] once mutual promises[23] and executory debts became commonly enforceable in assumpsit, it seemed logical that an executory accord contract ought to have been enforceable too, as with any other type of contract.[24] The courts seemed disposed toward that view of an executory accord for a while;[25] but, as the seventeenth century wore on, they altered their course and began following *Richards v. Bartlett*'s inclination toward a requirement of satisfaction, both because of confusion with the logic in debt and because of the rigidity of *stare decisis*' reluctance to throw out the "old books."[26]

Other suggestions, besides the old books justification, have been proffered to explain assumpsit's adoption of the satisfaction requirement of debt. One is that an accord had to be fully satisfied to bar a later suit by the plaintiff[27] because an accord was intended as a bar and not as a basis for enforcing an obligation created in an executory contract.[28] Another suggestion is that an accord usually entails a concession to the debtor, and so performance of the accord, and not merely the debtor's promise to satisfy, is the inducement for the concession.[29] A creditor would not be interested in granting a concession if he could not enforce the original claim, should the debtor not live up to his promise.[30] Nevertheless, one can't help but see debt logic lurking in assumpsit cases requiring property to pass to satisfy the defendant's duty, just as in debt.

The above distinction that an accord acts as a bar, while an executory contract creates an obligation, involves a recognition that the requirements for contract discharge are different from formation of the original agreement. Thus, if different rules can apply at formation and discharge of a contract modified by an accord, it would seem logical to apply a different test for formation of the original contract from that applicable to its discharge.

RULE REVIEWED: *FOAKES v. BEER*

Coke's dictum in *Pinnel's Caseo* (1602) wasn't much questioned until the nineteenth century, largely because the issue was rarely raised in the common law courts. Indeed, an overt adoption of the dictum in *Pinnel's Case* as the applicable rule did not occur until a reevaluation of its logic in

Foakes v. Beer (1884).[31] The failure to seriously question *Pinnel's Case* earlier can partially be explained by the way that general pleading, permitted under the common counts in *indebitatus assumpsit,* averted the opportunity for particularized discussions concerning the doctrine of consideration. The abolition of the common counts in the mid-nineteenth century in England and the United States[32] generated long overdue analyses about the meaning of consideration[33] and resulted in modified, and differing, judicial definitions of the doctrine on each side of the Atlantic.[34] In this climate, it was probably inevitable that there would be scrutiny of *Pinnel's* doctrinal flaws in failing to recognize, one, the difference between the "real" nature of debt and the consensual nature of assumpsit[35] and, two, the difference between the requirements for contract formation and those for contract discharge.[36]

A majority in *Foakes v. Beer* were of the opinion that *Pinnel's Case* had been the accepted rule since its announcement and that it would be unwise to overrule it after such a long adherence to the rule.[37] However, Ames's research, published fifteen years after *Foakes,* pointed out that *Pinnel's* dictum was only intended for debt actions and was not immediately accepted in assumpsit.[38] Moreover, several decisions from the late eighteenth century onward enforced promises based on preexisting duties. A reported judicial musing in 1798 was that an accord could "not only be fair but advantageous."[39] In 1794 the rule was not found to bar a creditors' composition.[40] Then in 1846, *Cumber v. Wane* (1721), the case most often cited as supporting *Pinnel's Case,* was nearly overruled on its facts in *Sibree v. Tripp.*[41]

In 1884, Lord Blackburn seemed inclined to dissent in *Foakes v. Beer* on the ground that Coke erred in his interpretative reporting of *Pinnel's Case* because businessmen recognize that prompt payment may be more beneficial than insisting on the whole,[42] but he elected to avoid dissension with his fellow lords and deferred to their ancient books argument. Ironically, the extended judicial discussions in *Foakes v. Beer* about *Pinnel's* shortcomings actually created both more awareness of the old dictum and closer adherence to it as precedent. The judicial reference to a wide variety of preexisting duty cases, many of which were not accords, resulted in a contribution to the unification of law movement then afoot by the consolidation of all promises based on preexisting duties under the accord rule in *Pinnel's Case.*[43] A generalized application of the preexisting duty rule in *Pinnel's Case* and *Foakes v. Beer* occurred in England and the United States.[44] Some portray *Foakes v. Beer*'s failure to reform the preexisting duty rule as signaling an ebbing of nineteenth century obeisance to the freedom of contractors to bargain for any desired objective.[45]

The arguments for and against the preexisting duty rule revolved around the doctrinal and functional roles of the doctrine of consideration. Objections to the rule stimulated the expansion of exceptions to the rule. New objections raised in the nineteenth century emanated from the consensual theory-inspired argument that the rule barred the enforcement of many voluntary consensual modifications in the process of barring the targeted coerced ones. A few state courts and legislaturesrocess of barring responded by outright rejection of the rule. Simultaneously, common law courts, now fused with equity, were developing the policing mechanisms of economic duress, unconscionability and good faith, which were more discriminating than the absolutist consideration bar in surgically thwarting abusive bargaining behavior. American courts of law and equity did develop equitable exceptions to the rule when unanticipated circumstances arose subsequent to the original agreement or when reliance on a modification agreement occurred. These scattered reforms notwithstanding, the preexisting duty rule was reaffirmed in England and in most American jurisdictions during the latter part of the nineteenth century.

JUSTIFICATIONS FOR RULE

Arguments in support of the rule included more than simply the old books justification in *Foakes v. Beer.* One justification flows naturally from the rule's long standing, however, since it was argued that the consistent application of this static rule afforded certainty for business planners when modifications were proposed. This was consistent with a strain of doctrine developed earlier which also reinforced predictable contract rights, e.g., parole evidence rule and the strict contract principle. The ruling in *Foakes v. Beer* fit the times in providing a formalistic defense of vested property rights acquired through deals negotiated by well informed bargainers; furthermore, it limited an entrepreneur's exposure to damages as a result of maneuvering done to cajole performance by a contractor now reluctant to complete a losing contract.

In justifying the rule from the perspective of the doctrinal demands of consideration, the application of that doctrine to an accord fact situation generated the conclusions that the promisor received no benefit, since he would receive nothing that he didn't already have a right to, and that the promisee suffered no detriment since he was already obligated under the original agreement. The earlier discussed assumpsit case *Richards v. Bartlett* (1584)[46] essentially made this analysis, and this remained the doctrinal view not only in England in *Foakes v. Beer* (1884) but also in contemporaneous American decisions.[47]

Advocates of the preexisting duty rule's applications to accords could point to abuses averted, such as unconscionability, coercion, bad faith, undue influence and deception employed to force an accord; for example, the perpetrator might employ such behavior to threaten cessation of performance unless a modification was agreed to.[48] Proponents of the rule also argued that the party with the bargaining leverage to abuse was not always the creditor since creditors could likewise find themselves in the weaker economic position, and further, that the preexisting duty rule afforded no incentive to stronger parties, like insurance or railway companies, to attempt unfair settlements since all modifications, including a pressured reduction, would be unenforceable.[49]

A special area of concern over coercion in modification agreements involved existing duties of employees and contractors, both public[50] and private, where advantage might otherwise be taken when the employer or owner was vulnerable. The decisions vacillated between policy and lack of consideration as the ground for rejecting employees' claims. The early cases involved seamen promised additional wages during a voyage to perform extra work during a storm or after desertions. These cases have a close parallel to accord agreements; in an accord the modified agreement is for the debtor to pay less, and in a wage case the modified agreement is for the employer to pay more. The lumping together of these two types of modification agreements in *Foakes v. Beer* caused the analysis of these employment and contractor cases to be subsumed under the consideration-based accord rule in *Pinnel's Case.*[51] In *Harris v. Watson* (1791), Lord Kenyon refused the additional seamen's wages for extra work done while a ship was in danger "on a principle of policy, for if sailors were in times of danger entitled to insist on an extra charge," it would "materially affect the navigation of the kingdom."[52] In oft-cited *Stilk v. Myrick* (1809), Lord Ellenborough doubted Lord Kenyon's policy ground, saying, "the agreement is void for want of consideration"[53] since they had a duty under the original contract to do all they could to assist after others deserted.

The pendulum then briefly swung back to policy logic in *Harris v. Carter* (1854) in a seaman's wages case when Lord Campbell declared: "I cannot agree with Lord Ellenborough . . . in discarding the ground of public policy on which Lord Kenyon relied . . . for I think it could be most mischievous to commerce."[54] The seaman's counsel said there was consideration for the agreement for extra wages because of his extra labor as a result of the desertions, but Campbell said, had the plaintiff been discharged and then entered into a "fresh contract," only then would there be consideration.[55] It may have been preferable for these employment cases to be handled under the public policy ground of averting economic duress; however, after consideration logic won out after *Foakes v. Beer,* these cases were eventually placed under the rule in *Pinnel's Case.* Despite the fact that only one of the holdings in the above three seamen's cases was based primarily on consideration, and none of the three cited *Pinnel's Case,* all three were cited in *Foakes v. Beer* as supportive of the rule in *Pinnel's Case.*[56] Thus, both increases and decreases in original contract obligations were becoming viewed as governed by a single doctrine to avert coerced modifications now referred to as the preexisting duty rule.

Chapter 3

Judicial Reform of Preexisting Duty Rule

During the generation after *Foakes v. Beer* (1884), many American judges raised objections to the ruling. In fact, objections to the rule in *Pinnel's Case* appeared in case reports from early in the nineteenth century onward.[1] In the 1840 Massachusetts decision *Brooks v. White*,[2] the court stated:

> [The preexisting duty] rule, which obviously may be urged in violation of good faith, is not to be extended beyond its precise import; and whenever a technical reason for its application does not exist, the rule itself is not to be applied . . . [to] any new consideration . . . which might raise a technical legal consideration.

In addition to Blackburn's misgivings in *Foakes v. Beer* itself, Lord Fitzgerald had lamented that "some of the distinctions which have been engrafted on it, make the law absurd."[3] American jurisdictions continued to apply the rule at the end of the nineteenth century, but not without objection. A representative case is an 1899 Washington judicial opinion imparting its dissatisfaction with the rule and its inclination to restrict it because: "It is certainly not in accord with ethics and ought not to be in accord with the rule of law."[4] The court said it might be better to change the rule but then didn't bother because it was able to find a modicum of consideration lurking in the facts. It is remarkable how the rule held on so tenaciously in the face of widespread opposition. Explanations for the vitality of the rule naturally begin with the aged and sanctified status of the doctrine of consideration. Support for the predictability of knowing what one's rights and duties were under the original contract cannot be ignored. Another force to take into account was the formalist urge of mid- to late nineteenth century commercial lawyers and judges to contend with uniformity problems in a federalized national market by adhering to landmark cases.[5]

OBJECTIONS RAISED TO RULE

A look at the influence of landmark cases is a good place to start in discussing the reasoning behind the judicial grumblings against the rule. In *Foakes v. Beer*, Lord Blackburn found solace in the support given to the rule in *Pinnel's Case* in the note to *Cumber v. Wane* (1721)[6] in John Smith's A SELECTION OF LEADING CASES.[7] Although Blackburn said he could find few cases taking a position on the issue, Smith's treatise declared that *Cumber v. Wane* had frequently been affirmed, "although the doctrine laid down by Pratt, C. J. in delivering the judgement of the court, has not been to its full extent sustained, [citing] *Sibree v. Tripp.*"[8] Pratt rendered a muddled opinion in *Cumber v. Wane* which began by saying a later modified agreement could be enforced but then backtracked since he became hung up on an inappropriate analysis of adequacy: "As plaintiff had a good cause of action, it can only be extinguished by a satisfaction he agreed to accept; and it is not his agreement alone that is sufficient, but it must appear to the court to be reasonable satisfaction."[9] One can't help but wonder if Pratt's clumsy reliance on inadequate consideration might not be the misguided sub-text in decisions keeping the preexisting duty rule alive. In *Sibree v. Tripp* (1846), Barons Parke and Pollock rejected Pratt's adequacy analysis;[10] Parke said: "It may be of equal value, but that we cannot enter into: it is sufficient that the parties have so agreed."[11] Chief Baron Pollock even doubted whether *Cumber v. Wane* was good law,[12] while still managing to say he was only distinguishing it since it wasn't clear the promissory note was negotiable in *Cumber v. Wane.*[13] This was a feeble distinction since, negotiable or not, the note was for a lesser amount.

Blackburn acknowledged Pollock's severe reservations: "Cumber v. Wane was certainly denied to be law in Sibree v. Tripp,"[14] and he recognized that *Cumber v. Wane* was the only case, of the two he found,[15] clearly following *Pinnel's Case.*[16] Nevertheless, Blackburn was groping for support to justify joining his more traditional brethren in ruling in favor of *Pinnel's Case.* He fell upon the gloss in Smith's note on *Cumber v. Wane,* that *Sibree v. Tripp* merely stood for the proposition that part payment in the form of a negotiable instrument was an exception to the rule.[17] Thus, despite the fact that the rule in *Pinnel's Case* was mere dictum, *Cumber v. Wane,* the case championed as a reiteration of the rule, was nearly distinguished to death. Just as Mansfield could not tame the central contract formation test of consideration, the preexisting duty rule offshoot of that fundamental theory would not be easily suffocated.

Before leaving Smith's treatise, it must be pointed out that the editor of the treatise was not without his misgivings; witness his barbed criticism of *Cumber v. Wane*, which the debtor's attorney in *Foakes v. Beer* raised,[18] but the law lords made no reference to Smith's point grounded on the consensual theory:

> [*Cumber v. Wane's*] doctrine is founded upon vicious reasoning and false views of the office of a court of law, which should rather strive to give effect to the engagements which persons have thought proper to enter into, than cast about for subtle reasons to defeat them upon the grounds of being unreasonable.[19]

Contrary to the atavistic clinging to Coke's dictum in *Pinnel's Case*, Professor Ames said he could deduce from the caselaw a definition of consideration that would overcome overly technical distinctions and fulfill Smith's stated goal of courts giving effect to accord bargains. He wrote that consideration could be defined as "any act or forbearance given in exchange for a promise."[20] An alternative proposal in line with Smith for jettisoning this reviled rule would be, putting it in Mansfieldian civilian terms,[21] to enforce commercial parties' freely consented-to accords.[22]

Were it not for the formalist tendencies in common law methods during the last quarter of the nineteenth century,[23] the fusion of law and equity and the abolition of the forms in the mid-nineteenth century[24] could have contributed to the emergence of a broad civilian approach in support of contract modification promises, based on consent, morality and business practices. After the fusion of law and equity, equity was to apply when the common law was inadequate or deemed unjust, and equity would not allow the promisor to go back on an accord if it were unfair.[25] An inequity could be found because of reliance, or unjust enrichment or in order to overcome Dewey, J.'s criticism in an 1840 Massachusetts case: "[a] creditor may violate with legal impunity his promise to his debtor however freely and understandingly made. This rule . . . obviously may be urged in violation of good faith."[26] Fusion of law and equity was a double-edged sword in that it facilitated the direct infusion of equitable principles into the common law on the one hand, but on the other it precipitated reactionary formalist judicial tendencies inhibiting the use of equity in order to provide the structure and certainty lost by the abolition of the traditional forms of action.

The plethora of judicially sanctioned exceptions to the preexisting duty rule made a mockery of the claim that the preexisting duty rule encouraged the predictability craved by commercial planners.[27] Take the tortured exception that a novelty ought to take a contract modification out of the rule; how did this make it any more of a bargain?[28] As Jessel, Master of the Rolls, declaimed in 1881: a creditor "might take a horse, or a canary, or a tomtit . . . but, by a most extraordinary peculiarity of the English Common Law, he could not take" less than the original price.[29] The long standing precedents recognizing some factual exceptions to the rule, but not others of seemingly equal or greater merit, fomented a perception of irrationality in the application of the rule and its exceptions.

The conservative judicial response to the straightforward argument that the parties had freely bargained for a contract modification was that it nevertheless must comply with the traditional consideration construct of there being a benefit to the promisor or a detriment to the promisee. Indeed, the inflexible application of this formula to contract modifications of preexisting duties was one of the main reasons some critics were opposed to the doctrine of consideration itself.[30] A study of appellate decisions earlier in this century indicated that over half of the cases where consideration was found lacking concerned performance of a prior legal duty.[31]

Critics of the way most courts applied the doctrine of consideration argue that benefits and detriments could be found in contract accord, not only in terms of logic but also in past caselaw. From the perspective of benefit, in *Reynolds v. Pinhowe* (1594) the court said the avoidance of trouble for the creditor in enforcement was good consideration, "for it is a benefit unto him to have his debt without suit or charge."[32] A 1639 decision acknowledged that if the creditor had part payment "in his hands without suit," this was "a good consideration to maintain this action upon the promise."[33] In *Foakes v. Beer*, Blackburn thought Coke was mistaken on the facts in denying the benefit to merchants of prompt part payment rather than needing to enforce the original debt and that this was all the more true if the debtor's credit was doubtful.[34] Other examples of this benefit logic include: when a financially beleaguered debtor pays more under an accord than he would after insolvency;[35] when a struggling debtor finds a third party to aid in coming up with part payment;[36] and when the debtor's reluctance to perform is overcome by the accord. After all, the creditor must have seen value in the part payment or he wouldn't have agreed to the accord.

As to the finding of consideration on the detriment side, critics argued this likewise could be found in an accord. In *Bagge v. Slade* (1616),[37] Coke himself said that an accord to pay £500 in satisfaction of a £1,000 debt was "upon a good consideration because he has paid money." In an 1846 Illinois case, consideration for a modification agreement was found because of the debtor's reliance on the extension of time.[38] Detriment to the debtor can be found in agreeing to the modification rather than using the money or providing a service, to greater advantage to the debtor, by directing it to another creditor.[39] These are detriments in fact, and it is reasonable that overly technical arguments should not bar them being detriments in law. Corbin urged that the application of the preexisting duty rule ought to move in the direction of modern contract law generally by finding sufficient consideration for an enforceable promise without becoming bogged down in intricate benefit and detriment tests.[40]

Finally, two concluding arguments in opposition to the preexisting duty rule, each suggesting that dwelling on consideration misses the point: the first argument is that the focus should be on whether the contract modification was coerced, and the second is that consideration should be irrelevant to contract discharge. As to coerced modifications, it is argued that judicial analysis prior to the twentieth century was so preoccupied with the doctrine of consideration that it overlooked what should be of paramount concern in regard to modifications, and that is whether the accord was the result of coercion.[41] The opinion in *Foakes v. Beer* doesn't even allude to the issue of voluntariness, let alone address it; for that matter, none of the cases decided before the twentieth century cited in this article, with the possible exception of one or two of the seamen's wage cases,[42] concern themselves with whether there was a modification coerced by an ill-intentioned threat of refusal to perform.

As to the requirement of consideration for a contract modification or discharge, the opposing argument is that consideration is irrelevant to a modification or discharge because a modification doesn't create a new claim but merely modifies an existing one. Consideration's raison d'être, from its inception, was to be the actionability test for assumpsit actions brought to enforce rights created under original contracts. Instead of creating a right, critics argue that a modification agreement acts as a bar or a defense to the enforcement of the original obligation.[43] This is the most fundamental doctrinal objection to the preexisting duty rule. Furthermore, unlike the creation of contract rights, the release of a right does not require the degree of formality and caution provided by consideration.[44] Nonetheless, courts have traditionally misperceived the bargain features of contract modifications to be the equivalent of those for the creation of an original contract right and hence have lumped both under the doctrine of consideration in order to maintain consistency.[45]

COMMON LAW REFORMS

As was discussed in the preceding chapter, the decision of *Foakes v. Beer* (1884) inadvertently infused the preexisting duty rule with a broader scope and an increased vitality. During the last two decades of the nineteenth century, it became abundantly clear that the requirement of consideration for a binding modification was going to stay stuck in the throats of most common law judges, despite the judicial grumblings of previous decades. Courts felt constrained to provide just results, when they could, but within the parameters of consideration, by: one, widening the types of doctrinal exceptions to the rule; two, a few jurisdictions turning the old rule on its head and either rationalizing that consideration was present or that it wasn't necessary in the typical contract modification; three, developing mechanisms to police against lack of consent on account of economic duress and unconscionability; and, four, developing modern equitable exceptions to the rule on account of reliance and unanticipated circumstances.

The mid-nineteenth century fusion of law and equity facilitated the injection of these equitable principles directly into the common law, as some courts began rejecting formalism. In Pennsylvania, where law and equity had uniquely been fused since colonial days, Tilghman, C. J. declared, in upholding a written cancellation of a debt: "But in this Commonwealth, where, for want of courts of equity, the courts of law have assumed chancery powers."[46] This emphasis on equity coalesced with the nineteenth century focus on the consensual will of the parties to effectuate the evolution of doctrines to ameliorate some of the harshness of the preexisting duty rule. This reform process was reinforced by contemporaneous judicial revisions in the way the doctrine of consideration itself was applied generally, based on modern notions of unconscionability, duress, frustration and impracticability, reliance, good faith and unjust enrichment. Although the foundation contract doctrine of consideration could not be dethroned from the law of contract modifications, activist courts of law and equity were becoming less inclined to blindly adhere to Coke's seventeenth century precedent when it failed to reflect fairness and modern commercial life.[47]

Whatever certainty the preexisting duty rule lent to contract law during earlier static economic periods, that role was seriously called into question in a modern commercial and industrial economy. The likelihood of the need for an amendment during the life of the contract increased by the latter part of the nineteenth century due to the longer term and relational nature of modern contracts, fraught with market unpredictability. Entrepreneurs needed the flexibility to jointly alter their agreement, should needs or minds change; however, the strictness of the traditional common law definiteness rule barred flexible, open-ended contract language that could have accommodated some of this uncertainty as it unfolded over the life of the contract.[48] The common law's tradition of support for certainty and formality was ill-equipped to accommodate this state of economic flux and uncertainty. Hence, a judicial movement unfolded for the partial reform of the preexisting duty rule.

Traditional Exceptions to Rule

So many exceptions to the preexisting rule were recognized by the turn of the twentieth century that one would have thought that the rule was moribund, yet many contract modifications continued to fail in the courts as the century wore on.[49] (Some of the exceptions listed in this section will be developed in more detail in succeeding chapters of Part I.) A discussion of exceptions to the rule begins with *Pinnel's Case* (1602) itself.

Three exceptions were suggested in Coke's dicta: (1) part-payment before the due date, which could be "beneficial" to the creditor; (2) payment, at the request of the creditor, in a different place than prescribed in the original contract was a "sufficient consideration" due to the detriment ("expense") of the debtor travelling elsewhere; and (3) the payment of a novelty, as a "horse, hawk or robe, etc. might be more beneficial."[50]

A stream of exceptions to the rule followed, and they grew as judges reacted against the rule in the nineteenth century. The remainder of this section lists some other important exceptions to the rule. (4) A variation in the debtor's performance was enough, and this sometimes was a mere novelty,[51] as payment in the form of collateral security or the providing of some security. (5) Part-payment in the form of a negotiable instrument, as discussed above.[52] (6) A third party's involvement by aiding the debtor was enough, as by providing security or making part-payment.[53] (7) A disputed claim was outside the rule since the actual debt due was not established, and an unliquidated sum, as the right to collect uncertain damages, was also outside the rule.[54] (8) Various fictions (not exceptions as such) were employed, the best known being a supposed rescission of the original contract and the subsequent creation of a new substituted contract. If the second agreement was simultaneous with the rescission, as most would have been were it not for the fiction, a preexisting duty would exist.[55] This approach will be developed in Chapter 5. (9) Written evidence of an accord and satisfaction was a widespread statutory exception, which will be covered in Chapter 4. It reflected Mansfield's urging that the existence of a writing supplanted the need for the formality that consideration lent.[56] The writing exception came in several versions. While the seal was still recognized in the United States during the first half of the nineteenth century, a sealed accord was sufficient.[57] Eventually, some jurisdictions deemed a written receipt of accord and satisfaction sufficient.[58] Jurisdictions recognizing an unsealed writing as sufficient usually required that the writing evidencing the accord be fully performed and satisfied.[59] (10) An unanticipated subsequent circumstance permitted an enforceable modification of the obligation. This exception, discussed in detail in Chapter 5, was widely applied when the modification, prompted by a refusal to perform, was fair and the new circumstances were substantial and unforeseen.[60] This exception did not apply simply because of a losing bargain or an adverse economic environment.[61] (11) A party's change of position in reliance on a modification agreement could be a basis for enforcement of a modification; this exception will be discussed in detail later in this chapter. (12) Creditors' compositions were enforceable, under several theories, as discussed above.[62] (13) A gift of a portion of the original amount due could be enforced. Some accords actually recited that there was a gift.[63] Some courts referred to it as a waiver of rights under the original contract.[64] (14) An accounting between a creditor and debtor of the balance due created a new contract, known as an account stated, based on preexisting debts and was enforceable without consideration.[65]

As the number of exceptions proliferated, an Ohio court observed in 1851:

> [Exceptions] so effectually undermined [the rule], and having neither rhyme nor reason to support it, ought to be at once overruled, and the whole matter placed upon the footing of reason and common sense, especially as the exigencies of modern commerce frequently compel. . . . In this case we aspire to nothing higher than to follow in the footsteps of sages of the law, and hold this one of cases "taken out of the rule" because [of an exception].[66]

A few courts, possessing less timidity, took the bull by the horns and overthrew the rule.

Rejection of Rule in Some Jurisdictions

A few American jurisdictions rejected the old books argument and abolished the rule. Of the four state supreme courts in the United States completely refusing to apply the preexisting duty rule, three rejected the rule of *Pinnel's Case* and *Foakes v. Beer* out-of-hand and the fourth accomplished the same result without referring to those hallowed precedents. There is a fifth jurisdiction to consider, but only as to executory contracts, and again no reference was made to the precedents.

Of the three jurisdictions forthrightly rejecting the "old books," only one of them ruled that consideration was unnecessary for a subsequent agreement changing the original contract. These developments reflected a waning of nineteenth century American majority support for English interpretations of the doctrine of consideration in particular and of common law contract doctrine in general. The initial outright rejection of the old rule came in the 1896 Mississippi case *Clayton v. Clark*.[67] This was the first common law decision to squarely reject the rule in *Pinnel's Case*, a decision which the *Clayton v. Clark* court denounced as a "mischievous and misleadingly reported case" where the ruling was on a pleading defect.[68] The court was "painfully impressed with slavish adherence" to the supposed precedent.[69] Commerce was noted to be less developed in Coke's time, but today the Mississippi court said, "[i]t is as ridiculous as it is untrue to say that payment of a lesser part of an originally greater debt, cash in hand, without vexation, cost, and delay or the hazards of litigation in an effort to collect all, is not often—nay, generally—greatly to the benefit of the creditor."[70]

Eleven years later in *Frye v. Hubbell*[71] the New Hampshire Supreme Court cited the analysis of benefit and detriment in *Clayton v. Clark* as it also rejected the rule in *Pinnel's Case*. The court said if the net after enforcement costs is always equivalent to cash-in-hand and if interest is always recompense for delayed payment, then there is no detriment or benefit to support an accord, but the present parting with money is a detriment to debtor and receipt of payment before enforcement is beneficial to the creditor. In paying homage to the consensual theory, the court declared: "No better guide for determination of the rights of the parties in a contract can be discovered than their purpose and intent in making it."[72]

The Minnesota position follows from the last mentioned point in *Frye v. Hubbell*: that intent should be the guiding principle. The Minnesota Supreme Court announced the most advanced common law position to date in both rejecting the rule in *Pinnel's Case*, and, more fundamentally, rejecting the proposition that an accord must be supported by consideration. This view was first announced in dictum in the Minnesota Supreme Court case *Rye v. Phillips* (1938),[73] and that dictum was later adopted as Minnesota law.[74] The *Rye v. Phillips* court declared: "The doctrine thus involved is one of the relics of antique law which should have been discarded long ago. It is evidence of the former capacity of lawyers and judges to make the requirement of consideration an overworked shibboleth rather than a logical and just standard of actionability."[75] The court drew a parallel to past consideration cases involving waivers of bankruptcy and statute of limitations where "judges have recognized the futility of their former efforts to create a synthetic consideration."[76] The court added that if an alternative theory was needed to enforce an accord, past the parties' agreement, then gift or waiver could be employed.

The fourth American jurisdiction no longer following the preexisting duty rule is Wisconsin. Wisconsin courts achieved this in an unconventional way. In *Brown v. Everhard* (1881)[77] the Wisconsin Supreme Court proclaimed that the consideration of the original contract was "imported" into the modified contract. The court achieved this result by misinterpreting a Lord Denman decision[78] and by making no reference whatsoever to Coke's report of *Pinnel's Case* or to *Foakes v. Beer* or to the preexisting duty rule for that matter. Sir Edward Coke had been the master of misconstruing and ignoring ancient precedents in order to obtain a happy modern result,[79] and, wittingly or unwittingly, the same had been done in turn. In Coke's day, early published court reports were not widely available and the records were in a confused state. In the United States, the confusion of the myriad of positions across the multitude of American jurisdictions, and the unavailability of out-of-state reports before the West Reporter System began in 1878, facilitated inexactitude in the use of *stare decisis* in order to obtain a desired result.

The fifth jurisdiction, which only partially rejected the requirement of consideration in modifications of contracts, was Alabama. Alabama courts took the position that a subsequent modification was enforceable by "mutual assent," before a breach occurred, so long as the original contract was executory. The early decisions vacillated between saying that the mutual assent constituted the consideration for the modification[80] and saying that no consideration was needed.[81] The more recent cases have settled on saying that: "Where a contract is still executory, no consideration is necessary to support a modification of such a contract."[82] Curiously, as in Wisconsin, none of these Alabama decisions make any reference to *Pinnel's Case, Foakes v. Beer, Stilk v. Myrick* or any other case supporting the traditional preexisting duty rule.

Economic Duress

When an agreed-to modification or discharge of a preexisting duty is alleged, the potential that the concession was obtained by coercion is always a possibility if it appears there was no viable alternative but to agree. As long as the preexisting duty rule was firmly in place, it averted the possibility of enforcing coerced, bad faith or unconscionable modifications, though the protection was by no means complete due to all the exceptions and fictions related to the preexisting duty rule. Courts focused on whether consideration was present, with little or no heed to the issue of coercion. Judicial equivocation regarding the possibility of coercion is reflected in the handling of the turn of the nineteenth century seamen's wage cases. Lords Kenyon and Ellenborough could not agree over whether the refusal to enforce these modified agreements made on distant voyages for higher wages should be based on policy (impliedly to avert suspected coercion by the seamen)[83] or on lack of consideration.[84] Unfortunately, the latter approach of presuming coercion prevailed, in the wake of *Foakes v. Beer.*[85]

Massachusetts courts aggravated the consequences of judicial inattention to finding whether there was coercion by enforcing a modification made because a contractor refused to proceed unless he was paid more. In the precedent setting case *Munroe v. Perkins* (1830),[86] the extra amount promised did not come from a request by the contractor, but later Massachusetts cases applied the precedent to modifications expressly because the contractor indicated he would not proceed unless he was paid more.[87] These decisions did not indicate the slightest hint of anxiety about a possible coerced concession exacted by a contractor in a category of cases that seemed ripe for such an inquiry. Some jurisdictions criticized the "Massachusetts Rule" because it "invites" coercion.[88] The Massachusetts courts found consideration for the promise to pay more in the surrender of the contractor's elective "right" to refuse to perform the first contract and pay damages, the modification accomplishing continuation of the contractor's performance.[89] This application of the consideration doctrine was criticized because it was morally unjustifiable[90] and because the contractor had no right to breach but rather had a duty to perform.[91]

Despite the failure of the influential decisions of *Munroe v. Perkins* and *Foakes v. Beer* to concern themselves with the issue of coerced consent, the contemporaneous nineteenth century intellectual construct now known as the consensual theory had its impact elsewhere in encouraging enforcement of freely consented-to original agreements and their modifications. The consensual theory emanated from civil law countries and opposed assumpsit's actionability test of consideration since it barred enforcement of proven voluntary modifications along with coerced ones. The development of the doctrine of economic duress aided in making the determination of whether the consent was voluntary or extorted, irrespective of the presence of consideration. Indeed, the role of consideration in barring coerced modifications had to be replaced as some jurisdictions, under the sway of the consensual theory, began rejecting the preexisting duty rule. The majority of jurisdictions retaining the preexisting duty rule began to use economic duress analysis to augment consideration's protective function; and, as economic duress became more refined, some courts would rationalize the presence of consideration if it was obvious the modification wasn't extorted. Once economic duress evolved enough, it freed some jurisdictions to either apply the preexisting rule more flexibly or entirely jettison it. As a means of depicting the role of economic duress in contract modification cases, attention will now be turned to the evolution of economic duress and its impact on contract modification cases.

The origin of economic duress is found in common law duress. In the medieval period, Bracton said the focus was on the means of the duress, and only fear for life or limb or fear of imprisonment were sufficient; fear of damage to property, and even fear of battery, were insufficient since "he may have satisfaction in damages."[92] Coke and Blackstone followed Bracton's lead.[93] The first clear departure from the strict rule toward a common law doctrine of economic duress came in the well known "duress of goods" case *Astley v. Reynolds* (1732),[94] where the plaintiff was compelled to pay interest in excess of the legal limit in order to recover pawned goods. The king's bench held for the plaintiff that he paid under compulsion of wrongful detention of his property. Roughly contemporaneous with this common law development, chancery was granting relief in similar cases and was quite willing to weigh lack of equivalence in a bargain under loose notions of duress, unconscionability, fraud and undue influence. Chancery's ease in mixing these ideas to obtain a fair result in cases of economic duress would make for a confused translation into the common law in the United States.[95] A third source in the development of economic duress began in the 1840s with the granting of restitution for payments of overcharges to public utilities when the utility threatened to refuse service unless excess payment was made.[96]

Despite these early glimmerings, nineteenth century notions of economic individualism and freedom of contract caused the focus in contract formation and modification cases to be on whether objective consent was present and not on the equivalency of the exchange in the modification.[97] So in *Skeate v. Beale* (1841),[98] it was seemingly irrelevant that an excessive distraint of goods caused the defendant to agree to pay rent in excess of the amount originally due because duress of goods did not destroy the free will of an individual of ordinary firmness, and further that *Astley v. Reynolds* should be narrowed to its facts of a wrongful detention of goods forcing an agreement in excess of the lawful limit.[99] With some exceptions,[100] this restrictive emphasis on presumed voluntary consent in duress of goods genre cases slowed the emergence of economic duress in the United States and halted it for a lot longer in England.[101] Nineteenth century obeisance to freedom of contract and individualism caused an American resistance to using economic duress when there was merely a threat to breach an existing contract, as exhibited in two Michigan decisions authored by Justice Cooley in the early 1880s. Still, some progress can be seen in that Cooley focused on the voluntariness of the modification rather than dismissing them out-of-hand under the preexisting duty rule.

In the first Michigan case of *Hackley v. Headley* (1881),[102] the defendant would only pay two-thirds the amount the plaintiff alleged was due on a contract for logging services, and the plaintiff accepted the lesser amount, rather than suffering the delay of suing, because he was near insolvency.[103] Since at the first trial there appeared to be a dispute, the preexisting duty rule was inapplicable.[104] The Michigan Supreme Court did much the same thing that the English court had done in *Skeate v. Beale* (1841) by containing *Astley v. Reynolds* (1732)[105] to its facts. Justice Cooley pointed out that the defendant hadn't caused the plaintiff to be in pecuniary straits and that the plaintiff would not have alleged duress had he been financially solvent. Cooley said that to accept the plaintiff's argument "would be a most dangerous, as well as a most unequal doctrine; and if accepted, no one could well know when he would be safe in dealing on ordinary terms of negotiation with a party who professed to be in great need."[106] Whereas *Hackley v. Headley* involved a threat to not pay money when due under a contract, the next year the Michigan case of *Goebel v. Linn*[107] involved an ice company's threat to not deliver ice contracted for delivery in the spring unless a higher price was paid by a brewer. The preceding mild winter had caused an extraordinarily low ice crop, and the buyer, fearful that a large quantity of beer would spoil if he didn't obtain ice soon, agreed to the increase. Justice Cooley cited his opinion in *Hackley v. Headley* as authority for the absence of duress in a "refusal to keep the previous engagements."[108] Cooley added that, even if there was duress initially, there was a waiver when the buyer "independently" and "freely" elected to abide by the higher price by continuing to pay it without a showing that later on a supply was unavailable elsewhere.[109] Although Justice Cooley's ruling in *Goebel v. Linn* denied the existence of economic duress, it arguably may be considered a harbinger of the modern view that the preexisting duty rule should not apply to modifications made on account of unanticipated circumstances.[110]

Judicial reluctance to recognize economic duress in cases like *Hackley v. Headley* and *Goebel v. Linn* represented the majority position until nearly the mid-twentieth century,[111] though there were emerging minority positions permitting relief from the preexisting duty rule based on notions of economic duress. Some of these early decisions gave relief from economic duress while labeling it as relief from bad faith. In fact, the remand of *Hackley v. Headley* exemplifies one of those approaches. The remanded economic duress case of *Hackley v. Headley* (1881) returned to the Michigan Supreme Court a second time in 1883 on an appeal from the remand hearing.[112] The plaintiff argued it was "bad faith" for the defendant to raise what the jury saw as unfounded claims in order to avoid full contract payment for the logging services and thereby extort a modification when it was obvious that the plaintiff needed his money.[113] (In the face of Cooley's first ruling for the defendant on the economic duress issue, the remanded trial verdict came back again in favor of the plaintiff.) This time the court overturned the "oppressively" obtained compromise agreement because the defendant had "acted unfairly."[114] This second review in 1883 supplied the equitable ground of bad faith in support of the second trial verdict, instead of applying the preexisting duty rule to the attempted modification of the liquidated debt. Under the nineteenth century consensual theory, the defendant's conduct had not been deemed egregious enough to apply economic duress in the first appeal, but the dishonesty was sufficient for a fused court of law and equity to find bad faith.

Eight years later in *Lingenfelder v. Wainwright Brewing Co.* (1891), the Missouri Supreme Court heard a contract dispute between a landowner and an architect.[115] The architect became angry when the landowner awarded a separate contract to a competing enterprise, and so he abused the advantage he had, because of the defendant-landowner's timetable, by refusing to proceed unless he was paid more. The court cited the seamen's wage cases as a basis for a holding there was *no consideration.* The court employed the policy-based logic of some of the seamen's wage cases in saying that the architect "took advantage of (defendant's) necessities, and extorted the promise" and that "to permit plaintiff to recover under such circumstances would be to offer a premium upon bad faith."[116] The Missouri Court said that strict enforcement of the preexisting duty rule averted duress, and it criticized Cooley for doing otherwise in *Goebel v. Linn.*[117]

Other minority positions soon squarely adopted economic duress. In *Fitzgerald v. Fitzgerald and Mallory Construction Co.* (1895),[118] the Nebraska Supreme Court heard a case involving a contractor on the verge of bankruptcy, who was forced by a railroad company to take less than agreed for work done and to be done. The court said the modified agreement "was procured under circumstances amounting to practical compulsion, which is nearly related to duress, and may be the ground of relief."[119] In *Thomas and Cross v. Brown* (1914)[120] the Virginia Supreme Court heard a case involving a landowner who refused, without any valid reason, to pay for construction work unless the contractors would accept less than agreed. The court found it necessary to take a position on economic duress in that an 1887 Virginia statute had abolished the preexisting duty rule. The court ruled that the modified agreement was made under "aggravated circumstances of constraint" and said that prior to the statute no part-payment would satisfy a debt but that the "statute was never intended to enable a party to perpetrate the wrong and injustice that the defendant has sought to accomplish in this case."[121] As a consequence of Virginia being one of the early states to abolish the preexisting duty rule, it became one of the first states to adopt economic duress in order to provide a safeguard against coerced modifications in place of the protective function consideration had formerly performed for modifications in Virginia. By the middle of the twentieth century, economic duress was recognized by a majority of American jurisdictions.[122]

Once the defense of economic duress was widely accepted by American courts, it became an important protection against coerced modifications, while affording an opportunity for restitution of any benefits conferred.[123] The availability of economic duress removed the objection that abandoning the preexisting duty rule would result in judicial enforcement of coerced modification agreements. The acceptance of the doctrine contributed to the increasing numbers of courts and legislatures that abolished the preexisting duty rule,[124] thereby facilitating analysis of the core issue of whether there was a freely assented-to modification.

Before leaving a discussion of the development of policing mechanisms, mention should be made of the complementary doctrine of unconscionability, which like economic duress concerns the question of lack of consent due to undue advantage taken against a party in a vulnerable position. Unconscionability likewise focuses on the negotiation procedures leading to formation of the modification. If one-sided modification terms are dictated on a take-it-or-leave-it basis by a party in a stronger bargaining position, a court can rationalize intervention on the grounds of unconscionability.

Unconscionability relief began by at least the eighteenth century in chancery,[125] and by the first quarter of the twentieth century, common law courts provided disguised unconscionability relief by manipulating traditional common law principles related to consideration, offer and acceptance, fraud, public policy, duress, etc.[126] Llewellyn sought to convert equity's individualized tool into black letter contract doctrine for modern standardized sales transactions covered by the Uniform Commercial Code;

the final version of the Code's unconscionability Section 2–302 applied to all sales contracts.[127] Restatement of Contracts Second Section 208 recognized the caselaw developments this century, some of which came from analogies drawn to the Code, by declaring that unconscionability applies to all contracts.

Judicial analyses of both unconscionability and economic duress find relevant inequality of bargaining positions and a victim's sense of a lack of a viable alternative course of action. Whereas the unconscionability doctrine analyzes the unfairness of the result flowing from the lack of choice, economic duress focuses primarily on lack of free will causing the unfairness. Both doctrines provide rescission relief; unconscionability's firmer rooting in equity facilitated greater flexibility in also allowing a questionable modification to stand if it is reformed or divided in a way that renders the transaction fair.

In sales contracts and in jurisdictions where consideration is not required for modifications of other types of contracts, unconscionability, economic duress and good faith complement each other in policing overreaching and sharp practices during the bargaining phase leading up to formation of a modification. Rather than absolutely barring contract modifications the way the preexisting duty rule would, fair modifications are enforceable. While economic duress provides relief for lack of free will and unconscionability protects against unfairness resulting from lack of choice, the good faith standard scrutinizes whether a good motive existed for seeking the modification; so, in tandem, the three principles police the instigating motive for the modification, the process of negotiating it and unfair results.

Reliance-Based Relief

The nineteenth century genesis of promissory estoppel in cases of justifiable reliance upon gratuitous promises is well enough known.[128] The spread of this ground for liability to bargain-based promises encountered some initial resistance,[129] but it became a widely accepted ameliorating doctrine in commercial law by the middle of the twentieth century.[130] Its use in support of contract modification promises would become an important reform removing some of the harshness from the preexisting duty rule.

During the nineteenth century, reliance-based relief in support of modifications began to appear in American caselaw, disguised as modification contracts supported by consideration. In *Wadsworth v. Thompson* (1846),[131] an Illinois court ruled that a debtor's reliance on a time extension, by not rushing to make the original deadline, constituted consideration for the extension. In the Iowa case *Maxwell v. Graves* (1882),[132] a three year lease of cows for breeding purposes was modified by providing that the lessor-defendant would replace any barren cows in the spring. The plaintiff-lessee returned ten barren cows the next May, which the defendant took possession of, but the defendant refused to provide replacement cows. In a later suit, the Iowa court found the modification to replace barren cows binding because the plaintiff's care and delivery of the barren cows constituted consideration in the form of reliance. The court stated: "[e]ven if there was no original consideration for the parol modification of the contract, the defendant cannot raise the question after the plaintiff has performed his part of it, and defendant has accepted such performance."[133] In the New York case *McKenzie v. Harrison* (1890),[134] lease payment obligations were lowered by agreement and were paid. The New York Court of Appeals said once the modification was performed and "fully executed,"[135] the preexisting duty rule didn't apply. The court said the lessor had made an executed gift, waiving the right to consideration,[136] thereby taking the case out of Coke's criticized rule, which the court noted had been reaffirmed in *Foakes v. Beer* six years before.[137] Nine years later reliance-based dictum appeared in an 1899 Washington accord case.[138] The court intoned: "Pleas of want of consideration are not favored by the law, especially where the relative positions of the parties have been changed by the transaction."[139] The court said it didn't need to overturn the rule, however, because it found consideration for the accord in the partial payment scraped together by the near insolvent debtor for what would have otherwise been, as a practical matter, a worthless claim.[140]

Before the turn of the twentieth century, reliance logic was also used to find consideration in another line of cases when contract modifications were made to pay more money for performance because of unanticipated circumstances increasing the burden of the performer, e.g., declaration of war making labor scarce or an excavator of earth running into granite. Performance had stopped in these cases once the unforeseen event occurred, and work was induced to resume in reliance on the promise of the increased price.[141]

After the publication of Restatement of Contracts Section 90 in 1932,[142] courts began to forthrightly state reliance as the sole basis for enforcement of modification agreements. A 1933 Massachusetts decision stated in dictum that promissory estoppel could be the basis for enforcement of a modification,[143] but the plaintiff failed since he didn't show actual reliance. The next year the Michigan Supreme Court applied estoppel to bar a life insurance company from denying inaccurate statements made about the remaining period of contract coverage;[144] the court inferred that since the insured didn't apply for another policy that he had relied on the misstatement.[145] Then in the Pennsylvania case *Fried v. Fisher* (1938)[146] promissory estoppel was applied directly in enforcing a discharge of a partner from liability on a partnership's lease obligation. The partner of a law firm told the lessor that he wanted to leave the firm and start a restaurant but only if he had no further liability on the lease; the lessor assured him that he would be released if he left. The lawyer then resigned. The Pennsylvania Supreme Court found justifiable reliance on the oral release of the three year written contract.

Nine years after *Fried v. Fisher,* the British House of Lords announced their decision in *Central London Property Trust Ltd. v. High Trees House Ltd.* (1947);[147] the decision has become the best known common law decision recognizing reliance as ground for enforcement of a contract modification.[148] The decision was widely discussed for several reasons: one, it was the first significant reform of the preexisting duty rule in England since the conservatism of *Foakes v. Beer;*[149] two, it is the fountainhead case for what limited recognition there is of promissory estoppel in English law; and three, the decision was rendered by Judge Denning,[150] perhaps the best known English jurist of this century. In the *High Trees* case, a landlord and tenant had agreed to a rent reduction on a lease during the war, but after the war the landlord sued for the full amount of future payments, and he also sued for the agreed deductions from past payments since the preexisting duty rule barred enforcement of the modification. Denning acknowledged the absence of consideration to support the landlord's promise[151] to reduce but said the promise was enforceable, for the wartime period anyway, because the landlord's "promise to accept a smaller sum in discharge of a larger sum, if acted upon,[152] is binding notwithstanding the absence of consideration: and if the fusion of law and equity leads to this result, so much the better. That aspect was not considered in *Foakes v. Beer.*"[153] The decision created the most significant English exception to date to *Pinnel's Case* and *Foakes v. Beer.*

Denning's dictum in *High Trees* went further, suggesting that a broader application of promissory estoppel might be possible.[154] Several years later, an English lower court took Denning at his word by employing reliance as a basis for creation of an obligation rather than merely for discharge or modification of an existing contract. However, perhaps due to conservative rumblings in the legal community against what extensions of *High Trees* might do to the doctrine of consideration,[155] Denning, L. J. himself reversed the lower court, saying: "The principle stated in the *High Trees* case . . . does not create new causes of action where none existed before. It only prevents a party from insisting upon his strict legal rights, when it would be unjust to allow him to enforce them."[156]

So promissory reliance logic is available in England as a defense to suspend a preexisting obligation but not as a basis for a new cause of action when consideration is lacking. In its narrowest sense, *High Trees* could be read to merely provide a reliance defense in support of a suspensory release from, or reduction of, a preexisting contractual obligation. It did lend support to the proposition, argued in accord cases generally, that a contract discharge was not necessarily governed by the same rules applicable to the formation of a contract.[157] This anemic English version of promissory reliance has not been able to move past this welcomed partial reform of *Foakes v. Beer* because: one, the continued presence of the seal in England arguably provides a mechanism for modifications and discharges without the need to show consideration; two, consideration is easier to establish in English law today than it is in the United States;[158] and three, the reverence for precedent is stronger in the single jurisdiction of England and Wales than in the multiplicity of American common law jurisdictions. It has been suggested that England needs a restatement of the law, as a means of urging the accomplishment of what Restatement of Contracts Section 90 did in the United States, in order to facilitate a broader usage of promissory estoppel in England past its narrow application to modifications and discharges.[159]

Returning briefly to the American use of promissory estoppel in enforcement of modifications of contracts, that usage grew by the 1960s to the extent that the drafters of the Restatement (Second) of Contracts included Section 89(c), separate from Section 90, expressly recognizing reliance as a ground that made a contract modification binding.[160] A myriad of types of relied-upon modifications could qualify for this exceptional relief. One of the most frequently litigated categories of cases involves reliance on an informal waiver of a formal, often technical, contract condition, such as requirements concerning a restriction on renewal[161] or a notice of termination[162] or an extension.[163] These tend to be long term contracts, e.g., leases, employment and financing, where an informality develops and informal modified practices are detrimentally relied upon. Courts are reluctant to allow a later demand for technical compliance with the letter of the original contract to wreak such an unfair result.[164] Today, there is a broad acceptance of this reform of the preexisting duty rule when there is justifiable reliance on a modification promise. As a practical matter, a contract modification may not be enforceable when made because of the preexisting duty rule, but it may become enforceable if there is justifiable reliance on the modification.

Chapter 4

Legislative Reform of Preexisting Duty Rule

Before the end of the nineteenth century, ten state legislatures became restive with the failure of the common law to cure itself and adopted Benthamite solutions by breaching the legislative tradition of not intruding upon the common law of contract, with the major exception of the Statute of Frauds,[1] by partially or totally repealing the preexisting duty rule.[2] Later, during the economic shifts of the 1930s,[3] the continuing debate over the need for the law to accommodate necessary adjustments of contracts due to economic change stimulated legislative law revision commissions in the United States and England to reconsider the issue. In 1936 the New York Law Revision Commission recommended reform of the rule to permit binding written contract modifications, without consideration, in order to avoid hardship and to realize the parties' expectations when they entered into the modification agreement.[4] The next year the English Law Revision Committee recommended abrogation of the rule in *Pinnel's Case* and *Foakes v. Beer* because of its injustice and inconvenience and because the Committee agreed with Blackburn's criticism in *Foakes v. Beer* that prompt payment could be more beneficial than insisting upon the whole.[5]

SCATTERED LEGISLATIVE REFORMS

Various legislatures chose between two modes of reforming the preexisting duty rule: one, total abrogation of the rule or, two, enforcement of a contract modification if it was in writing. Beginning with those jurisdictions totally abandoning the rule, the first common law jurisdiction to legislatively reject the rule completely was neither in the United States nor in England but in India in 1872.[6] (The Indian Contract Act, and the

California Field Code passed the same year, represented the first major codifications of common law contract principles since the thirteenth century;[7] major portions of both were borrowed from Field's proposed substantive law code for New York.[8]) Virginia passed legislation in 1887 abolishing the preexisting duty rule: "Part performance of an obligation . . . when expressly accepted by the creditor in satisfaction . . . though without any new consideration, shall extinguish such obligation."[9] Georgia, Maine and North Carolina achieved the same result as Virginia, each with its own verbiage.[10]

The second major category of legislative reforms provided for a binding modification of a contract without consideration so long as the modification was evidenced by a signed writing. The cautionary function of a writing averted the concern that loose negotiations about possible adjustments during the performance phase could be misunderstood as modifications. Four types of writings were recognized as a substitute for consideration in the various statutes: (1) Four jurisdictions resuscitated the seal by treating sealed and unsealed instruments the same,[11] and Massachusetts declared that an instrument that recited it was sealed would be treated as a sealed instrument.[12] The analogy to the seal fared poorly since the anachronistic seal did not mesh well with modern legal doctrine; thus some cases even stated that a sealed instrument required consideration.[13] (2) The Uniform Written Obligations Act, drafted by Williston,[14] was approved by the Commissioners on Uniform State Laws in 1925 and provided:

> A written release or promise hereafter made and signed by the person releasing or promising shall not be invalid or unenforceable for lack of consideration, if the writing also contains an additional express statement in any form of language that the signer intends to be bound.

Only Pennsylvania[15] in 1927 and Utah[16] in 1929 ever passed the Uniform Act, and Utah subsequently repealed it. The fact that the seal still has much of its original force in Pennsylvania[17] makes it largely redundant. The Act's attempt to fill a gap created by the loss of the seal has not been favorably received because the inadvertent use of promissory language, which might later be construed to fit under the Act, could cause one to be liable on a gratuitous promise not intended as binding.[18] (3) In 1936 New York adopted its Law Revision Commission's[19] recommendation by declaring binding a written modification or discharge of an obligation "signed by the party against whom it is sought to enforce the change" without the need to show consideration.[20] Unlike the California accord-type statutory reform, this New York language would cover both accords for decreased amounts due (as in *Pinnel's Case*) and modifications for increased amounts (as in the seamen's wage increase cases). In 1941, Michigan followed New York's 1936 statute verbatim,[21] though fickle New York repealed its law in 1963 and then later readopted it.[22] As mentioned, in 1872 the California legislature overturned the rule that an accord must be supported by consideration, so long as the accord was in writing, and three Northern Plains states, which had followed California's lead in codification in other areas, adopted California's verbiage.[23] (4) The final type of writing statute was a nineteenth century variety that did not specifically exempt a written release or discharge from the consideration requirement but could arguably be construed to do so by an agreement "according to the intentions of the parties."[24] This odd approach naturally led to litigation since it did not clearly exempt the changed agreement from consideration.[25] Tennessee and Alabama statutes were of this type, but because of confusion generated, they have been amended to specifically allow a written contract modification to be binding without consideration.[26]

Problems continued, however, in the enforcement of modifications in jurisdictions with statutes declaring that a writing supplanted consideration because modifications often arise as oral assurances that the naive promisee will be covered against losses he's suffering in completion of a difficult performance cojoled by the promisee. Other problems surfaced under the statutes. These statutes did not deal with actions which were enforceable by strangers. Difficulties arose when a statute's requisite contractual intent was not clearly stated in the written modification agreement.[27] The variety of state statutory positions, ranging from total abolition of the rule to relief if there is a writing plus the absence of reform in a majority of jurisdictions caused uniformity problems for business planners operating in a national market.

U.C.C. REJECTS PREEXISTING DUTY RULE

Uniform Commercial Code Reporter Karl Llewellyn successfully urged an adoption of reasonable commercial usage[28] by abolishing the preexisting duty rule, despite the fact that it still enjoyed judicial support in a majority of common law jurisdictions in 1952. American legal realists were attracted to the commercial practice of adjusting past relations, through settlement, in order to preserve ongoing relations. U.C.C. Section 2–209(1) provides: "An agreement modifying a contract within this Article needs no consideration to be binding." This realization of a uniform, nationwide rejection of the preexisting duty rule for sales contract modifications, and since 1987 for leases of goods, will be analyzed here in terms of, one, its requirements for formation, and two, what impact bad faith might have on its enforcement.

Formation of Modification Agreement

Formation of a modification under the Code adheres to the consensual theory viewpoint in focusing on the issues of intent[29] and whether any written formality is required "without regard to the technicalities which at present hamper such adjustments."[30] The policy reasons in support of reform have already been explored. The doctrinal genesis of this reform can be found in the earlier discussed caselaw and statutory reforms of the preexisting duty rule in some jurisdictions. The Code effectively adopted Minnesota's "logical and just standard" in *Rye v. Phillips* (1938) that no "overworked shibboleth" like consideration[31] should bar enforcement of the contractors' consensual modification. What should this standard be? As the New Hampshire court said in *Frye v. Hubbell* (1907), there is "no better guide for determination of the rights of the parties" to a modification than their "purpose and intent."[32]

As to prior statutory reforms that would be considered a model for U.C.C. Section 2–209, the Virginia-type statute[33] is closest since it abolishes the requirement of consideration for formal and *informal* modifications; however, unlike the Code, Virginia covered a modification decreasing a debtor's obligation but it did not cover an increase in the obligation owed. The New York–type statutory reform[34] covered both increases and decreases in obligations, but the modification agreement had to be in writing.[35] The unsuccessful Uniform Written Obligations Act of 1925 is naturally a forerunner of the U.C.C. rule since it was the only prior attempted uniform statute on point,[36] but, as to modifications, the U.C.C. of course goes further, since the Code has no independent writing requirement.[37]

The U.C.C. and the writing requirement genre of statute grappled with the loss of the protective formal functions performed by the doctrine of consideration, each in its own way.[38] The U.C.C. drafters did give special attention to the cautionary function for consumers signing standardized contracts to assure they didn't unknowingly lose in the fine print the right of a later informal method of changing the relationship.[39] U.C.C. Section 2–209 does acknowledge the place of written formality in modifications, as required by the Statute of Frauds and by any private statute of frauds.[40] The Code Comments indicate that these writing rules "are intended to protect against false allegations of oral modifications"[41] and assist in establishing "mutual consent"[42] to the modifications. However, informality in making waivers was assured by providing that any writing requirements for modification or rescission could not limit the effect of the parties' later conduct.[43] The distinctions made in U.C.C. Section 2–209 between modification, rescission and waiver indicate that the rules for each vary in terms of the formalities of consideration and writing.[44] Unlike most of the earlier state statutes reforming the preexisting duty rule, U.C.C Section

2–209(1) allows informal modifications since the cautionary concern is not so great when a right is being surrendered rather than created.[45]

The U.C.C. accomplished for sales contracts what Blackburn would have liked to have done in *Foakes v. Beer* for all contracts by allowing the parties to form contract modifications free of the fetters of consideration. The ground for enforcement of sales modifications was now the parties' manifestation of consent. But what assurance was there that the outward consent to a change in the original contract was free of overreaching or duress? The removal of the consideration impediment to contract modifications left the courts with the burden of policing to assure that modifications were not coerced or exacted in bad faith. The existence in the law merchant of developed sales standards of fair dealing in the trade made it easier for the Code drafters to justify abandoning consideration's protective role in sales contract modifications than has been the case for courts applying the common law of contract to all other types of contracts.

Good Faith Modification

Until modern reforms, the preexisting duty rule barred contract modifications generally, whether coerced,[46] unconscionable or voluntary, though in some hardship cases courts employed fictions and other exceptions to manipulate the doctrine of consideration to allow enforcement. The U.C.C. guarded against improperly induced modifications by replacing consideration's positive contribution of thwarting coercion with the good faith policing mechanism.[47] The use of good faith here is a deviation from the objective standard of classical contract law favored by Holmes; the finding of a bad motivation or reason[48] for seeking a modification could now override an outward manifestation of consent.[49] Good faith indicates the good reason, or *causa*, for making the modification promise.

The genesis of the notion of good faith in contracting can be isolated as early as the seventeenth century in chancery practices and mercantile usages. The more immediate American inspiration for Llewellyn's inclusion of the good faith standard[50] to police contract modifications[51] can be seen percolating in late nineteenth century decisions of now fused courts of law and equity along four related equitable strands. One strand is found in a couple of late nineteenth century modification cases discussed earlier, where economic duress elements were present,[52] and bad faith was given as a reason for refusing enforcement. In *Headley v. Hackley* (1883), a case returned to the Michigan Supreme Court a second time, the plaintiff argued it was "bad faith"[53] for the defendant to trump up a dispute to extort a lower price when the plaintiff was near insolvency. The court agreed and overturned the unconscionable modification because the defendant acted "unfairly" in "oppressively" obtaining the modification.[54] In *Lingenfelder v. Wainwright Brewing Co.* (1891), the Missouri Supreme Court applied policy-based logic in finding no consideration for the modification because the architect was aware of the defendant's deadline and "took advantage of (defendant's) necessities, and extorted the promise" and "to permit plaintiff to recover under such circumstances would be to offer a premium upon bad faith."[55]

A second strand of cases involved another aspect of the coerced modification case of *Headley v. Hackley*, i.e., when a party tries to position himself outside the preexisting duty rule by feigning a dispute. In an 1887 Minnesota case, the court said: "A person cannot create a dispute sufficient as a consideration for a compromise by a mere refusal to pay an undisputed claim. That would be extortion and not a compromise."[56] And in a similar 1923 California case, the court said: "An arbitrary refusal to pay, based on the mere pretense of the debtor, whether for the obvious purpose of exacting terms which are inequitable and oppressive, is not such a dispute as will satisfy the requirements of the rule."[57] In the next chapter there will be a discussion of how good faith dispute ideas were also influential in rationalizing an exception to the preexisting duty rule in unanticipated circumstances cases.

A third development influencing the use of good faith to police modifications was the recognition that contracts could be excused from performance when the purpose was frustrated[58] or performance became commercially impracticable[59] due to an unforeseen change in a fundamental assumption, shared by the parties, upon which the contract was based. The translation of these excuse ideas into modification cases involved two logical extensions. One, if the original contract could be entirely excused from performance on the account of a failure of a basic assumption, then couldn't unforeseen circumstances justify a modification of the contract without requiring fresh consideration?[60] And, if that was possible, then couldn't the magnitude of the unanticipated circumstance be somewhat less substantial than that required for an excuse from performance[61] since the relationship will continue on the basis of the parties' common consent?

A fourth strand stimulating the application of good faith to contract modifications was the recognition of a general good faith standard applicable to the performance and enforcement of all contracts. During the last quarter of the nineteenth century, interrelated equitable notions drawn from established practices in chancery, were invoked by recently fused courts of law and equity to ameliorate one-sided transactions made between parties of unequal bargaining power. These ideas culminated in a recognition of a duty of good faith in all contracts before 1920.[62] One group of cases influencing this development involved the failure of a party to cooperate in the contract's common purpose.[63] A second group concerned a lack of good faith in contract enforcement, such as unreasonable demands for full performance in cases of frustration and impracticability and bad faith failure to mitigate damages.[64] Furthermore, as interrelated ideas fed off each other, the early forced modification cases mentioned under the first strand, which were overturned on account of bad faith and coercion,[65] also contributed to the recognition of a generalized standard of good faith in performance and enforcement of all contracts.

The good faith duty owed under U.C.C. Section 2–209 for modifications both overlaps and goes beyond the general duty of good faith required in the performance and enforcement of all contracts[66] because it also requires good faith in negotiating a contract modification.[67] While the requirement of good faith negotiation of an original contract is only an emerging notion in contract law,[68] the Code's drafters employed it to replace the policing function that the doctrine of consideration had crudely performed with a meat cleaver at the bargaining and formation stage of a modification agreement. Today, no general duty exists for entrepreneurs in the marketplace to negotiate the original contract in good faith; in fact, it is irrelevant whether there is a legitimate commercial reason for the formation of the original contract. Objections that the original contract was not negotiated and formed on the basis of honesty-in-fact and fair dealing will not be considered by courts, short of duress, fraud, unconscionability or other invalidating cause. Once the original bargain is struck, however, there exists today a common law duty to cooperate during the performance phase; and, under the Code, this duty continues through any renegotiation of the ongoing relationship for the purpose of modifying the contract.

Since the standard of good faith described in Comment 2 to U.C.C. Section 2–209 is more stringent than the general duty of good faith in the Code because it covers the negotiation phase, it is both curious and regrettable that the drafters didn't bother to include good faith verbiage in the statutory language of Section 2–209. Of the 400 or so sections of the U.C.C., 60 make specific reference to good faith, but here, where the standard needs to be specific, there's no reference to it.[69] It is difficult to see how Section 2–209(1) can operate without the good faith bargaining standard specified in the Comments. Assuming, then, that the Comment's gloss on the statute applies, who has the burden of proving the presence or absence of bad faith? Does the proponent of the modification have a duty to show good faith as a part of his case-in-chief or is it only necessary to establish good faith in rebuttal if evidence of bad faith is raised by the opponent? Again, the Code is silent. The caselaw suggests that good faith is not a point of discussion unless abuse is suggested from the surrounding circumstances; plenty of appellate opinions applying the Section 2–209 make no reference to good faith one way or the other, sometimes even when the facts hint at questionable motivations.[70] Nevertheless, some courts do place an affirmative burden on the proponent of the modification to prove good faith in order to shift the burden of proof.[71]

If bad faith becomes an issue, the proponent of the modification must prove, one, under the subjective standard of honesty-in-fact, that he or she was motivated by a good reason in seeking the modification,[72] and two, under the objective standard of fair dealing in the trade, that an ordinary and reasonable merchant would have done the same thing.[73]

The good faith standard applicable to Section 2–209 is augmented by the doctrines of unconscionability and economic duress. Comment 2 to Section 2–209 prohibits the "extortion of a 'modification' without legitimate commercial reason." Unconscionability and economic duress supplement the policing role played by good faith in focusing on the fundamental concern here for lack of consent caused by overreaching. Unconscionability was clearly made applicable to sales contracts and their modifications by the Code drafters codifying common law and equitable notions of unconscionability.[74] Although economic duress is not specifically referred to in the Code, it applies to coerced sales modifications under U.C.C. Section 1–103, which supplements the Code with "principles of law and equity, including . . . duress [and] coercion." Some decisions simply assume that economic duress is a breach of honesty-in-fact and fair dealing under Comment 2 of Section 2–209[75] or that a bad faith extortion of a modification constitutes economic duress.[76]

In concluding remarks on the role of good faith in policing modifications, it should be remembered that the preexisting duty rule effectively presumed bad faith and in the process excluded good faith modifications that parties desired and voluntarily agreed to. After the Code reform, consented-to modifications made for good reasons were binding but bad faith and coerced ones of course were not. The Code drafters could have gone further and declared modification agreements binding, even in the absence of good faith negotiations, in order to be consistent with undiluted notions of individualism and freedom of contract. The justification for not doing that seems to be that after the original contract is formed, the parties must cooperate and drop their former arms' length relationship since they have been permitted to enter each other's camp and have become aware of any vulnerability of the other, such as a deadline or financial exigency.

The abrogation of the preexisting duty rule by the Code can be criticized for creating uncertainty, but then an industrial economy foments uncertainty and change, and to say that parties may not make adjustments to their contractual relations in response to the hurly burly of modern markets is unrealistic and inefficient.[77] The U.C.C. replaced the uncertainty of the convoluted exceptions to the preexisting duty rule with the moderate uncertainty of good faith, but now inefficiencies later found in the original contract terms may be cured under the governing principles of consent and fairness.

Chapter 5

Restatement Second Position

Given the fact that only a handful of state supreme courts and legislatures had completely abolished the preexisting duty rule when the first Restatement of Contracts was being prepared in the 1920s, it is hardly surprising that the drafters elected to reaffirm the old rule in 1932.[1] The drafters, led by Williston, might have pointed the way to modernization by adopting the impulse in the scattered reforms, as they did in converting nineteenth century cases of justifiable reliance on gratuitous promises into the broad principle of promissory estoppel, but they resisted departure from the entrenched preexisting duty rule defense.[2] When a second crack at restating contract law was undertaken in the 1960s and 1970s, the restaters incorporated the expanding equitable exceptions for reliance and unanticipated circumstances, which were present in the caselaw in greater proportions than at the time of the first restatement, but they still did not see a sea change in the common law of contract law generally to justify total abrogation of Coke's enduring dictum.

TENACIOUS RULE REAFFIRMED

Restatement Second Section 73 retained the preexisting duty rule except for the long recognized instances of a doubtful or disputed claim and a promise of a different performance.[3] The Restatement Second was in fact stricter than the application of the classic preexisting duty rule on two counts. The restaters rejected the device of a novelty, when it was a mere "pretense of a bargain,"[4] and they likewise rejected the sometimes recognized fiction of a rescission coupled with a new agreement because its routine use, without adequately weighing fairness and voluntariness, could uphold "inequitable modifications."[5] In another respect, however,

Section 73 was more lenient in allowing an "honest dispute" to qualify as an exception without demanding, as the first Restatement had, that it also be "reasonable."[6] Overall, however, were it not for the soon-to-be-discussed Section 89 reforms, the Restatement Second position taken in Section 73 would have, ironically, actually barred more modification agreements than under the first Restatement by purging the law of the impurities of the traditional fictional bargain exceptions.

The rationale the restaters gave for reaffirming the preexisting duty rule was that contract modifications raised suspicions of duress, unconscionability and mistake, and the best way to render "unnecessary any inquiry into the existence of such an invalidating cause" was to refuse enforcement without fresh consideration.[7] Thus, if averting duress is a higher goal than the parties' realizing their adjusted consent, it would be illogical to ground relief on apparent consent or to permit the pretense of consideration in the form of a peppercorn.[8]

A different perception of the role of consideration in relation to coercion, suggested recently by an English justice, might encourage the finding of consideration in the absence of coercion: "The modern cases tend to depend more on the defense of duress in a commercial context rather than lack of consideration for the second agreement."[9] The Missouri decision *Rexite Casting Co. v. Midwest Mower Corp.* (1954)[10] provides an example of how consideration can be employed as a tool to avert suspected duress. A manufacturer of aluminum casting made a take-it-or-leave-it offer to modify its contract by raising the price 50%, due to a false claim of an increase in the cost of metal. The buyer protested but acquiesced since it was in the middle of production and didn't have time to find the castings elsewhere. The modification smacked of coercion, but instead of struggling with whether the facts fell under the abstraction of economic duress, the court simply declared that consideration was absent.[11] In this way a modern court can act as a chancellor in equity and find consideration lacking if the factual pattern raises a strong suspicion of coercion; but if the modification seems fair, the court can either find a benefit or a detriment or find an exceptional ground applicable.[12] As an example of an exception, had the *Rexite Casting Co. v. Midwest Mower Corp.* modification been free of coercion and the claim of a price increase legitimate,[13] the court could have pointed to the increase in the price of metal as an instance of the now recognized exception of an unanticipated change in circumstances.[14] A more straightforward way would of course be to analyze whether there was a voluntary consensual transaction made in good faith, as is done under U.C.C. Section 2–209(1).

The application of Restatement Second Section 73's general bar on contract modifications, and its attendant presumption of duress, will obviously dash the parties' common intention more often than if the common law starts with the presumption that a consented-to modification is binding, subject to countervailing proof of coercion or bad faith. The drafters of Section 73 were torn between a presumption of coercion and the acknowledged merit of enforcing the parties' "equitable adjustment in the course of performance of a continuing contact."[15] The recent opinion of an English justice on the subject of the preexisting duty rule and consideration might provide a guidepost for judges to work their way through this issue:

> Consideration there must still be but in my judgement the courts nowadays should be more ready to find its existence so as to reflect the intention of the parties to the contract where the bargaining powers are not unequal and where the finding of consideration reflects the true intention of the parties.[16]

The drafters of Section 73 confessed in their schizophrenic Comment (c) that there were criticisms to retaining the preexisting duty rule since it was based on "scholastic logic" and it did not admit the benefit of modifying an agreement by offering a "bonus to a recalcitrant promisor to induce performance without legal proceedings." But then the Comment quickly retreated by adding that "an unscrupulous promisor may threaten breach in order to obtain such a bonus."[17] The modern shift in common law approach in England announced in *Williams v. Roffey Bros. & Nicholls (Contractors) Ltd.* (1990)[18] overcame the traditional reticence exhibited in Comment (c) to Section 73 by allowing realization of the parties' intent, when coercion isn't suggested, by finding consideration in the "commercial advantage to both sides" of continued performance of the contract.[19]

In *Williams v. Roffey*, a sub-contractor who had bid a job too low had little incentive to continue because continued performance placed him in mounting financial difficulty by increasing his losses. The general contractor felt motivated to offer more than originally agreed both because of a penalty clause for late completion in his separate contract with the owner and because of the commercial advantage to himself of finishing the project. No concern was expressed about coercion because the general contractor in fact offered to pay more in order to induce the disheartened sub-contractor to continue performance; so it wasn't a case of the performer holding the other party up. In its rationale, the English Court of Appeal reaffirmed as good law the nineteenth century precedents of seamen being barred from recovery on a promise to pay more;[20] but, unlike those cases, there was "some other consideration,"[21] to support the promise to pay the sub-contractor more, found in the benefit[22] to the general contractor of securing himself commercially both by avoiding the penalty and by answering his obligations to the owner of completing the project without the hassle of finding another sub-contractor for more money.[23] Despite the talk about receiving something extra, in avoiding costs and the penalty, this case comes very close to relegating the seamen's wage increase cases to the public policy arena of coerced price increases. Justices Russell and Purchas stated they saw consideration solely in the mutual benefit of continuation of contractual performance,[24] something that could be found in almost any voluntary commercial contract modification.

At first glance, it might seem that the logic of *Williams v. Roffey* provided a comprehensive overhaul of *Foakes v. Beer*'s preexisting duty rule and consequently of the rule in *Pinnel's Case* (1602). Amongst Commonwealth jurisdictions, an Australian court has come to this conclusion;[25] but an English judicial reaction soon exhumed the pre–*Foakes v. Beer* dichotomy of *Stilk v. Myrick*'s modified promise to pay for contractual services and *Pinnel*'s modified promise to pay money. English judicial dictum in 1994 and in 1995 resisted extending *Williams v. Roffey*'s reform of *Stilk v. Myrick*–type modified promises to encompass modified promises to pay money; the English court preferred that Parliament consider the proposal, as if the rule in *Pinnel's Case* was a Parliamentary mandate.[26] In 1884, *Foakes v. Beer* brought together the two categories of modification promises represented in the seamen's wage case *Stilk v. Myrick* and *Pinnel's Case*, but the recent English decisions' narrow reading of *Williams v. Roffey* atavistically resurrected the fragmented view prior to 1884. It is reminiscent of Denman, C. J's reactionary resuscitation of a moribund, century-old application of the past consideration rule[27] in order to largely smother Mansfield's moral obligation reforms, as will be discussed in Chapter 8. Given this English judicial conservatism in the wake of the most electrifying common law contract departure in decades, a further narrowing of the impact of *Williams v. Roffey* could come in the form of restricting its applicability to modifications made on account of difficulties in performing contractual services precipitated by the eruption of unanticipated circumstances.[28]

Returning to the logic in *Williams v. Roffey*, the benefit found was not the bird-in-the-hand or the avoidance of collection costs,[29] as has often been argued for unsuccessfully. Instead, the bargained-for benefit to the promisor–general contractor[30] was the avoidance of costs and the continuation of timely performance. The sub-contractor's continuation of performance, rather than cutting his business losses and breaching, provided the general contractor with the added, or different, benefit of continuation of contract performance in order to avoid the penalty and other commercial costs of complying with his obligations to the owner.

The approach followed by the English Court of Appeal is very similar to the solution to the preexisting duty rule conundrum devised by Massachusetts in *Munroe v. Perkins* (1830);[31] indeed, if the English court was aware of the Massachusetts rule, and English courts were not so loath to reference American precedents, it surely would have been discussed in *Williams v. Roffey*.[32] As in the English case, the contractor in *Munroe v. Perkins* had made a losing construction contract, not caused by unanticipated circumstances,[33] and was in resulting financial difficulty. The contractor had not demanded more money but was discouraged about continuing. In order to keep the construction project going, the owner's agents informally promised the contractor more, and the court enforced the price increase by finding consideration to support the second promise in the contractor's forbearance from exercising his right to breach, thereby accomplishing continuation of construction.[34] There was a benefit to the promisor–owner in the project continuing and a detriment[35] to the promisee–contractor in forbearing from simply breaching and paying damages. The Massachusetts rule has been criticized for inviting coercion,[36] being morally unjustifiable[37] and doctrinally unsound on the grounds that the claimed rescission was a fiction and that there was no right to breach.[38] Justice Purchas admitted his own unease in *Williams v. Roffey* with the court's unorthodox use of the right-to-breach logic.[39] Nevertheless, this is the consideration-based logic Massachusetts and, to a degree, England have created to free themselves from the preexisting duty rule impediment to enforcing the modified intent of the parties.

EXCEPTION FOR SUBSEQUENT UNANTICIPATED EVENT

Pursuant to the equitable doctrine developed by courts of law and equity over the preceding century, the drafters of the Restatement Second created a new, separate[40] Section 89 for equitable exceptions to the preexisting duty rule when there is either a subsequent unanticipated circumstance or a modification agreement subsequently relied on. Comment (b) to Section 89 states that the preexisting duty rule was justified in cases of mistake or coercion; but, instead of narrowing the rule to those situations of lack of assent, exceptions were recognized only in the cases of reliance and unanticipated circumstances. Section 89(b) also adopted state statutory reforms of the common law rule. Since this study covered the development of reliance-based relief, recognized in Section 89(c), in Chapter 3 and statutory reforms in Chapter 4, the following discussion will focus on relief isolated by the restaters on account of unanticipated circumstances. Section 89 provides:

> A promise modifying a duty under a contract not fully performed on either side is binding (a) if the modification is fair and equitable in view of circumstances not anticipated by the parties when the contract was made.[41]

While Restatement Second Section 73 constitutes the continuing majority common law position by reaffirming the preexisting duty rule, Section 89(a) reflects an emerging minority position that modifications made on account of unanticipated circumstances should be enforceable without consideration. The ensuing discussion in this section will cover: (1) the logic and origins of the unanticipated circumstances exception; (2) why consideration is not required; and (3) the elements of this exception.

Unanticipated Circumstances Exception: Logic and Origins

The reasoning behind granting exceptional relief for a contract modification precipitated by unanticipated circumstances rests on the notion that a contract includes fundamental assumptions about surrounding circumstances impacting the parties' rights and duties. A bargain involves shouldering risks based on certain jointly anticipated possibilities, and, if such a foreseeable change occurs, that is a risk to be borne; but, if the change is unanticipated, fairness and consensuality support allowing either an excuse or a modification,[42] especially if enforcement of the letter of the contract causes a substantial loss.

Modern contracts are more susceptible to unexpected circumstances because these contracts tend to be long term and market swings can be more dramatic than during the preindustrial period. These longer term modern contracts are exposed to substantial, unanticipated circumstances, like strikes, shortages, depressions, war, weather, changed construction conditions and a myriad of other unanticipated circumstances not as likely to have arisen in Coke's day. Comment (a) to Section 89 recognized the "utility" in "adjustments to on-going transactions." An efficient and equitable continuation of a contract might only be possible under modified terms.

The inefficiency, unfairness and potential loss precipitated by an unanticipated shift in conditions provide good motives for the modification; unanticipated circumstances provide a *causa* or reason for seeking the modification.[43] These circumstances establish a justification for the modification and consequently help overcome the usual suspicion of coercion that a modification otherwise engenders.[44] Under this logic, the nineteenth century seamen's wage increase promises might have been binding if it had been established that an unanticipated risk, rather than coercion, had stimulated the requests for wage increases.[45]

The origins of the exceptional treatment given contract modifications made on account of unanticipated circumstances are found in decisions rendered during the second half of the nineteenth century based on notions of: the consensual theory, actual or near impossibility, settlement of bona fide contract disputes and fundamental fairness. These reasons for exceptions to the preexisting duty rule were usually rationalized within the parameters of the doctrine of consideration.

The civilian-influenced consensual theory[46] spawned several contract doctrines that fed off each other. Modern emphasis on free consent inspired such rules as remoteness of damages and impossibility; and these rules, along with general support for consent-based obligations, contributed to the recognition of the unanticipated circumstances exception to the preexisting duty rule. Before the middle of the nineteenth century, proponents of the consensual theory argued that parties to a contract should not be liable for consequences not "foreseen" and not "contemplated at the time of the contract.''[47] An early implementation of this idea appeared in 1854 in the rule governing remoteness of damages, which rule stated that damages were not recoverable unless they were the consequence of what was in the ''contemplation of both parties, at the time they made the contract.''[48] If it wasn't within their contemplation, then it wasn't consented-to, and therefore it wasn't a part of the bargain. This logic, and accompanying verbiage, was translated into American decisions enforcing contract modifications made on account of unanticipated circumstances; these judicial opinions reasoned that the parties should be permitted to consent to an alteration of the terms of their original contract if it no longer reflected the conditions upon which their original consent was based.

The first case recognizing the unanticipated circumstances exception to the preexisting duty rule was the New York decision *Meech v. City of Buffalo* (1864),[49] wherein the city agreed to pay a sewer contractor more than originally agreed to when quicksand was unexpectedly encountered. Since it was then twice as expensive to complete the project and the contractor would have abandoned the work, the city agreed to a modification thereby settling the matter. In *King v. Duluth Ry. Co.* (1895), the Minnesota Supreme Court cited *Meech v. City of Buffalo* with approval and declared that a modification increasing the payment due to a contractor should be enforced because of the ''additional burden not contemplated by the parties.''[50] The 1907 Maryland decision *Linz v. Schuck*, involving a construction contract disrupted by unforeseen soil conditions, ruled a modification binding on the same basis; the court stated: ''[t]he difficulties were substantial, unforeseen and not within the contemplation of the parties when the original contract was made.''[51] By enforcing such modification agreements, these decisions were effectively allowing the parties' modified consent to accomplish what the remoteness of damages rule did in efficiently limiting or mitigating the damages and loss otherwise sufferable, due to the unforeseen circumstances, under the original contract.[52]

Another application of the consensual theory facilitated an excuse from performance of the strict terms of the contract[53] when performance became impossible due to unanticipated circumstances. Blackburn, J. enters the picture again here in 1863 in recognizing a physical impossibility excuse from the terms of a contract, when the subject matter was destroyed by fire, because the parties had ''contemplated'' its ''continued existence'' as ''essential for the fulfillment of the contract.''[54] Early in the twentieth century, excuse was further liberalized to discharge contracts frustrated in their purpose because ''the foundation or basis of the contract,'' which was ''assumed by the parties,'' ceased to exist[55] and also to discharge contracts on account of unanticipated circumstances short of physical impossibility when performance was commercially ''impracticable.''[56] The logic employed in these excuse cases was adjusted to justify contract modifications along similar lines. The degree of foreseeability and of altered circumstances for a contract modification didn't need to be as great as for an excuse discharge because of the consensual continuation of the relationship and also because, as stated in *King v. Duluth Ry. Co.* (1895), the facts "are sufficient if they are of such a character as to render the party's demand for extra pay manifestly fair," thereby quelling concern about coercion.[57]

The settlement of a bona fide dispute, an exception to the preexisting duty rule,[58] was another source drawn on for the development of the unanticipated circumstances exception to the same rule.[59] Enforcement of a modification made on account of unanticipated circumstances was sometimes rationalized as simply falling under the established exception of settlement of a bona fide dispute; the eruption of an unanticipated circumstance would create a controversy as to who bore the risk under the terms of the contract, and the modification agreement would specify the settled-upon adjustment. In the Minnesota case *Michaud v. McGregor* (1895),[60] the controversy over who bore the risk of removing unanticipated rocks from the soil under the terms of the contract was settled, and the court ruled that the settlement of the controversy over the unanticipated circumstance was consideration for the modification.[61] In *United Steel Co. v. Casey* (1920),[62] a court concluded that a modification made because of unanticipated weather conditions was a settlement of a dispute over a party's delays in failing to fully perform before wintertime.

Courts tended toward mixing the emerging, independent exception of unanticipated circumstances and the bona fide dispute exception together. As recently as 1958 in *Pittsburgh Testing Laboratory v. Farnsworth & Chambers Co.*,[63] a court ruled that the assurances of extra compensation for additional, unexpected work required was enforceable on the two-pronged rationale of the "unforeseen difficulties exception" to the preexisting duty rule and the bona fide dispute exception.[64] The unanticipated circumstance discovered during the performance of this contract to provide materials testing services was that twice as much earth as had originally been expected would need to be moved in order to do the testing.

Caselaw Support for Not Requiring Consideration

Restatement Second Section 89(a) does not require consideration to enforce a modification made on account of circumstances not anticipated when the original contract was formed. Of the many cases cited in the Reporter's Note to Section 89, only two decisions enforced modifications without requiring consideration, and one is partially,[65] and the other totally,[66] rationalized under the rescission fiction rejected in Section 89.[67] The remainder of the decisions cited were rationalized under the doctrine of consideration. In *King v. Duluth Ry. Co.* (1895), the most influential unanticipated circumstances case stating that consideration could be found to support a modification, Minnesota Supreme Court Chief Justice Start opined that when:

> unforeseen and substantial difficulties in the performance . . . cast upon him an additional burden not contemplated by the parties, and the opposite side promises him extra pay or benefits if he will complete his contract, and he so promises, the promise to pay is supported by a valid consideration.[68]

Start, C. J. added: "Cases of this character form an exception to the general rule that a promise to do that which a party is already bound to do" is not consideration to support the promise to pay more.[69] Start rejected the position of the Minnesota court taken in 1876[70] that a modification to pay more for excavation, due to the discovery of unexpected rocks, was unenforceable under the strict contract liability view that he was obligated to excavate at the original price no matter what difficulties arose subsequently.[71] Start, C. J. cited with approval the 1864 New York case *Meech v. City of Buffalo.* The New York court had ruled the modification promise binding because the contractor proceeded with the work on the faith of the additional compensation promised on account of the unanticipated circumstances; the New York court declared that the completion of the project at the necessary increased expense constituted sufficient consideration for the promise to pay more.[72]

The logic and language of *King v. Duluth Ry. Co.* was adopted by some courts verbatim.[73] Other courts found consideration to support modifications using different analyses. In *Goebel v. Linn* (1882), Michigan Supreme Court Justice Cooley isolated a mutual benefit in both the ice company and the brewery preserving their interests by raising the original price of the ice after the failure of the ice crop.[74] In the wartime labor shortage case *Blakeslee v. Board of Water Commissioners* (1927),[75] the Connecticut court found a detriment to the promisee both in doing the unanticipated extra work and in the risk that the cost of work could increase, and the court saw a benefit[76] to the promisor in completion of the contract, thus avoiding delay and attendant cost. And in *Pittsburgh Testing Laboratory v. Farnsworth & Chambers Co.* (1958),[77] the court simply stated that the extra and unforeseen difficulties constituted consideration for the promise to pay more.

The drafters of Section 89(a) found comfort in the broader stroke of U.C.C. Section 2–209 (1), and of some other state statutes, which did *not* require consideration to support a modification,[78] but a search of the caselaw unearths a paucity of support in the common law for Section 89's position. The only case very directly on point is *Watkins v. Carrig* (1941),[79] and it is partially rationalized on the bases of a gift and the fiction of a rescission;[80] moreover, this New Hampshire decision emanated from a jurisdiction following a minority common law position, announced early in the century, that had rationalized the presence of consideration to support any contract modification, changed circumstances or not.[81] The modification promise to pay more in *Watkins v. Carrig* was made on account of unanticipated solid rock encountered in excavating a cellar. Putting the gift and rescission reasons to the side, the New Hampshire decision can be read to have also enforced the modification without consideration on the independent grounds of common intent, business practices and fairness. The court found the higher price to be based on the "intention of the parties"[82] and their "mutual understanding . . . that the contract price was not to control."[83] The court said: "The defendant intentionally and voluntarily yielded to a demand for a special price for excavating rock."[84] The defendant didn't protest but agreed, and so, "fairly," he should be held to the new arrangement under principles of "fundamental justice and reasonableness."[85] The court emphasized that this approach is "considered to meet the reasonable needs of standard and ethical practices of men in their business dealings with each other."[86] The realist court added that the enforcement of contract "changes to meet changes in circumstances and conditions should be valid if the law is to carry out its function and service by rules conformable with reasonable practices and understandings in matters of business."[87]

The reasons given in *Watkins v. Carrig* for not requiring consideration seem sound not only for modifications made due to unanticipated circumstances but also for modifications generally. There would appear to be other reasons for concluding that the traditional functions of consideration are adequately fulfilled in *Watkins*. One of the functions of consideration is to determine if the promise is motivated by a good reason; unanticipated circumstances evidence such a reason, or *causa*, for a modification.[88] The cautionary and channeling functions of consideration are supplied by the fact that the modification itself is a bargain and one regularly made as a matter of business practice; indeed, while not requiring consideration, the Comments to Section 89(a) are themselves rationalized within the parameters and logic of the bargain construct.[89] Furthermore, the protective function of consideration safeguarding against coercion can be fulfilled by the now developed common law doctrines of good faith, unconscionability and economic duress.[90]

The evidentiary and cautionary functions performed by the reliance element[91] are also often present in a modified relationship made on account of unanticipated circumstances, whether the modification is justified on the basis of consideration, the unanticipated circumstances exception, estoppel or some other theory. The early consideration-based rationales often allude to how reliance by the promisee contributed to the finding of detriment consideration[92] for the modification promise in much the same way that later courts were comfortable with invoking the maturing ground of promissory estoppel.[93] In fact, very few of these modification agreements stimulated by changed circumstances enter the courts until after the promisee has relied on the promise of extra compensation by resuming performance under the more burdensome conditions.[94] *Watkins v. Carrig*, which is neither an estoppel nor a consideration-based decision, exemplified the relevance of the reliance factor when the New Hampshire court emphasized: "The plaintiff on the strength of the promise proceeded with the work."[95]

Elements of Unanticipated Circumstances Exception

In order for a promise modifying an original contract obligation to be binding under Restatement Second Section 89(a), it must: one, relate to "a contract not fully performed on either side;" two, be precipitated by "circumstances not anticipated by the parties;" and, three, be "fair and equitable."

Executory Contract

Why must the original contract be at least partially executory at the time of the modification? Some earlier cases say that a wholly executory contract may be rescinded but an executed one may not be; these are typically rescission cases[96] focusing on whether or not consideration has passed. But then Section 89(a) does not require consideration. It's true that often little harm is done when there is a modification, or even a breach, of a wholly executory contract, since there has been no reliance or unjust enrichment.[97] Section 89 allows a modification as long as "not fully performed on either side,"[98] which opens up the possibility of a binding modification on a contract that has been partially performed and thus could involve potential reliance or unjust enrichment. As a practical matter, however, this reform would have little meaning if it only covered purely executory contracts because unanticipated circumstances are typically not discovered until performance has commenced, as in the common example of granite discovered during construction excavations. If Section 89 is going to permit a modification of a partially executed contract, then why not permit modification when it has been fully performed on one side or the other? U.C.C. Section 2–209 does not impose any restriction on the degree of performance when a modification without consideration is binding. The chance of extortion should usually no longer be much of a concern once the work is done, but it is something to weigh when a partial performer refuses to proceed unless he's paid more.[99] If a modification is freely consented-to after a party has fully performed, why not enforce it if the promisor finds a benefit or in fairness consents to higher recompense because of the unforeseen difficulties overcome? The mixing of notions appropriate to consideration[100] with a principle not requiring consideration needlessly defeats consent.

Circumstances Qualifying for Exception

Start, C. J. stated, in the influential Minnesota case *King v. Duluth Ry. Co.* (1895), that a modification agreement was binding when made on account of "unforeseen and substantial difficulties in the performance of the contract."[101] The consensual theory–influenced requirement that the circumstances be unforeseen by the parties, and hence should not be considered a part of the original bargain, was discussed earlier under the origins of this exception and will not be repeated here. The focus here will be on the circumstances qualifying for what Start, C. J. characterized as "substantial difficulties." Comment (c) to Restatement Second Section 73 stated that "slight variations of circumstances" take the case out of the preexisting duty rule; however, that comment must be read guardedly since it was a part of the drafters' agonized justification for retaining the preexisting duty rule. The caselaw does not support a slight variation providing a good reason for a modification.

Start elaborated on what "substantial difficulties" meant: "[t]hey are sufficient if of such a character as to render party's demand for extra pay manifestly fair, so as to rebut all inferences that he is seeking to be relieved from an unsatisfactory contract" or is guilty of coercion.[102] Start continued: "Inadequacy of the contract price which is the result of an error of judgement, and not some excusable mistake of fact, is not sufficient."[103] So the mere fact of losing money on a contract is not enough.[104] Courts try to ferret out feigned substantial difficulties manipulated to exact a concession because of the concern over coercion. In *Rexite Casting Co. v. Midwest Mower Corp.* (1954),[105] it was relevant to the Missouri court in ruling the modification unenforceable that the manufacturer's refusal to sell except at a higher price was based on an apparently false assertion that raw metal costs had substantially increased.[106] Here bad faith and insubstantiality converged.

Although the unanticipated circumstance must be substantial, it need not be so great as to qualify for an excuse discharge based on impossibility, frustration, impracticability or mistake. The first Restatement required facts sufficient for excuse before a modification was binding,[107] although there was caselaw by that time saying lesser circumstances would suffice.[108] In *King v. Duluth Ry. Co.*, it needed to be enough to be "manifestly fair" so as to rebut coercion.[109] In *Watkins v. Carrig* (1941), it could be short of excuse, so long as the promisor consented, since he found value in avoiding delay.[110] In an 1895 bona fide dispute generated by unanticipated circumstances, the court said the facts need not show an impossibility excuse but only enough to show a dispute.[111] Comment 2 to U.C.C. Section 2–209 states that a legitimate commercial reason for modification may include a market shift short of excuse. And Comment (b) to Section 89 suggests that more foresight by a party of a potential frustrating event may be permitted for a modification than would be allowed for an excuse.[112] Because a modification, unlike an excuse discharge, includes consent and a continuation of the relationship, the degree and foresight of an unanticipated circumstance should logically be permitted to be less, so long as it is fair, in order to realize the contractors' attempt to update their agreement.

Fair and Equitable Modification

An inquiry into whether a modification is "fair and equitable in view of the circumstances not anticipated"[113] scrutinizes the motivation for, and the process of, negotiating and forming the modified agreement. In the early New York case *Meech v. City of Buffalo* (1864), the concurring judicial opinion approved of the modification because its purpose was to create "a new agreement on a more just and equitable basis."[114] In *Linz v. Schuck* (1907), the Maryland court said the refusal to perform under the original contract, unless the price was increased, must be "equitable and fair"[115] in light of the unanticipated circumstances. The unanticipated circumstances help rebut suspicion of abuse and suggest a good motive for seeking the modification.[116] Since being fair and equitable is a higher standard than the arms' length negotiation of the original contract, it is relevant and permissible to determine whether a party in a stronger financial or market position than the other abused that advantage to pressure an unfair modification.[117]

The modification is equitable if the unanticipated circumstances evidence an absence of coercion[118] or of a bad faith attempt to escape the original performance obligation. Fairness means that maneuvering for a modification without being guilty of coercion may not qualify as fair since, as the court declared in *Watkins v. Carrig* (1941), the basis for a modification needs "to meet the reasonable needs and ethical practices of men in their business dealings with each other."[119] Comment (b) to Section 89 states that the standard "requires an objectively demonstrable reason for seeking the modification," which could include a good commercial reason or that it be consistent with fair dealing; however, for contracts not between merchants, general contract law does not have the benefit of the tightly developed principles and usages available as safeguards in commercial sales law.[120] Moreover, the narrowness of the unanticipated circumstances exception does not encompass all possible modifications that can be shown to be fair and made for a good reason.

Chapter 6

Remaining Vitality of Outdated Rule

The capacity of the preexisting duty rule to survive the onslaught of criticism and reform attempts over the past century is perhaps only surpassed by the impregnability of the underlying doctrine of consideration mandated for formation of the original contract. In this final chapter on the preexisting duty rule, there will be an overview analysis of the extent to which the reforms have failed to defeat the old rule and a discussion of ways to cure the rule's remaining deficiencies. The discussion is divided into three parts: a comparison of when a modification is enforceable under the U.C.C. and Restatement Second, when the rule still applies today, and possible common law solutions.

COMPARISON OF U.C.C. AND RESTATEMENT SECOND POSITIONS

The Code and Restatement positions on the binding nature of contract modifications differ in two fundamental respects: one, the Code does not require consideration, and two, the good reasons the Code recognizes for the parties seeking a modification are not limited to cases of reliance or unanticipated circumstances. The Code's rejection of the preexisting duty rule and subsequent caselaw did, however, influence the drafters of the Restatement Second to recognize exceptional relief, without the requirement of consideration, for cases of reliance and unanticipated circumstances.

As to unanticipated circumstances, the black letter text of Restatement Second Section 89(a) states the modification must be "fair and equitable," and its Comment (b) "requires an objectively demonstrable reason for seeking a modification." The text of U.C.C. Section 2–209 makes no reference to good faith, though its Comment 2 states that there is a good faith requirement to give a "legitimate commercial reason" and further that between merchants, the observance of fair dealing in the trade is needed, which "may" require giving "an objectively demonstrable reason for seeking a modification." Unanticipated circumstances would be a good reason, but any other legitimate commercial reason could also be a basis for a modification under the Code. Under Section 89(a), the judicial analysis invariably includes a focus on the affirmative duty of the plaintiff to establish that the modification was fair and equitable.[1] However, under Section 2–209, unless the issue of bad faith is raised, it is not uncommon for the court to make no reference to good faith,[2] even though the facts in some of these cases don't particularly appear to suggest a very good motive for seeking the modification.[3]

Sales law has an advantage here over contract law generally because of two centuries of development of a tight body of legal doctrine, bolstered by the regularity of trade usage which includes the self policing mechanism of fair dealing in the trade.[4] Good faith and mercantile fair dealing, along with the economic duress and unconscionability doctrines, provided control mechanisms to supplant the protective functions formerly performed by consideration.[5] Given that there is no such developed standard of fair dealing for the sprawling field of general contract law, courts and, as a consequence, restaters have been more reticent to abandon the preexisting duty rule.

In attempting to decipher how far the common law, as reflected in the Restatement Second, has come in finding modifications binding, an analysis will now be made applying the Restatement's rules to six selected cases covered earlier, five being well known English preexisting duty rule cases and the sixth being a modern American case. Four famous traditional English cases have been selected: *Pinnel's Case* (1602),[6] *Stilk v. Myrick* (1809),[7] *Foakes v. Beer* (1884)[8] and *Central London Property Trust v. High Trees House Ltd.* (1947).[9] The two more recent cases selected, one American and the latter English, are *Farmland Services Coop v. Jack* (1976),[10] a Nebraska decision which involved a modification made because a farmer changed his mind about his sales agreement with a grain elevator company after the market price had increased, and *Williams v. Roffey* (1990),[11] which involved a promise to increase the payment because a construction sub-contractor found himself in a losing project that he was reluctant to complete. Under the American common law, as reflected in Sections 73 and 89 of the Restatement Second, only the modification in the *High Trees* case would be binding both because the rent reduction modification was relied on and because the rent reduction was precipitated by the unanticipated circumstance of World War II. The modification in *Stilk v. Myrick* would probably not be enforceable, even if the desertions of two of the ship's crew was found to be unanticipated, because of the coercive bad faith of the remaining seamen in taking advantage of the ship captain's vulnerable position. The modifications in the remaining four cases would not be enforceable because there was neither reliance nor a qualifying unanticipated circumstance.

Applying U.C.C. Section 2–209 to the six above selected cases, only the modification in *Farmland Services Coop v. Jack* would be binding because only that one involves a sale of goods; and, whether or not the farmer seemed to have a legitimate commercial reason, the court in fact upheld the modification. Were it not for the sale of goods factor, all of the modifications would be enforced under the Code's approach, except for probably the arguably bad faith modification in *Stilk v. Myrick.* This little exercise exhibits how far the common law still is today from broadly enforcing voluntary consensual modifications. Until non-sales modifications receive a treatment similar to sales, many modifications will continue to be found wanting in the courts.

One way for the common law of contract to come in line with the Code would be for courts to use the common law reform technique of drawing an analogy to U.C.C. Section 2–209(1) as a vehicle for rationalizing abandonment of the preexisting duty rule. In fact, starting in the 1950s, many changes in principles from the first to the second Restatement reflected intervening judicial reform based on analogies to Code reforms.[12] However, in order for a court to adopt the principle in Section 2–209(1), it must reject the sacred liability test of consideration for contract modifications, something only one common law court has ever had the courage to do over the past half millennium.[13] Take the service contract modification case *Angel v. Murray* (1974)[14] as an example of judicial reluctance to deviate from consideration-based precedent. The Rhode Island court approvingly made reference to the binding nature of contract modifications generally under Section 2–209(1), but, in the end, the court did not leave consideration's domain, nor has that jurisdiction done so since. Instead the court in *Angel v. Murray* relied on a tentative draft of the Restatement Second to rationalize its holding under the unanticipated circumstances exception to the requirement of consideration. With the exception of promissory estoppel, U.C.C. Section 2–209(1) is perhaps the boldest nationwide rejection of consideration.

WHEN PREEXISTING DUTY RULE APPLIES TODAY

Despite all the judicial and legislative reforms, the preexisting duty rule can still present a formidable barrier for a party trying to enforce a non-coerced modification if it fails to fall under a statutory or common law reform. There is a significant array of exceptions and reforms, it's true, but one doesn't have to search hard in the reporter systems to find modern courts refusing to enforce modifications as courts pay obeisance to the preexisting duty rule, as the sample of cases in the following endnote reflects.[15] The Restatement Second's doctrinal clarification of the rule has actually broadened the rule's applicability in at least one jurisdiction.[16]

Briefly, when does the preexisting duty rule apply today? A reply to this question entails an overview summary of the gaps left by the reform attempts. In order to answer the question, the response has to be divided into contract subject matter and the exceptions to the rule. As to subject matter, non-sales transactions are still generally subject to the rule. When one contemplates the burgeoning service sector of the economy, it represents an enormous volume and range of contracts, but it's more than just services. It encompasses contracts for transfers of interests in real property, security interests, licenses, franchises, transfers of intellectual property, royalties, sales of securities and the residual black hole of general contract subject matter.

A contract fitting within one of the above types of non-sales contracts is not, however, subject to the preexisting duty rule if it falls under one of the statutory or common law exceptions to the rule. Seven general categories of exceptions come to mind. One, there are a myriad of traditional exceptions to the rule, as discussed above, like a novelty or a bona fide dispute. Two, fictions, like rescission and importing consideration facilitate enforcement of voluntary modifications, but also run the risk of enforcing coerced ones. Three, four or five state supreme courts have largely abolished the common law rule for all types of contracts, though in all but one jurisdiction, consideration must still be rationalized present. Four, some state legislatures have tried to abolish the rule for all types of contracts, but one must read the wrinkles in a particular statute carefully since, for example, it may apply to decreases in obligations but not to increases and it may cover duties to pay money but not other types of obligations. Five, some state legislatures have provided that the preexisting duty rule does not apply if the modification agreement is in writing. These requirements of formality provide no solace for one claiming under the typical modification made in the form of an oral assurance given to induce a disheartened performer in a losing contract, e.g., "I'll make sure you don't lose if you finish the work" or "Keep on with the work and I'll cover for your extra time and materials." These special state statutes notwithstanding, the Statute of Frauds will usually require a written modification if the original contract must comply with the Statute. Also, U.C.C. Section 2–209(2) allows the parties to exclude oral modifications in the original contract. Six, courts will enforce a modification if there has been detrimental reliance on the modified promise. Even if the reliance facts do not qualify for promissory estoppel, they may help establish equitable estoppel or that the reliance facts are an indicator of detriment consideration. And, seven, if the modification was made on account of circumstances not anticipated by the parties when the contract was made, a growing number of courts will enforce the modification without demanding consideration.

All of these exceptions to the preexisting duty rule may cause one to think that the rule has been excepted to death, but the caselaw reports indicate to the contrary. The sheer volume of modifications necessitated by a rapidly changing economy makes it one of the most frequently litigated consideration-related issues reaching the appellate courts. The result of the continuation of the preexisting duty rule is that many non-coerced modification agreements still fall through the cracks and are found unenforceable; and, even when a court finds that a modification fits under an exception, the process of proving it causes delay, cost and inefficiency.

POSSIBLE COMMON LAW SOLUTIONS

Consent and Fairness

The comments to Restatement Second Sections 73 and 89 justify the judicial retention of the preexisting duty rule on the basis of the "suspicion" a modification was mistaken, coerced or unconscionable, and the Comments to Section 89 acknowledge the criticism of the rule when one of these invalidating causes is absent.[17] The obvious rejoinder is that therefore the bar should be limited to those types of misbehavior so the voluntary modified consent of the parties can be enforced in all other cases. This is the approach employed in civil law countries[18] and under U.C.C. Section 2–209(1). The resistance to reform cannot be because of the absence of adequate policing mechanisms against abuse since, unlike the time of *Pinnel's Case* (1602), there exist the developed doctrines of economic duress, unconscionability and good faith. The approach of a strong majority of courts and the Restatement Second may stop overreaching but it does not separate coercion and greed from legitimate reasons for the parties adjusting their relationship.

The preexisting duty rule promotes inefficiency in refusing the parties the freedom to modify their agreement pursuant to the perceived economic needs of the present situation. No one should be forced to change his or her agreement, but once the parties voluntarily agree to a change without protest, reasonable expectations should be realized. In a commercial context, once a voluntary promise is proven, accepted business practice and fairness suggest one should cooperate and conform to the adjusted agreement.[19]

The preexisting duty rule tends to be unfair to some economic underdogs, who would benefit from the enforcement of a modification. For the inexperienced small contractor or tradesman, a low bid may be made because of a lack of appreciation of the magnitude or intricacies of the job; without an adjustment, the contractor will be either unfairly under-compensated or will be forced to breach. The preexisting duty rule can actually aggravate the naive contractor's losses because, rather than cutting his losses by breaching, he or she may be induced by a promise of more compensation to pour more time and material into a losing project, thereby generating an ever increasing loss if the terms of the original contract are enforceable under the preexisting duty rule.[20] The doctrine of consideration can act as a guard against improvidence at the original contract's creation, but the requirement of consideration for a modification can cause harm here. That is not to say that it is invariably the weak who are urging enforcement of modifications in the face of the rule, but those parties with legal representation and bargaining leverage are less likely to need a modification[21] and are more likely to be able to structure the adjustment of the contractual relationship in a way that avoids the bite of the rule, as by incorporating some extra duty in the modification to establish fresh consideration and by assuring that it doesn't violate the Statute of Frauds or any other writing requirement.[22]

The writing provisions in U.C.C. Section 2–209(2) may likewise work against an underdog in allowing the original written contract to bar an informal modification.[23] It may cause harm to the weak in much the same way that strict enforcement of the parol evidence rule can work against the underdog.[24] It is commonplace for signatures and initials to be scribbled on various parts of a standardized contract without a consumer being cognizant that it would bar a later informal modification.[25] A consumer or small business could later, during the performance phase of a contract, be informally induced by a proffered lowered obligation or increased payments to commit scarce resources, which could better be applied elsewhere,[26] and then subsequently the underdog would discover that he or she has nothing in the end since the informal modification is unenforceable.

Reform with or without Consideration

The obvious choice in devising a common law rule that renders modifications generally binding is either to develop a general theory rationalizing consideration present or to declare modifications enforceable without consideration. The U.C.C. has taken the latter route for sales contracts, but, unfortunately, there is no uniform statute for general contract law to amend. The most recent restatement rejected the Code's example of changing the law; only in a few instances, like Section 90, have contract restaters engaged in law reform.[27] Since courts have proved reticent, for over 400 years, to jettison the doctrinally flawed preexisting duty rule corollary to the doctrine of consideration, courts should at least consider more flexible interpretations within the consideration construct in a way that would make modifications binding generally, and leave the policing of coerced or predatory modifications to economic duress, unconscionability and good faith. Some American courts accomplished it earlier in the century by finding in a modification a detriment or a benefit,[28] and the English courts have edged in that direction as of late.[29] Exchange values should be left to the parties' bargained-for adjustments; what was valuable to them at one time may change, and they should be free to make that later assessment.[30]

Minnesota is the only subscriber to the alternative common law solution of completely rejecting the "overworked shibboleth" of consideration for modifications in favor of a "logical and just standard of actionability."[31] The modification bargain satisfies cautionary[32] and channeling form functions, and so rather than dwelling on the ancient mysteries of consideration, the Minnesota courts focus on whether there was voluntary consent. Experience over the past half century has witnessed no hue and cry over the coerced or bad faith modifications fomented under either Minnesota law or the U.C.C.[33] Continental civil law has managed for centuries to control abuses while enforcing contract modifications and discharges on the basis of agreement alone.

Common law contract possesses the tools to police modifications, if modifications were generally recognized to be binding either without the need for consideration or under a flexible application of consideration. Economic duress and unconscionability are both developed common law doctrines. Good faith is required in the performance and enforcement of all contracts and is enthroned in the Restatement Second[34] and could naturally be extended to modifications, as it has been under the U.C.C. 2–209. Methodology for analyzing the motivation for and negotiation of modifications can be drawn from common law trends requiring good faith bargaining[35] and from analogous caselaw requiring a good reason for a modification under U.C.C. Section 2–209(1) and Restatement Second Section 89(a). Thus, the notion of reason or *causa* for a promise, which is bundled up in the meaning of consideration,[36] would still need to be established by the proponent of a modification.

Contextual Needs

Whether the shortcomings of the preexisting duty rule are overcome by rationalizing the presence of consideration to support most modifications or by dropping the consideration requirement, a flexible manner of accommodating the unavoidable adjustments to modern contracts is needed. This necessity is spurred by dramatic market fluctuations and by a degree of uncertainty unparalleled during the preindustrial times of *Pinnel's Case.* This urgency for flexible contract adjustments has been accentuated by a tendency toward longer term and more complex contractual relations undertaken by corporations with perpetual life.[37] Contract doctrine must be malleable enough to permit an integration of unforeseen events and behavior as the future unfolds.

Unlike the non–common law legal systems of many competing national economies, the doctrine of consideration thwarts the realization of contractors' amended consent necessitated by fluctuating economic circumstances. European civil law does not require consideration and does not have an impediment to enforcement of modification agreements like the preexisting duty rule. Since Japanese law is based on the German civil code, it likewise does not have a preexisting duty rule; moreover, Japanese commercial practice favors informal negotiated settlements of contract modifications and disputes and, failing that, prefers mediation and arbitration over actions in the courts.[38] The United Nations Convention on International Sales of Goods also allows consensual modifications of international sales contracts without the need for consideration.[39] The commercial law governing our major trading partners, outside the common law, facilitates realization of necessary adjustments and is better suited to efficiently accommodate the dynamics of the modern marketplace.

CONCLUSION: REFORM OF PREEXISTING DUTY RULE

The application of Coke's dictum in *Pinnel's Case* (1602) to assumpsit actions was doctrinally flawed from inception in requiring consideration, a doctrine developed to determine whether an original contract had been formed, to also act as the test to determine whether a contract modification or discharge was binding. Since consideration became inextricably linked with the meaning of assumpsit in the sixteenth century, it was perhaps understandable that during the generations immediately following the emergence of consideration as the test for actionability of the new contractual action of assumpsit that consideration would be required when assumpsit was brought to enforce a contract modification. Despite the preexisting duty rule's doctrinal shortcomings, it would remain largely intact until the twentieth century.

The interest in the consensual theory starting by the early nineteenth century eventually stimulated the criticism that the rule in *Pinnel's Case* thwarted parties' free consent to alter their agreements as they saw fit. As the nineteenth century wore on, this consent-based critique was bolstered by equitable arguments raised in now-fused courts of law and equity regarding the unfairness of precluding realization of adjusted expectations founded on legitimate motivations. These arguments, and the end of the ancient forms of action, forced courts to dwell on the reasons for the old precedent. From the perspective of the meaning of consideration, the accepted rejoinder to a proposed contract modification was that it held no value for the promisor who was now opposed to its enforcement. This argument came very close to engaging in an analysis of the adequacy of the consideration to be found in the modification rather than leaving value to the contractors' adjusted appetites, as expressed in their consent. If the explanations afforded by the mysteries of the doctrine of consideration seemed unconvincing to modern skeptics, there remained the defense that the old rule barred coerced modifications. But if barring coercion was the reason for requiring consideration, then shouldn't the bar be adjusted to analyze whether abusive behavior in fact occurred, and then in fairness shouldn't the remaining voluntary modifications be enforced in fulfillment of the legitimate expectations raised by the parties' voluntary modified consent?

The pressure for abandonment of the preexisting duty rule intensified during the early stages of the industrial revolution as uncertainty increased in the context of longer term complex contracts set in more volatile markets. Contractors needed the capacity to efficiently adapt as the future unfolded, but the traditional rule, which developed in a static economy, failed to respond to the reality of the tumult of the modern age. Starting in the last quarter of the nineteenth century, a handful of state courts and legislatures reformed the preexisting duty rule to accommodate reasonable contractual modifications. In those jurisdictions removing the consideration bar, the substitute policing mechanisms of economic duress, unconscionability and good faith were contemporaneously emerging to protect against coercive modifications. The development of these safeguards made it easier for these and subsequent jurisdictions to rationalize removing, or at least reforming, the consideration barrier to contract modifications.

Nevertheless, despite the emergence of reforms in a minority of jurisdictions by the late nineteenth century and the widespread criticisms based on doctrinal, equitable and commercial reasons, judicial insecurity over tinkering with the core contract test of the doctrine of consideration rendered a majority of courts impotent to act boldly. Instead, the *Foakes v. Beer* (1884) decision in England and the American Uniform Sales Act of 1906 reaffirmed Coke's dictum under a now consolidated preexisting duty rule encompassing attempted modifications to increase or decrease promissory obligations to pay money or to perform services. Fused courts of law and equity did, however, develop equitable exceptions to ameliorate the unfairness of the rule for instances of reliance or unanticipated circumstances; the hardship context of these new exceptions lessened concern about coerced modifications.

The cataclysmic economic events of the 1930s revived demands for efficient legal means of realizing contractors' joint desire to adjust their agreement as new circumstances arose. Due to the continuing inability of judges to reform the consideration-based preexisting duty rule, legislatures renewed their attempts to reform the rule. A smattering of state statutory reforms followed and culminated in the Uniform Commercial Code abolishing the preexisting duty rule for good faith modifications of contracts for sales of goods. Subsequent experience has shown that abuse of the statutory right to freely modify contracts has not erupted, because of the safeguards provided by workable modern policing mechanisms.

These scattered reforms have failed, however, to suffocate the indomitable preexisting duty rule. Voluntary modification agreements still frequently fail because of gaps left in the partial reforms of the preexisting duty rule. The exceptions to the rule may have increased, but the instances where contract modifications are needed in a shifting modern economy have also increased. Since no uniform statutory vehicle exists for the complete abolition of the rule for the common law of contract generally, scattered reform will continue to appear sporadically, but a national overruling of the preexisting duty rule will not happen unless a judicial ground swell develops, perhaps encouraged by a restatement of the law declaring either that a good faith modification agreement does not require consideration or that a bargained-for benefit or detriment can be found in a good faith modification.

Part II

Past Consideration Rule and Moral Obligation Principle

Chapter 7

Origins of Past Consideration Rule and of Moral Obligation Principle

Just as courts have long struggled with permitting enforcement of contract modifications, the question of enforcement of a promise grounded on a past moral obligation has confounded common law courts for centuries. Although no legal system enforces all promises, much less a moral obligation in the absence of a promise, some voluntary promises grounded on moral obligations have long been enforced in civilian jurisdictions and in chancery. For example, if a plaintiff provided unrequested aid to a creditor in successfully collecting a debt and the creditor later promised to pay the plaintiff for his beneficial efforts, should that promise be binding? The equitable view that in fairness one ought to honor promises to make restitution stimulated a few common law judges to grant occasional relief. Mansfield articulated support for moral obligation even beyond such restitutionary promises.

As long as common law and equity courts were separated, common law judges usually emphasized the predictable market test requiring a bargain and left exceptional relief to equity; but, once law and equity were fused, American courts tried to reconcile these opposing viewpoints. In attempting to realize parties' consent and achieve a fair result in cases where restitutionary promises were made, some nineteenth century American judges began to question whether the bargain paradigm should be the sole test for determining contractual liability in such cases. Certain American courts began to take up this challenge, but in designing a limited moral obligation principle, American courts found it necessary to narrow the scope of Mansfield's sweeping remarks.

Part II of this book provides a historical analysis of the logic employed by common law lawyers and judges in connection with: one, the emergence of early moral obligation exceptions to the past consideration rule;

two, the conservative reaction to Mansfield's moral obligation ideas; and three, American adaptations of Mansfield's ideas, and of ideas found outside the common law, in creating the modern American moral obligation principle.

ORIGINS OF PAST CONSIDERATION RULE: *HUNT v. BATE*

Even before the doctrine of consideration appeared, the action of debt was unavailable for a past benefit that a plaintiff provided to a defendant.[1] Rejection of recovery on a past benefit surfaced in a 1490 action on the case for deceit where a plaintiff was barred from recovering on breach of a warranty because the warranty was not bargained for but was given after the sale.[2] Then in the harsh, precedent-setting 1568 assumpsit action *Hunt v. Bate,*[3] the plaintiff paid the bail for the defendant's imprisoned servant "in consideration that the master's business should not go undone." The defendant later promised "upon the said friendly consideration" that he would reimburse the plaintiff, his friend. The plaintiff brought an assumpsit action for failure to pay, but the court held for the defendant because "the master never requested the plaintiff to do it, on behalf of his servant, but he did it of his own head."[4] It seemed a meritorious cause of action in that the master obtained the benefit of the availability of his servant and the master acknowledged the benefit by promising to pay. It appeared a logical case for assumpsit to perform its early interstitial role of providing justice when a traditional writ like debt was unavailable,[5] but the continuing nature of the friendship in *Hunt v. Bate,* which existed prior to the promise, made it a past consideration. Indeed, insufficiency of love and affection was a source of the past consideration rule.[6]

More generally, the rule that consideration must move from the plaintiff in reliance on the defendant's request in all assumpsit actions follows from the past consideration rule. Concomitantly, this request and reliance paradigm presented a challenge for sixteenth century plaintiffs, who were trying to take advantage of preferred procedures in assumpsit including its enforcement procedures and trial by jury, by alleging a fictional subsequent promise in order to create the impression that it did not overlap the jurisdiction of the entrenched action of debt. The alleged subsequent promise made the consideration past, but this objection was overcome by the *indebitatus assumpsit* pleading form[7] which alleged the sale was at the previous request of the defendant.[8] After *Slade's Case* (1602)[9] defeated the objection that assumpsit overlapped debt, the allegation of the subsequent promise was no longer necessary. It also meant that the need no longer existed to establish the linkage that consideration provided between the promise and the prior debt. The consideration test might then have been replaced[10] by a more flexible one like the notion of *causa* used in equity[11] or perhaps, as Mansfield later tried, by moral obligation.[12]

Slade's Case notwithstanding, plaintiffs' lawyers continued employing the *indebitatus assumpsit* pleading formula during the seventeenth century because of the generalized pleading advantages provided by this form; this form of pleading would evolve into the common counts. As a consequence of the continuation of *indebitatus assumpsit,* two lingering past consideration issues were resolved during the second decade of the seventeenth century. One involved the *indebitatus assumpsit* formula itself and the other concerned the difference between past and executed consideration. First, didn't the subsequent promise in the *indebitatus assumpsit* formula make the consideration past,[13] just as it had in *Hunt v. Bate* (1568),[14] when the defendant promised to pay after his servant was bailed out? The issue was raised in *Hodge v. Vavisour* (1617),[15] but it was overruled because the debt "always continues." It was a quibble employed to distinguish a case of true past consideration on its facts, like *Hunt v. Bate,* from the artifice of *indebitatus assumpsit's* fictional subsequent promise.[16] However, the court was unwilling to set the clock back at this late date by entertaining the defendant's argument that the "promise is grounded upon a consideration that is past, and so not good to raise a promise. And here he may have debt for his goods."[17]

The second past consideration issue concerned whether the prohibition on past consideration also precluded executed consideration. *Lampleigh v. Braithwait* (1616)[18] settled the law for good by making a distinction between past and executed consideration. In *Lampleigh,* the defendant, a felon, requested the plaintiff to obtain a pardon from the King. After the plaintiff exerted himself diligently, though to no avail, the defendant promised him 100 pounds. The plaintiff later sued the defendant, who pleaded *non assumpsit;* the court held for the plaintiff because the plaintiff's act was preceded by a request from the defendant, unlike in *Hunt v. Bate* (1568),[19] and because it was based on a business transaction rather than merely on friendship. The court stated: "the execution of the act must pursue the request, for it is like a case of a commission for this purpose."[20] The defendant's request, the plaintiff's act and the defendant's subsequent promise of payment might be described as elements of a single transaction.

EMERGENCE OF MORAL OBLIGATION PRINCIPLE

Holt's Exceptions: Waiver and Ratification

In the latter part of the seventeenth century, Holt, C. J.[21] made adjustments to the past consideration rule in cases involving the special defenses of infancy and statute of limitations. In *Ball v. Hesketh* (1697),[22] Holt held: "Ruled, that where the defendant under age borrowed money of the plaintiff, and afterwards at full age promised to pay it him, this is a good consideration for the promise, and the defendant shall be charged." An infant's promise had formerly been deemed void,[23] but Holt made it voidable in order to enforce an adult ratification supported by the past consideration of the loan. Holt did not look kindly upon such a special defense when there was a prior benefit and an unquestioned ratification in adulthood. Then *Ball v. Hesketh* was cited in *Heyling v. Hastings* (1699),[24] wherein Holt said the debtor's promise to pay, after a statute of limitations had run, was "in consideration that" the sale had occurred and thus "waived the benefit of the statute" and thereby revived the original debt. (This special statutory defense, enacted earlier in the century, had not existed during the early history of assumpsit and consideration.) Holt's exception now generated anomalous results: if a promise were made to pay half of a debt after a statute of limitations had run, it would be binding, but a promise to pay half before a statute had run would still be barred under the preexisting duty rule of Part I herein. In comparing Holt's exceptions to the past consideration rule for adult ratification with statute of limitations waiver, the ratification precedent went further because the infant's debt was at no time enforceable prior to the ratification.

This stretched invocation of consideration verbiage in both *Ball v. Hesketh* and *Heyling v. Hastings* constituted unadmitted exceptions to the prohibition on past consideration, since the debtor received no fresh benefit in exchange for his promise to pay for the otherwise unenforceable prior obligation. The strained consideration logic could not mask the reality that the subsequent promise to pay for a past benefit received was only supported by a felt moral obligation to pay for the benefit received. Holt's moral obligation exceptions to the past consideration bar would later be invoked by Mansfield in support of his bold assault on the doctrine of consideration.[25]

Mansfield's Moral Obligation Ideas

King's Bench Chief Justice Mansfield, a civilian at heart,[26] attempted a dramatic civilian-style reform of common law contract based on the principles of logic and equity. Since he perceived consideration as an irrational impediment to the enforcement of serious promises, which in justice should be binding, he made a frontal assault on the doctrine. He conducted a three-pronged attack, arguing, first, that commercial promises did not need consideration; second, that written contracts generally did not need consideration; and third, that a moral obligation alone could fulfill, if not supplant, the traditional requirement of consideration.

All three of these notions are found in Mansfield's reasoning in *Pillans v. Van Mierop* (1765),[27] his best known and most aggressive foray against the doctrine of consideration. In *Pillans*, a past consideration objection was raised in an action brought on a commercial undertaking to honor a bill of exchange.[28] Instead of trying to rationalize a narrow extension of

Holt's precedents, Mansfield boldly declared that, past consideration or not, the usage of merchants did not require consideration for a binding contract and further, that consideration was not required in an unsealed written contract since the passage of the Statute of Frauds (1677).[29] The civilian Mansfield was impliedly saying that once the defendant's promise was established, the defendant was under an enforceable obligation because of his consent to either perform or pay breach damages. Mansfield's decision in *Pillans v. Van Mierop* was followed in his court over the ensuing thirteen years[30] until his reform ideas were flatly rejected by the House of Lords in *Rann v. Hughes* (1778),[31] an action on an administrator's individual promise to pay an heir his legacy. Lord Skynner proclaimed *Pillans v. Van Mierop* bad law because all unsealed contracts must be supported by consideration under the common law.[32] The core contract doctrine of consideration, by then in place for over two centuries, would not fall so easily.[33]

Mansfield's most direct extensions of Holt's moral obligation precedents came in a couple of decisions rendered in the mid-1770s. The one staying closest to Holt was *Trueman v. Fenton* (1777).[34] This debtor's waiver of bankruptcy case was an obvious descendant of Holt's waiver of a statute of limitations decision, and Mansfield cited *Heyling v. Hastings*[35] as precedent. In ruling for the creditor, Mansfield cited chancery precedents, stating: "all the debts of a bankrupt are due on conscience, notwithstanding he has obtained his certificate; and there is no honest man who does not discharge them, if afterwards he has it in his power to do so."[36] The second case, which did not roam very far from Holt, was *Goodright ex dim. Elizabeth Carter v. Straphan* (1774).[37] A widow promised to honor her earlier mortgage obligation; the prior obligation was unenforceable because she made the mortgage while contractually incapacitated as a married woman. In an extension of Holt's enforcement of an adult ratification of a debt made during infancy,[38] Mansfield held the widow's subsequent promise binding because "in conscience she has confirmed this security."[39] It was an extension of Holt's precedent for ratification of a voidable obligation in that a married woman's obligations had been reaffirmed as void in 1719.[40]

Mansfield's willingness to cite chancery practices was out of step with common law tradition. He developed a strain of moral obligation decisions, which utilized ideas from chancery, and went beyond the scope of Holt's precedents. He instigated this line of reasoning in *Atkins v. Hill* (1775).[41] Again, it as a case of an executor's duty to pay a legacy, the executor "in consideration thereof" individually promised to pay the heirs their legacies. Mansfield said the promise to pay for the past obligation[42] is: "made upon a good and valuable consideration. . . . It is so in cases of obligation which, without such promise, he could not be compelled to pay."[43] He then cited the examples of an adult ratifying a contract made during his minority, but the enforcement of the executor's moral obligation to pay the legacy was an extension of the infancy precedent (and also of the waiver precedents) because the executor wasn't committing himself to satisfy a moral obligation by promising to pay for a benefit received pursuant to an earlier agreement.[44] It was an extension of the waiver cases in another respect because this estate duty did not involve a debt once due at common law but later barred by a positive law like a statute of limitations or of bankruptcy.

Subsequent to his setback in *Rann v. Hughes* (1778), Mansfield pursued the moral obligation logic of *Atkins v. Hill* (1775) in *Hawkes v. Saunders* (1782),[45] again a case of an executrix individually promising to pay a legacy. Mansfield distinguished *Rann v. Hughes* because *Hawkes v. Saunders* had not included an averment of the existence of estate assets to pay the legacy. Following a more conservative approach, he did not raise the usage of merchants or the written contract arguments. His position in *Hawkes v. Saunders* was less radical than in *Pillans v. Van Mierop*, since he didn't deny the need for a contract to have consideration. Rather, he said a moral obligation constituted good consideration, something not at issue in *Pillans* and *Rann*. He declared that the rule of law as to whether there is a "good consideration in law goes upon a very narrow ground indeed; namely, that to make a consideration to support an assumpsit, there must be either an immediate benefit to the party promising, or a loss to the person to whom the promise was made. I cannot agree to that being the only ground of consideration sufficient to raise an assumpsit."[46] He gave examples of promises grounded on past consideration in Holt's infancy and statute of limitations precedents and in his own bankruptcy waiver precedent and said: "An equitable duty is a sufficient consideration for an actual promise. Where a man is under a moral obligation, which no Court of Law or Equity can enforce, and promises, the honesty and rectitude of the thing is a consideration."[47] Furthermore, he declared: "as the promise is only to do what an honest man ought to do, the ties of conscience upon an upright mind are a sufficient consideration."[48] The potential range of instances of moral obligations falling under his dictum was arguably broader than the past consideration category. Buller, J., Mansfield's disciple, wholeheartedly concurred with Mansfield's moral obligation argument and cited *Atkins v. Hill*[49] as a precedent. Buller claimed, in the alternative, that, even under the traditional narrow definition of consideration, he could find a loss to the plaintiff and a benefit to the defendant.[50] He also made an analogy to equity by citing a decision by Chancellor Hardwicke.[51] Mansfield's moral obligation cases had two common equitable ingredients: one, the benefit of the past consideration received was not officious and was grounded in conscience and, two, the subsequent promise was enforceable in chancery when specific relief was available.[52]

The civilian Mansfield approached the problem with a legislative mind. Mansfield's verbiage about a moral obligation being sufficient consideration was more sweeping than the facts of the cases he actually decided, but there is little doubt that he envisioned applications of moral obligation logic beyond Holt's precedents to facts beyond what Mansfield had accomplished himself.[53]

In making an overall assessment of whether authority existed to justify Mansfield's attempts to reform the doctrine of consideration, it must be admitted that slim authority existed for his views on written contracts[54] and merchant's contracts,[55] but decisions at law and in equity did support his stand that a moral obligation could constitute a sufficient consideration to support a subsequent promise to pay for an earlier benefit received.[56] In addition to respected common law thinker Holt's recognition of exceptions to the past consideration rule, English courts prior to Holt had rendered decisions at law and in equity enforcing moral obligations.

The earlier precedents at law involved enforceable moral obligations arising in charitable and familial contexts, some of which went beyond Holt's precedents in binding promisors to obligations not originally enforceable. In *Style v. Smith* (1587)[57] a moral obligation constituted sufficient consideration for a defendant's promise to pay £20 to his friend, a physician, after the physician had cured the defendant's son. The physician had heard of the son's illness and had gone to him in the defendant's absence and treated him. The decision in *Marsh and Rainford's Case* (1588)[58] cited *Style v. Smith* (1587) as precedent for a case where a father promised the plaintiff £200 if he married his daughter, but the plaintiff and daughter secretly eloped. The father acquiesced to the *fait accompli* and promised the plaintiff £100 in consideration of the earlier marriage. The past consideration rule objection was raised by the father's counsel, but Wrey, J. said: "Although the consideration be precedent, yet if it were made at the instance of the other party, the action would have lien. But here the natural affection of his daughter is a sufficient matter of consideration."[59] Then in 1682, Pemberton, C.J. rendered a precedent based on the moral obligation principle, which Mansfield cited as precedent on similar facts in 1763.[60] Pemberton ruled: "An *indebitatus assumpsit* will lie for meat and drink for a bastard child. And it was said by counsel to be my Lord Hale's opinion that where there was a common charity and a charge it would lie."[61]

Equity practices prior to Mansfield also facilitated enforcement of a promise supported by a prior moral obligation, which practices had migrated into earlier common law decisions. During the early sixteenth century, common law courts were familiar with chancery practices and were ready to encroach upon the expanding jurisdiction, commercial and otherwise, of this competing court.[62] Chancery gave contract relief when "reason and conscience," "natural justice" or the law of God demanded.[63]

Chancery provided gap-filling hardship relief when procedural technicalities and lack of precedent precluded relief at law. Chancery cured inequities caused by abuse of wager of law and provided remedies when none were available at law in cases involving *quantum meruit*, sureties, executors and parol nonfeasance.[64] Chancery's approach was more effective than the common law because chancery took a purely contractual viewpoint in emphasizing the defendant's promise and was not burdened by tort logic and the attendant historical procedural quirks at law, including consideration.[65] The clerical chancellors generally followed canon law principles and procedures[66] and applied the general notion that a promise ought to be enforced if a good reason, or *causa*, existed for the promise, even if the promise was non-commercial, e.g., a potentially gratuitous promise of a surety, a promise in consideration of marriage or on a past consideration.[67]

Mansfield was familiar with chancery's enforcement of promises grounded on moral obligation since earlier in his career he had actively practiced law before the chancery bar. For example, during his time at the chancery bar, chancery rendered *Reech v. Kennegal* (1748).[68] In that case, the executor raised the Statute of Frauds to defend against his promise made to his testator to pay a bequest to the testator's nephew out of the residuary, the executor being the residuary legatee. Chancellor Hardwicke ruled that the Statute of Frauds couldn't be used to protect the defendant from liability on his promise because of the fraud of representing that there was no need to amend the will in order for the testator to effectuate the bequest since the executor would pay it.[69] Two forms of moral obligation are present here: one, the moral obligation to fulfill the promise that the testator relied on; and two, the moral obligation recognized by the promise to pay for the earlier benefit of being named residuary legatee.

However overreaching Mansfield's ideas seemed, he had not launched his reforms based on the moral obligation principle in a vacuum. In light of the prior rulings at law and in equity, Mansfield's natural extensions of these ideas did not seem so radical. The issue had been pried open by common law and equitable decisions prior to Holt, by Holt's precedents and by Hardwicke's equitable logic. Indeed, as common law courts gobbled up equity's contract jurisdiction, it became incumbent upon common law courts to infuse doctrine with ideas from equity.

Chapter 8

Initial Support for Mansfield's Ideas Squelched

In 1840, the English judge Denman, C. J. would complain that if Mansfield's iconoclastic statements in support of the moral obligation principle were taken literally, they "would annihilate the necessity for any consideration at all, inasmuch as the mere fact of giving a promise creates a moral obligation to perform it."[1] Denman indicated a willingness to accept the moral obligation principle within the strict confines of the actual facts in Holt's and Mansfield's precedents, but he objected to decisions during the first quarter of the nineteenth century that took Mansfield's loose moral obligation dictum seriously; Denman claimed these later decisions enforced promises to pay moral obligations which at no prior time would have been considered enforceable promises at common law. In Denman's view, these extensions went beyond trimming the rough edges off the past consideration rule and came precariously close to discarding the ancient doctrine of consideration generally.[2] These early nineteenth century caselaw tendencies fit neither under the old consideration rule that the defendant must make a request before a benefit was provided[3] nor under the accepted narrow exceptions for a waiver of a statutory bar to enforcement of a prior enforceable debt[4] or for a ratification of a voidable obligation.[5]

EARLY NINETEENTH CENTURY ENGLISH SUPPORT FOR MANSFIELD'S IDEAS

After Mansfield's retirement,[6] English justices sympathetic to his equitable and rational perspective, such as Buller and Ellenborough, continued his practice of looking to developed civilian and equitable ideas for guidance. Not since the twelfth century had the insular common law system looked to continental ideas to such a degree. Under the civilian consensual theory, precedent was irrelevant to the central inquiry of whether the parties' common consensus existed. Under civil law, a promise to pay subsequent to receipt of a benefit was enforceable, in the absence of consideration, if an agreement was made for a good reason or "*cause*."[7] Civilian law enforced promises to pay for past benefits and even promises to make gifts if made for a good cause, such as a promise of a father to support an illegitimate child or a promise to a retiring employee for his past services.[8] During Mansfield's tenure through the early nineteenth century, these consensual ideas altered common law analysis of the past consideration rule. For the first time in the history of the common law of contract, judges were focused on whether an agreement supported by a good moral obligation existed rather than dwelling strictly on whether the case was "on all fours" with precedent or on whether it conformed to the intricacies of the doctrine of consideration and the formulary system's common counts. This perspective continued through about the first quarter of the nineteenth century, until Benthamite ideas caused a shift in policy-making and prerogative from the courts to the legislature;[9] whereupon reactionary judges like Denman and Parke then sounded a retreat.

Early nineteenth century judicial support for the moral obligation principle can be seen in the three following English decisions. In the first case, *Cooper v. Martin* (1803), an adult stepchild's promise to pay his stepfather for maintenance provided during his infancy was enforced because Ellenborough, C. J. reasoned that since the stepfather had no maintenance duty to the stepchild, "[t]he plaintiff having done an act beneficial for the defendant in his infancy, it is a good consideration for the defendant's promise after he came of age."[10] In order to pay nominal obeisance to consideration dogma, he added: "In such a case the law will imply a request."[11]

On its facts, the obligation found binding in *Cooper v. Martin* went beyond the factual holdings in Holt's precedents and in Mansfield's better known decisions for two reasons: one, the obligation wasn't binding originally, since the stepchild incurred no implied obligation to repay benefits provided during his infancy, and two, the stepchild made no request or promise to pay, voidable or otherwise, before maintenance was provided to him during his infancy. This decision fell somewhere between a narrow reading of the precedents and Mansfield's dictum that "[a]s the promise is only to do what an honest man ought to do, the ties of conscience upon an upright mind are a sufficient consideration."[12]

Cooper v. Martin could have been a better reasoned common law opinion since none of Holt's or Mansfield's precedents were even cited. It did, however, contain the essential ingredients of the modern moral obligation principle of a promise to honor a felt moral obligation to pay for a nonofficious past benefit received, which obligation would not have been enforceable at common law without the subsequent promise.[13] The fact that the opinion read like a decision in chancery disturbed Denman all the more because the loose use of consideration logic employed in finding liability in *Cooper v. Martin* was the kind of malleable analysis that a conservative common law thinker feared could lead to amorphous civilian-like notions of moral obligation swallowing up the hallowed assumpsit test of consideration.[14] This moral obligation decision, along with others of the first two decades of the nineteenth century, was rendered during a period, running from Mansfield's tenure until the mid-nineteenth century, of unprecedented judicial borrowing from the more organized and rational continental civil law[15] in order to remove lingering impediments to free consent still found in medieval precedent.

In the second early nineteenth century case, *Barnes v. Hedley* (1809),[16] a formerly usurious contract was corrected by the parties, once the illegality was discovered, in order to conform to the usury laws; the defendant, having earlier received the loan, again promised to pay under the reformed agreement. The court enforced the defendant's subsequent promise, seeming to adopt the plaintiff's attorney's argument: "That notwithstanding an usurious security agreement given, the money lent is a debt in equity and conscience, and ought to be repaid with legal interest, has long been acknowledged in courts of equity."[17] This decision falls under the precedents enforcing ratifications of void promises of former married women and infants, but it goes further in enforcing a promise on a former undertaking that was against public policy. The plaintiff's lawyer inaccurately said it was "indistinguishable" from Mansfield's bankruptcy waiver case[18] since a bankrupt's debt would have formerly been enforceable at law, but a usurious contract was void at law *ab initio.*

A third early nineteenth century case following Mansfield's lead was *Lee v. Muggeridge* (1813),[19] a case that became well known during the first half of the nineteenth century. Mansfield's precedent *Goodright ex dim. Elizabeth Carter v. Straphan* (1774)[20] was directly on point in support of enforcement of a widow's promise confirming a bond that was void since originally made while she was a married woman under coverture. Mansfield's precedent and *Lee v. Muggeridge* were of the same genre as Holt's adult ratification precedent.[21] Unlike the case of a waiver of a statute of limitations, the obligation of a married woman or an infant was not formerly enforceable at law. Something else remarkable about the decision was the broad support for Mansfield's liberal moral obligation dictum[22] expressed in the opinions of all of the common law judges sitting. Denman later complained of the opinions in *Lee v. Muggeridge*: "The language . . . of the whole Court of Common Pleas is very large, and hardly susceptible of any limitation."[23] The broad support of the common law court for Mansfield's moral obligation principle makes one wonder how Denman later managed to return contract law to the facts of Holt's and Mansfield's precedents.

Justice Chambre, sitting in *Lee v. Muggeridge*, said, "There cannot be a stronger or clearer case of moral obligation than this. The gentleman has done this lady a great favour, in going to this expense, and accepting an invalid security; and when she could give a better security, it became her duty so to do and she has done it."[24] The other justices sounded the same theme. Sir James Mansfield, C. J. said, "[i]t has been long established, that where a person is bound morally and conscientiously to pay a debt, though not legally bound, a subsequent promise to pay will give a right of action. The only question therefore is, whether upon this declaration there appears a good moral obligation?"[25] The answer to this question would ultimately set the parameters of actionability under the modern moral obligation principle.

The question ending the last quote underlines a fallacy in Denman's reactionary arguments against Lord Mansfield's moral obligation principle and the cases that applied it. Denman asserted: "[t]he mere fact of giving a promise creates a moral obligation to perform it."[26] Denman elaborated that it was "hardly susceptible of any limitation."[27] But that was not so, as was reflected in Sir James Mansfield's inquiry regarding whether a subsequent promise was supported by a worthy moral obligation.[28] Parameters were being set by the early nineteenth century for when the moral obligation principle applied. Common law judges did not read, nor did they apply, Lord Mansfield's dictum as though any promise was enforceable under the principle. There were three basic elements: One, the defendant-promisor had received an earlier non-officiously bestowed benefit.[29] Two, any possible prior obligation of the defendant to pay was now unenforceable at law, though it may have been enforceable in equity.[30] Three, the defendant subsequently promised to pay for the benefit that he felt morally obligated to satisfy.[31] Under this form of moral obligation principle, the antecedent moral obligation was sufficient consideration to support the subsequent promise.

The subsequent promise was an essential ingredient for contractual liability since courts would not find implied-in-law liability to pay for the benefit received. A benefit received might occasionally qualify for recovery under the emerging quasi-contract action for unjust enrichment, but the moral obligation principle would not create liability under the contractual action of assumpsit without a promise. Ellenborough, C. J., a devotee of Mansfield's ideas, said, "A moral obligation is a good consideration for an express promise; but it has never been carried further, so as to raise an implied promise in law."[32] The scope of liability was not based simply on the mere fact of giving a promise since boundaries existed with reference to bargain notions—the subsequent promise completed the circle of reciprocity of a promise given in return for the prior benefit received.

In the absence of defendant's promise to repay, Mansfield's complementary doctrine of quasi-contract could provide relief if fairness and natural justice required the defendant to disgorge the unjust enrichment received,[33] as when a benefit passed under a failed contract or by mistake or due to misconduct like coercion. Whereas a binding moral obligation is based on consent and enforced as a contractual obligation, restitution for unjust enrichment is effectively constructive trust relief, implied-in-law, for a benefit the defendant should not equitably be allowed to retain. Mansfield distinguished quasi-contract from a promise on a moral obligation by explaining that quasi-contract "does not lie for money paid by the plaintiff, which is claimed of him as payable in point of honor and honesty, although it could not have been recovered from him by any course of law;"[34] as examples of obligations "payable in point of honor," he cited Holt's moral obligation waiver and ratification precedents. In modern times, Mansfield's unjust enrichment ideas have been followed more literally and expansively than his moral obligation ideas because, unlike moral obligation, restitution is an equitable ground implied-in-law and truly independent of the constricting principles of contract and its attendant bargain consideration. Nevertheless, the influence of Mansfield's broad support for restitutionary notions contributed to the growth of the moral obligation principle, which was in effect "promissory restitution."

Mansfield's inspiration for the reforms of moral obligation and unjust enrichment, providing plaintiffs with consensual and implied-in-law restitutionary relief, came to a large degree from analogies to practices found in competing non–common law courts and from civilian notions of consent. While common law courts had successfully absorbed much jurisdiction from chancery, ecclesiastical courts, mercantile courts and local courts during the seventeenth century and earlier, ameliorating principles and practices related to the exercise of jurisdiction in those courts of conscience were not necessarily assimilated into the common law in the process of usurpation of jurisdiction. Mansfield tried to fill those hardship gaps in the common law by introducing exceptional equitable relief. In the process of this borrowing to liberalize the common law of obligations, Mansfield caused some confusion and rancor as he inevitably further intruded upon the jurisdiction of these competing courts, as by enforcing what were traditionally treated as unenforceable gratuitous promises.[35]

In many moral obligation scenarios, a gratuitous or charitable instinct may have originally been a part of the motivation for the plaintiff to provide the benefit for a friend or associate. Unless a donee's right to retain a completed gift is no longer going to be recognized, a donee has no legal obligation to pay for such a benefit; but if a person of honor assumes an obligation by extending a subsequent promise in recognition of a perceived moral obligation, stimulated by circumstances clearly indicating that a gift was not intended, then shouldn't the law accord a remedy? Such a perceived moral obligation is often generated by extraordinary aid, which the beneficiary would not naturally expect to receive as a gratuity, either directly or indirectly, as for example, a neighbor preserving the defendant's property during a flood occurring during his absence or a friend paying for the defendant's infant son's emergency medical expenses while the defendant was overseas.[36]

Returning to the liberal moral obligation decisions of the early nineteenth century, the common law courts continued to support moral obligation, sometimes without using the principle by name,[37] during the generation following the above three decisions rendered in 1803, 1809 and 1813.[38] In *Wing v. Mill* (1817),[39] a pauper became ill in a parish away from his normal residence. The apothecary, who treated him for twelve months before he died, obtained a judgment on a subsequent promise of payment for his services from an overseer of the defendant-parish, where the plaintiff treated the pauper. Ellenborough, C. J. said, "In this case both the legal and moral obligation obtain."[40] This was not merely a case of statutory liability because, without the promise, only the parish of residence was liable. Ellenborough said that *Watson v. Turner* (1767)[41] was "decisive," but in fact it was an extension of that decision, since the promise to the apothecary in *Watson v. Turner* came from an overseer of the pauper's parish of residence. The promissory liability in *Wing v. Mill* on a past perceived obligation, which had not been enforceable at any point in time prior to the promise, continues to this day to represent the area of both growth and debate under the moral obligation principle.

The stream of moral obligation decisions did not end with Ellenborough's retirement. In *Wells v. Horton* (1826),[42] an oral promise to make a testamentary legacy to repay a loan of money of eight years before, was enforced because, as Best, C. J. explained, "I think there is plenty of consideration. There was a moral obligation to pay; and I hope that the judges of Westminster Hall will always hold, that a moral obligation to pay is a sufficient consideration for a promise to pay."[43] Later, it would appear that such overly broad language, as that employed by Best, would unwittingly put the kiss of death on liberalization of the moral obligation principle in England. The next year, the plaintiff in *Nicole v. Allen* (1827),[44] who had boarded defendant's acknowledged illegitimate daughter for a number of years, brought an action against the father to collect for maintenance provided. Defense counsel stated: "There is, I admit, a moral obligation to found a promise, but there is no evidence of any such promise being made."[45] Tenterden, C. J., at *Nisi Prius,* responded: "There is not only a moral, but a legal obligation on the defendant, to maintain his child; he knows where she is, and he expresses no dissent, and he does not take her away."[46] This restitutionary rationale had gone too far. The Roman doctrine *negotiorum gestio,* which created an implied-in-law obligation to pay for such a benefit even in the absence of a promise, was never adopted by the common law. The defendant in *Nicole v. Allen* did not promise to pay nor did a benefit pass directly to him.[47]

The inevitable denial of Tenterden's justifications came in the Exchequer Court in 1840, the same year that Denman, C. J. strenuously criticized the growth in the moral obligation principle. In *Mortimore v. Wright* (1840),[48] the plaintiff, a London lodge owner, sued the defendant, who lived in the provinces, for board, necessaries and nursing services provided to defendant's ill twenty-year-old son. The trial judge instructed the jury that they could not find for the plaintiff unless they found that the father bound himself by his letter to the plaintiff, wherein he said that his son could pay from his own funds when he became twenty-one. Nevertheless, the jury found for the plaintiff. In ordering nonsuit, Abinger, C. B. rejected both the moral and the legal obligation prongs of Tenterden's trial level decision in *Nicole v. Allen* because a father was no more liable for benefits supplied his infant child than a stranger would be unless he agreed to pay. The argument of defense counsel in *Nicole v. Allen* was vindicated. Abinger explained:

> From the moral obligation a parent is under to provide for his children, a jury are [*sic*], not unnaturally, disposed to infer against him an admission of a liability in respect of claims upon his son, on grounds which warrant no such inference in point of law . . . but the mere moral obligation on the father to maintain his child affords no inference of a legal promise to pay his debts; . . . it would bring the law into great uncertainty, if it were permitted to juries to impose a liability in each particular case, according to their own feelings or prejudices.[49]

The courts of this period were reining in juries to avert unpredictable verdicts,[50] as here on the basis of an amorphous moral obligation principle, and they certainly were not going to open Pandora's box to the enforcement of perceived moral obligations floating around in the absence of a subsequent promise by the defendant to pay from his own funds. The loose language and slack logic employed in such moral obligation cases as *Wells v. Horton, Nicole v. Allen* and *Cooper v. Martin*[51] could compromise needed predictability and could sometimes cause wrong-headed outcomes if the parameters of the moral obligation principle were not recognized and applied as they had been in earlier cases which had logically extended the moral obligation principle. The zeal of some judges in making sympathetic applications of the moral obligation principle in an undisciplined fashion opened the door for reactionary opponents to shut off the natural, and undoubtedly desirable, extensions of liability based on moral obligation.[52]

NEGATIVE REACTION SETS IN

In contrast to the early nineteenth century support for extending Mansfield's reforms in England and in some jurisdictions in the United States, the influential Massachusetts Supreme Court decision *Mills v. Wyman*

(1825)[53] rejected the liberalization of the doctrine of consideration. That court ruled unenforceable a father's promise, communicated in a letter, to pay plaintiff's expenses in earlier caring for his ill adult son for a few weeks. Parker, C. J. reasoned it was only an obligation "of conscience" to pay for something the father originally had no duty to pay,[54] unlike a later promise removing an impediment to enforcement of a once enforceable obligation now barred by positive law, such as a bankruptcy discharge or a statute of limitations.[55] The *Mills v. Wyman* court ignored earlier English precedents allowing recovery on promises similar to its facts. In 1763, Mansfield held a father to his promise to pay for previous maintenance given to his bastard child.[56] In 1682, Pemberton, C. J. allowed an assumpsit action on a father's promise to pay for food and drink provided to a bastard child.[57] And in the sixteenth century, a physician recovered on a father's subsequent promise to pay for curing his son in his absence.[58]

It has been suggested that the rejection of Mansfieldian flexibility in some American jurisdictions such as Massachusetts, at an earlier point in the nineteenth century than occurred in England, may have been due to the split among American judges between Federalists and Jeffersonians; the latter, although supportive of Natural Law solutions, were opposed to what was perceived as uncontrollable judicial prerogative.[59] Early nineteenth century opponents of broad judicial discretion preferred legislative solutions along the lines of the relatively recent republican experience of translating Natural Law theory into the positivist legislation of a constitution.

Not long after the Massachusetts reaction, English common law conservatism returned. Most nineteenth century English judges succeeding Mansfield lacked his civilian perspective, since they were trained solely in the common law at the inns of court moots rather than at university; they focused on the methods and controls of the common law system of precedent and forms of action rather than on consent. As the aura of Mansfield's presence on the king's bench faded, the common law retreated before the middle of the nineteenth century as a result of a professional reaction against his attempt to rationalize away the doctrine of consideration. The legislature was also influenced by this conservative judicial perspective and passed Lord Tenterden's Act[60] in 1828. Inspired by Tenterden, C. J., this statute required that a waiver of a statute of limitations would no longer be enforceable unless it was in a signed writing; American jurisdictions adopted the same formality.[61] The main reaction came, however, from the protectors of the ancient common law.

As discussed at the beginning of this chapter, in *Eastwood v. Kenyon*,[62] Denman, C. J. came to the same conclusion that the Massachusetts Supreme Court had in *Mills v. Wyman* (1825)[63] by adopting an 1802 case Reporters' Note,[64] which was critical of certain extensions of Holt's waiver and ratification precedents. The Reporters, Bosanquet and Puller, argued that, "[h]owever general the expressions used by Lord Mansfield may at first sight appear," a careful reading of the facts of Mansfield's actual decisions showed that he did not go outside Holt's exceptions.[65] Denman agreed with the 1802 Reporters' statement that:

> an express promise . . . can only revive a precedent good consideration, which might have been enforced at law through the medium of an implied promise, had it not been suspended by some positive rule of law; but can give no original cause of action, if the obligation, on which it is founded, never could have been enforced at law.[66]

Although it is undoubtedly true that Mansfield intended for moral obligation to have a broader scope than the facts of the cases actually decided, the Reporters' Note adopted by Denman did not encompass all the factual categories of moral obligations enforced by Holt and Mansfield. Mansfield's sweeping remarks in support of moral obligation had become a lightning rod for conservative opposition. Denman made it a black and white choice between Mansfield's dictum and the position taken in the Reporters' Note, when the caselaw precedents were in fact somewhere in between. The Reporters claimed that the principle only applied to obligations "which might have been enforced at law,"[67] but several of Holt's and Mansfield's precedents enforced obligations not originally enforceable at law. Holt's exception to the past consideration rule for adult ratification of an infant's debt[68] and Mansfield's exceptions, such as a widow's ratification of her agreement made while she was an incapacitated wife,[69] a father's promise to pay for prior maintenance of a bastard child,[70] and an executor's individual promise to pay legatees,[71] each involved an obligation originally unenforceable at law. Bosanquet and Puller and Denman were aware of these precedents but conveniently glossed over them in their legislative construction of a positive black letter limit on extensions of promissory liability grounded on moral obligation. They tried to preserve the strict sixteenth century limitations on promissory liability, subject to the narrow exceptions fashioned by the respected common law thinker Holt, by only allowing enforcement of subsequent promises on either obligations which would have been enforceable were it not for some positive statutory bar or ones which were voidable. Denman wanted to insure that, outside the waiver's precedents, adult ratification and some very limited extensions thereof, the law retained *Hunt v. Bate*'s[72] ancient bargain paradigm of the consideration moving from the plaintiff in reliance on the defendant's request. Denman emphasized that the mere fact that a promise was made does not create a moral obligation to perform it. Denman wanted to preserve the integrity of the common law doctrine of consideration, which generated predictable results for businesses planning market transactions.

Despite the fact that, unlike the bold heresy of Mansfield in *Pillans v. Van Mierop*, none of the early nineteenth century cases following and extending Holt's and Mansfield's precedents made a frontal assault on the doctrine of consideration, Denman could not come to terms with some of the natural extensions of the waiver and ratification precedents. Nor did Denman accept, or fully appreciate, the fact that common law judges of the early nineteenth century had already corralled the moral obligation principle within parameters which only permitted comparatively predictable and narrow exceptions to the past consideration rule. The term *moral obligation* itself may have put Denman off; however, as it was applied, it was not a fuzzy civilian principle binding promisors to a seemingly limitless range of promises grounded on moral obligation. By the early nineteenth century, the preponderance of reform-minded judicial opinions made it clear that the moral obligation principle would only be applied to the facts of the precedents and to natural and logical extensions thereof. The moral obligation principle was simply an equitable exception, which removed the past consideration rule bar, when a promisor reasonably felt morally obligated to commit himself to pay for an earlier benefit received. Thus defined, the principle could not unseat consideration from its central role in market transactions; its very definition was drawn to mesh with notions bundled up in the history of the doctrine of consideration. Moreover, by the very nature of the unique moral obligation factual settings found in the eighteenth and nineteenth century cases, it had negligible impact on the predictability needed in regular commercial transactions.

Denman contained any imagined or real lingering support for carrying forward Mansfield's open-ended equitable and civilian ideas expressed in dictum in *Atkins v. Hill* and *Hawkes v. Saunders*. He latched onto Bosanquet and Puller's reassuring summary of the state of the law, despite the fact the Reporters' Note failed, if not refused, to recognize the full extent of precedents permitting common law actionability on moral obligations. Denman exuded confidently: "In holding this declaration bad because it states no consideration but a past benefit not conferred at the request of the defendant, we conceive that we are justified by the old common law of England."[73] Denman, C. J. not only halted further extensions of moral obligation, but he also implicitly denied the validity of prior decisions falling outside the outlines of his rationale and of the exceptions found acceptable in the Reporters' Note.

There seem several possible explanations for Denman's strong reaction to these equitable and civilian ideas. The obvious one is that conservative common law judges felt a self-serving compulsion to preserve and reinvigorate their revered common law system by reinforcing the traditional core test of contract actionability. Two, it has been suggested that an increased strictness in pleading, put into effect six years prior to *Eastwood v. Kenyon* (1840), caused common law lawyers and judges to study and become more aware of the historical and procedural bases of consideration hidden behind the common counts, ultimately forcing the retreat from Mansfield's revisionism.[74] Three, influential nineteenth century Benthamite positivist ideas held that policy and morals were the province of legislatures rather than the prerogative of courts and that courts were simply to apply formal rules.[75] And four, Denman's rejection of moral obligation reflected the nineteenth century view that entrepreneurial business planning and market bargains left no place for the uncertainty of amorphous moral obligations. Market forces and the concept of individualism opposed equitable and civilian notions of morality found so attractive earlier in the century, when the influence of continental legal writers was stronger. Yet, had Mansfield's suggestion in *Pillans v. Van Mierop* (1765) been pressed that consideration was not required by the law merchant, it might have received a more receptive hearing during the commercially instrumental nineteenth century.[76]

Denman's attraction to a general black letter principle, deduced from the caselaw rationalized by Bosanquet and Puller in their Reporters' Note to *Wennall v. Adney*, reflected a trend beginning in the second half of the eighteenth century of common law judges seeking guidance from the new common law treatise writers and case annotaters as a means of dealing with changes generated by the emerging industrial economy. The civilian judicial practice of relying on the organizing ideas of treatise writers had been introduced to the common law by the Enlightenment thinker Mansfield, though, ironically this rational technique was employed by mid-nineteenth century judges to combat his ideas. Although the doctrine of consideration was deemed unassailable, civilian ideas would contribute to the nineteenth century elaboration of what are now known as classical contract rules developed in accommodating economic change. Common law writers prior to Blackstone abridged isolated cases without any attempt to distill general rules from the scattered caselaw. Blackstone and the writers following him[77] deduced general principles from the detail of the yearbook reports. For the first time in the history of common law contract, a civilian practice entered the common law of inspiration coming from writers rather than earlier judges.[78] Once Bosanquet and Puller's tightly drawn general principle found support among the judiciary, the door seemed closed on prior occasional judicial relief based on moral obligation as granted earlier amidst the jumble of disorganized caselaw.

So where did the opinion of Denman, C.J. in *Eastwood v. Kenyon* leave the moral obligation principle? Two years later Denman confirmed that he did not reject all of the principle's applications providing for exceptions to the past consideration rule. Denman declared in *Roscorla v. Thomas* (1842)[79] that the Note to *Wennall v. Adney* and his opinion in *Eastwood v. Kenyon* delineated when subsequent promises were enforceable, as follows: "They are cases of voidable contracts subsequently ratified, of debts barred by operation of law, subsequently revived, and of equitable and moral obligations, which, but for some rule of law, would of themselves have been sufficient to raise an implied promise."[80] It soon became obvious that other English courts supported Denman's conservatism. In 1848, Baron Parke, an influential and technically exacting common law judge, reaffirmed Denman's restrictive position by adopting "the very able note to the case of *Wennall v. Adney.*" Parke stated: "The strict rule of the common law was no doubt departed from by Lord Mansfield in *Hawkes v. Saunders* and *Atkins v. Hill.*"[81] Pollock, C. B. agreed with Denman and Parke in *Flight v. Reed* (1863);[82] nonetheless, he was somewhat adventurous in drawing an analogy to *Barnes v. Hedley* (1809),[83] a decision that had extended Holt's precedent of an adult ratification to a promise to perform an earlier void usurious contract.

So by the middle of the nineteenth century, the moral obligation principle had retreated, though life remained in the principle, at least to the extent Holt and Mansfield's ideas had been approved by Bosanquet, Puller and Denman.[84] The first decades of the nineteenth century still represent the high-water mark of moral obligation in England since, by the last quarter of the nineteenth century, further restraints on moral obligation began to crop up. In England, moral obligation became even more diluted than the anemic version surviving Denman's atavism due to legislation interpreted to require new consideration for waivers of bankruptcy discharges and statutes of limitations.[85]

In English law, the moral obligation principle never recovered from the atrophy that set in during the middle decades of the nineteenth century. In contrast, as the century wore on, some American jurisdictions like New York and Pennsylvania, which were more sympathetic to moral obligation than Massachusetts, continued the process that they had begun in tandem with early nineteenth century English decisions of implementing Mansfield's ideas. One reason given to explain why English judges became more reluctant than an increasing number of their American counterparts to allow the infusion of equitable principles into the common law[86] was that the English judiciary became more formalistic by the middle of the nineteenth century because of the Benthamite legacy of policy being left to the legislature.[87] These positivist tendencies meant strict adherence to black letter law in the single jurisdiction encompassing England and Wales, as contrasted with the multiplicity of jurisdictions found in the United States,[88] where a state like Massachusetts could lead a nineteenth century majority position to rein in moral obligation while jurisdictions like New York and Pennsylvania allowed it to grow.

As the industrial revolution heated up in the United States, differences in the American and English approaches were accentuated by the resuscitation of an earlier egalitarian republican reaction against static legal principles perceived to favor vested rights and to be inconsistent with natural law and fairness.[89] The resultant decline in reverence for *stare decisis* at the state level gradually overcame the prevailing nineteenth century conservative judicial formalism in the United States, while formalism prevails in England to this day. American judges eventually became more amenable to the urging of legal realists that judges look to the substantive and policy reasons behind precedents and reject or revise doctrines that caused unfair results.[90] Thus, the story of the modern growth of Mansfield's moral obligation ideas must focus on developments in American caselaw.

INITIAL AMERICAN RECEPTION MIXED

With the formation of the American republic, "reception" clauses in state constitutions provided for the continued application of that English law which had been "adopted, used and approved" prior to the onset of the Revolution.[91] By 1776, the moral obligation principle had been recognized as an English common law notion. Holt's waiver of statute of limitations and adult ratification precedents[92] were accepted, and the core of Mansfield's moral obligation ideas had been suggested, including his open-ended language in *Atkins v. Hill* (1775)[93] and the cases upholding a widow's ratification of her void contract made while married (1774)[94] and a father's promise to pay for maintenance provided to his bastard child (1763).[95] Moreover, *Pillans v. Van Mierop* (1765)[96] was officially English law, since it would not be rejected by the House of Lords until 1778.[97] Indeed, a smattering of American cases took *Pillans v. Van Mierop* seriously in permitting a written contract to act as a substitute for consideration,[98] but this heterodoxy was soon squelched.[99] Nonetheless, the broad, equitable verbiage of *Atkins v. Hill*, and its cousin *Hawkes v. Saunders*,[100] were cited with approval in the United States by a determined minority during the nineteenth century.[101]

American state courts readily accepted Holt's and Mansfield's moral obligation precedents for waivers of statutory bars, as statutes of limitations[102] and bankruptcy,[103] and for ratifications of voidable obligations due to infancy[104] and other reasons.[105] As to those English moral obligation precedents disapproved of by Lord Denman,[106] because they went beyond the waiver and ratification precedents to enforce promises to pay for prior unrequested benefits, the nineteenth century American reception was mixed. Some state courts would follow precedents at variance with the restrictive Reporters' Note to *Wennall v. Adney* (1802),[107] but whether they were followers of Mansfield and Ellenborough or they followed Kenyon, Denman and Parke in opposing further development of the moral obligation principle, there is no denying that English decisions, rendered both before and after the War of Independence, carried weight in nineteenth century American caselaw. The American position on whether or not the moral obligation principle should be restricted to the scope of the waiver and ratification precedents was scattered and inconsistent throughout much of the nineteenth century; however, the claim of American treatise writers during the second half of the century that near unanimous support existed for Denman's position[108] was plainly inaccurate, as will be seen in the next two chapters.

Throughout the nineteenth century, disagreement existed in the United States over whether the moral obligation spin on the doctrine of consideration should be contained within the waiver and ratification precedents, as urged by Denman and the Reporters of *Wennall v. Adney*, or whether extensions should be permitted along the lines of Mansfield's equitable notions regarding obligations to pay for benefits received under the complementary grounds of the moral obligation principle and quasi-contract. Mansfield's ideas about moral obligation and quasi-contract fell on more fertile soil in the United States, where mature doctrines of a moral obligation principle and restitution would blossom. Most American courts would not, however, break free of the *Wennall* Note during the nineteenth century as a majority adhered to English doctrine. Massachusetts became a leader in this conservatism by rendering its earlier-mentioned influential decision in *Mills v. Wyman* (1825).[109] Although growth of the moral obligation principle seemed impeded, that didn't mean that opposition to extensions of moral obligation could be counted as unanimous, since New York and Pennsylvania courts contemporaneously led a minority position in support of the growth of moral obligation.[110]

By trumpeting *Mills v. Wyman* as the definitive American position opposed to moral obligation, some treatise writers[111] did, however, contribute to slowing the development of the moral obligation principle. Ironically, the *Mills v. Wyman* facts even fell outside the boundaries of binding moral obligation in the most liberal early nineteenth century American and English cases. The father in *Mills v. Wyman* had no legal obligation to pay for the costs of medical care given to his indigent adult son, and the father's promise to pay was not for the promisor's personal benefit.[112] Even today, the father would not be bound under American law since he received no direct benefit himself. A trio of nineteenth century contract law writers from Harvard denied the growth of moral obligation in favor of a strict common law paradigm of bargain and consideration. Parsons wrote in 1855:

> [The widow's ratification case] Lee v. Muggeridge is clearly wrong, and inconsistent with many subsequent cases in England and this country, where the doctrine is now almost universally recognized, whatever it may have been in some earlier cases, that a mere moral obligation is not sufficient to support an express promise. Thus [the decision in] Mills v. Wyman.[113]

Langdell, formerly Parsons' research assistant in writing the above contract treatise, included *Mills v. Wyman* as a leading case in his pedagogically innovative 1871 casebook.[114] Williston, who edited later editions of Parsons' treatise, wrote in its eighth edition in 1893: "In this country the doctrine that a moral obligation would support a promise seems never to have been generally accepted. A leading case is Mills v. Wyman."[115] On the preceding page, in referring to the Note to *Wennall v. Adney*, Williston wrote: "At the present time, it may be doubted whether even this statement of the law does not concede too much."[116] Williston repeated Parsons' 1855 quote of Baron Parke: "a mere moral consideration *is nothing*."[117]

The overkill of promoting a decision like *Mills v. Wyman*, with facts which even today would not qualify under the moral obligation principle, as the leading case opposing the moral obligation principle furthered these treatise writers' interest in containing the unpredictability of moral obligation during an individualistic entrepreneurial age. However, treatise writers of the common law have never had the degree of influence on judicial decision-making that their academic counterparts enjoy in civil law countries. Those American judges sympathetic to the moral obligation principle quietly went about extending the suggestions found in earlier precedents. Ultimately, realist judges would follow Mansfield's lead in fashioning an independent ground of promissory restitution liability based on the American moral obligation principle.

Chapter 9

Case Precedent for Mansfield's Notion of Liability without Prior Legal Obligation

As discussed in the preceding chapter, the 1802 Reporters' Note to *Wennall v. Adney* stated:

> A promise can only revive a precedent good consideration, which might have been enforced at law . . . had it not been suspended by some positive rule of law, but can give no original right of action if the obligation on which it is founded never could have been enforced at law.[1]

Lord Denman, C. J. invoked this passage in *Eastwood v. Kenyon* (1840) to rebut Mansfield's notion of moral obligation and confidently declared that it was "justified by the old common law of England."[2] It was one thing for Denman to decree that the Reporters' interpretation would be the law thereafter, but it was simply not true that recovery on a moral obligation at common law had been restricted to promises on obligations once enforceable at law but which were now barred by some stubborn rule of law. As mentioned earlier, decisions can be found as early as the sixteenth century, within several decades after the genesis of the doctrine of consideration, which enforced promises on prior moral, but not legally enforceable, obligations. No precedent prior to Denman had declared that the moral obligation principle applied only to formerly enforceable legal obligations.

ENGLISH PRECEDENTS NOT REQUIRING PRIOR LEGAL OBLIGATION

The crux of the Reporters' argument in their Note to *Wennall v. Adney* was that the moral obligation principle had not been applied at common law to prior obligations which had not formerly been enforceable at law. This interpretation justified supporting the waiver precedents, but it foreclosed Mansfield's broader civilian moral obligation ideas. The key factor that the Reporters emphasized must be present in order for the past obligation to have been enforceable at law was the presence of a request of the defendant previous to the plaintiff providing the benefit. The reciprocity of the bargain was fulfilled by the defendant's request inducing the plaintiff to provide the benefit. Without the previous request, the plaintiff was a mere volunteer since the defendant had not bargained for the plaintiff's performance. This idea, which was bundled up in the doctrine of consideration, emanated from the ruling in *Hunt v. Bate* (1568),[3] the case of the plaintiff paying to bail the defendant's servant out of jail while the defendant was away. The court held for the defendant, despite his subsequent promise, because he "never requested the plaintiff to do it, on behalf of his servant, but he did it of his own head."[4] The Reporters in *Wennall* claimed that no precedent truly fell outside that rule; however, a closer look at the precedents during the two centuries after *Hunt v. Bate* indicates that not all decisions fell neatly within the previous request formula.

The first case found to deviate from the *Hunt v. Bate* bargain paradigm of a previous request was *Style v. Smith* (1587).[5] A father promised to pay a physician friend who had cured his ill son in the father's absence. Because the father made a promise, assumpsit could be brought, and the court held in favor of the physician despite the fact that the father could not have requested the treatment since he was absent. A father's sense of moral obligation to pay for necessaries provided to his child arose again in a 1682 action brought on a father's promise to pay the plaintiff for comestibles previously given to his bastard child. Once more, no previous request was alleged. Still, Pemberton, C. J. ruled: "An *indebitatus assumpsit* will lie for meat and drink for a bastard child."[6] Mansfield came to the same conclusion in *Scott v. Nelson* (1763)[7] by holding a father bound by his promise to pay for the previous maintenance of a bastard child. Without the fathers' promises in the last two cases, they would not have been liable for their bastards' necessaries; even if a statutory action was brought against them, they would only be liable prospectively. A fourth example of a father being liable on a promise to pay for a prior benefit provided a child is *Best and Jolly's Case* (1660).[8] The father was held liable on his own debt *and* his son's debt, both due the same creditor, because he promised to pay them both if the plaintiff would forbear from suing. The court said, "he was not liable for his son's debt," but having induced forbearance, he was liable.[9]

Another batch of precedents enforcing a defendant's subsequent promise, without his request previous to the plaintiff providing a benefit, involved cases of plaintiffs financing the burial of a defendant's spouse or child in the absence of the defendant. In *Church v. Church* (1656),[10] the court "ruled that *assumpsit* would lie for the expenses of defendant's child, buried by plaintiff without request." And in *Jenkins v. Tucker* (1788),[11] a father paid for a relatively lavish burial, according to the wealth and station of the absent husband, who had left his wife in order to run a plantation in Jamaica. Loughborough, J. said: "[t]here was a sufficient consideration . . . though there was neither request nor assent on the part of the defendant, for the plaintiff acted in discharge of a duty which the defendant was under a strict legal necessity of himself performing."[12]

Two final examples of precedents recognizing liability on promises to pay for a moral obligation, which were unenforceable at law, come from Mansfield's tenure as Chief Justice. Mansfield held executors liable on promises to pay out legacies to heirs even though they had no obligation to pay legacies at law.[13] Executors did have such a duty in equity and canon law, however, and Mansfield adapted these principles to the common law. Also Mansfield held a widow liable on her promise recognizing a moral obligation to satisfy a debt which was void because it was incurred while she was disabled as a married woman.[14]

In the Note to *Wennall*, the Reporters denied that the above cited precedents enforced promises on past moral obligations; they justified the rulings for the plaintiffs by disingenuously arguing that, despite the absence of evidence in the reports, the defendants must have made requests prior to the plaintiffs' actions. Their strained justification for *Style v. Smith* was:

> From the expression "in the absence of a father," used in that case, it may be inferred that the son lived with the father, and that the medicine was administered to the son in the house of the father, while the latter was absent, from whence it results that the physician's debt, though not founded on any immediate benefit to the father, or on his request, was most probably founded on his credit; which credit, it fairly inferred from circumstances by the physician, might operate to charge the father in the same way as his request would operate, the physician having sustained a loss in consequence of that credit.[15]

The Reporters disposed of the cases of fathers promising to pay for victuals provided to bastard children by saying: "Although the latter case does not expressly say that there was a previous request by the Defendant, yet that seems to have been the fact."[16] Their retort to the cases of promises to pay for funeral expenses of a child or spouse paid by the plaintiff was: "[t]hough no request was laid in the declaration. Of which case it may be observed that possibly after verdict the Court presumed a request proved."[17]

By the *Wennall* Reporters inferring that plaintiffs had made previous requests in the above precedents, they were rationalizing them under the rule in *Hunt v. Bate*, thereby denying that common law precedent had ever bound defendants to subsequent promises supported only by felt moral obligations to pay for the prior receipt of unrequested benefits. The monist urge of common lawyers to insist upon a single bargain test of liability, applicable to all promises,[18] made it unfathomable that there could be permitted even this narrow exceptional sub-category of the doctrine of consideration for promises based on the moral obligation of paying for necessary, and thus non-officious, maintenance provided to dependents.[19] Since these precedents did not accord with their view of consideration, they explained them away. They disingenuously overlooked the reality that these were types of obligations that a promisor would have requested or paid for himself originally, had he been available to do so, and he ought to pay, previous request or not.

Thus, as early American courts began to build their own common law on the foundation of English law inherited at the Revolution, English precedents existed to support the application of the moral obligation principle to prior obligations that had not once been enforceable at law. Denman's atavistic 1840 ruling in *Eastwood v. Kenyon* was of course not a precedent that American courts were bound by; however, a majority of American judges and writers were probably sympathetic to Denman's restrictive view. Nevertheless, a persistent minority of judges and writers were not persuaded. For those who supported the growth of the moral obligation principle in the United States past the waiver and ratification precedents, the first step was to accomplish what the early nineteenth century English decisions had done, under Ellenborough's leadership, in enforcing subsequent promises on certain prior void contracts. Once that position was consolidated, an emerging nineteenth century minority, less deferential to English decisions, would expand the moral obligation principle beyond what English law was ever able to achieve.

VOID CONTRACTS COVERED

Two of the main applications of the moral obligation principle during the period of liberalization in early nineteenth century England were for enforcement of promises subsequent to contracts deemed void on account of usury and the disablement of married women. In *Eastwood v. Kenyon,* Denman effectively denied the enforceability of a former married woman's ratification of a contract made under coverture, as had been enforced in *Lee v. Muggeridge* (1813).[20] Although Denman thought the upholding of a second promise curing a usurious one in *Barnes v. Hedley* (1809)[21] was "consistent" with the *Wennall* Note,[22] the ferocity of his general attack against deviations from the old waiver and ratification precedents left in doubt enforcement of formerly usurious contracts in England until *Flight v. Reed* (1863) approved a somewhat similar promise curing usury.[23] Pollock, C. B. articulated in 1863 what Denman probably meant, in saying *Barnes v. Hedley* was consistent with the precedents, when Pollock said the case fit under the exceptions for promises waiving positive statutes which barred the plaintiff from recovering for what the defendant had received.[24] American courts now had to decide for themselves whether they found these post-Independence English decisions persuasive. Langdell thought Denman should have overruled *Barnes v. Hedley* before *Lee v. Muggeridge* because at least in *Lee* there was "a clear moral obligation" which was more than what could be said about a promise in the "face of the statute of usury."[25]

Later in the same year that *Barnes v. Hedley* was decided in England, a Connecticut court upheld a second promissory note, which replaced the usurious original, in *Kilbourn v. Bradley* (1809).[26] Defense counsel argued that a claim originating in an illegal transaction is merely a substitute and just as void.[27] The court pointed out that equity would order repayment of the sum owed at the lawful interest and said: "The moral obligation of the borrower to repay the principal sum actually loaned, with the lawful interest is unimpaired. If the lender will expunge the usury, and the borrower voluntarily assents to repay the sum loaned with lawful interest, it is an act of justice forbidden by no principle of public policy, and which constitutes a good consideration for a new contract."[28] Twelve years later in *Early v. Mahon* (1821), Chief Justice Spencer of the New York court stated: "*Barnes v. Headley* [*sic*] . . . in my opinion places validity of the promise and the sufficiency of the consideration, beyond a doubt."[29] Although the usurious contract was "void," he said: "It has been repeatedly decided in this court that an equitable or moral duty is a sufficient consideration for an actual promise to pay. In *Hawkes v. Saunders* . . .",[30] the court emphasized the equitable duty to pay for the benefit received and stated: "[t]he defendant having had the plaintiff's money, without any consideration . . . the promise subsequently to repay this money, was founded on a moral and equitable duty."[31]

Langdell went against the tide in opposing subsequent promises on illegal usurious contracts since enforcement was supported by a majority of American jurisdictions by at least the early twentieth century.[32] The common law followed equity's lead by enforcing the subsequent promise for the non-usurious amount since the debtor had received the benefit of the loan.[33] Subsequent promises on other illegal contracts were treated the same,[34] unless sensitive policy concerns existed.[35]

Langdell was likewise out-of-step with the position of a majority of American jurisdictions in thinking that perhaps a subsequent ratification of a married woman's promise should be binding.[36] Subsequent promises of divorcees and widows recognizing their moral obligation to honor agreements made during marriage were first enforced by Mansfield in 1774; Mansfield said she had received the benefit of the original agreement and "in conscience" she should abide by her ratification made after she was out from under coverture.[37] When the reaffirmation of Mansfield's view in *Lee v. Muggeridge* (1813) was quashed in *Eastwood v. Kenyon*, it was probably more on account of the broad judicial support of the moral obligation principle articulated in *Lee v. Muggeridge* than for the merits of the plaintiff's claim.

In the United States, statements supportive of enforcing a former married woman's ratification of her agreement made during coverture can be found by the 1820s.[38] In the oft-cited Pennsylvania case *Hemphill v. McClimans* (1855), a wealthy married woman induced the plaintiff to provide services to her son by promising she would pay; she later ratified her original promise after she divorced. The court baldly stated: "But the rule is a very familiar one, that an existing moral duty, not enforceable by law, is a sufficient consideration for an express promise to perform that duty."[39] The court acknowledged a subtle legal difference between a promise of a married woman and a promise of an infant, but, in conscience, the court saw no difference in the morality of their conduct. In enforcing the subsequent promise even in the absence of a direct benefit to the woman, the court emphasized that the creditor relied upon her sense of justice in that she had the money and she wouldn't rely on a disability defense. Dictum in *Wilson v. Burr* (1841)[40] gave a doctrinal justification for enforcement of a subsequent promise on a void promise of a married woman. The New York court suggested that the overall transaction complied with the bargain paradigm because her unenforceable promise made while married, though not enforceable at law, constituted the equivalent of a previous request inducing the plaintiff to provide the benefit. Denman admitted as much, in an aside to his lambasting of *Lee v. Muggeridge*, when he said: "It should however be observed that in that case there was an actual request of the defendant during coverture, though not one binding in law."[41]

Kent v. Rand (1886)[42] is a representative case for the majority American position that a former married woman's subsequent promise lacks consideration. The court cited the dictum in well known precedents opposing enforcement,[43] while distinguishing the traditional exceptions to the past consideration rule. The New Hampshire Supreme Court distinguished bankruptcy and statute of limitations since they "only suspend the remedy" and distinguished voidable infants' contracts since married women's contracts were "[v]oid, no debt ever existed, and hence they furnish no consideration for a subsequent promise made during widowhood."[44] Thus, unlike the majority American position enforcing subsequent promises to cure usurious contracts, a majority did not eventually adopt the above-discussed minority position, held by New York and Pennsylvania, enforcing a former married woman's ratification.[45] A majority of jurisdictions did, however, enforce a former married woman's subsequent promise if the promise during her marriage bound her separate estate in equity;[46] through this analogy to equitable enforcement, the presumption of voidness was overcome.

Why did a majority of American jurisdictions never come over to enforcing a former married woman's subsequent promise generally? The prime reason seems to be that American courts have taken the doctrinal difference between void and voidable agreements seriously.[47] There were of course policy reasons behind this void status. In contrasting the treatment of former married women with debtors under usurious contracts and ratifying young adults, widows and divorcees had their own special problems. Earlier in this century, a woman, finding herself out on her own, might not have been of an active age or employable status to realistically shoulder a perceived past moral obligation. Policy concerns exhibited in reservations in nineteenth century married women's acts also suggest reasons. Although these statutes conferred contract and property rights to married women, married women were exempted from contract liability in certain instances for fear they may have agreed involuntarily; for example, some statutes did not hold married women for agreements to act as a surety, an accommodation party, an assumer of her husband's debts or even a contract not for her benefit.[48]

In enforcing some subsequent promises on prior void obligations, American law had more or less regained the ground lost in English law as a result of the decision in *Eastwood v. Kenyon.* In order to further expand the range of binding promises on prior obligations, reform-minded American judges had to surmount the doctrinal impediment of reciprocity and its required presence of a previous request. In finding ways to rationalize away doctrinal demands, American enforcement of promises based on moral obligations would surpass the liberalizing English decisions of the early nineteenth century.

Chapter 10

American Promissory Restitution Supported by Consideration

The concluding two chapters analyze the evolution of the modern American moral obligation principle. All exceptions to the traditional past consideration rule recognized today include the common feature of the defendant-promisor's felt moral obligation on account of the prior receipt of a material benefit. The first three stages of recognition of exceptions were rationalized within the confines of the bargain construct: one, that the subsequent promise constituted what Holt characterized as either a waiver of an impediment to enforcement or a ratification of a prior imperfect transaction; two, that the circumstances surrounding the receipt of the benefit raised the promisor's implied previous request; and three, that the moral obligation to pay for the prior benefit received constituted consideration to support the subsequent promise. Under a fourth exception, twentieth century American courts abandoned the bargain consideration construct entirely in declaring that a moral obligation to pay for a prior benefit supported a subsequent promise, in and of itself, without the need to rationalize the existence of consideration. The first of the above exceptions, dealing with waiver and ratification, was discussed previously. The remainder of this study analyzes the development of the last three of the above exceptions, which comprise the field of promissory restitution, wherein courts focused directly on the legal meaning and efficacy of a promise grounded on a prior receipt of a material benefit. This penultimate chapter concerns the second and third exceptions rationalized under the doctrine of consideration, and the final chapter focuses on the fourth exception of promissory liability in the absence of consideration.

IMPLIED PREVIOUS REQUEST

The broad support which the conservative common law community afforded the *Wennall v. Adney* Note's doctrinal criticism of Mansfield's moral obligation ideas during the nineteenth century made it necessary for plaintiffs' lawyers to come into technical compliance with what the Note's Reporters declared the traditional rule of liability to be. A plaintiff thus had to establish that the defendant had incurred a prior legal obligation, as for example a debt now barred by a statute of limitations. The key doctrinal burden for plaintiffs' lawyers since *Hunt v. Bate* (1568), in showing that the promisor-defendant had a prior legal obligation, was to establish that plaintiff's action on behalf of the defendant had been preceded by the defendant's request that the plaintiff act,[1] thereby completing the circle of the bargained-for exchange. In attempting to provide the rationale for growth in this area, past Holt's waiver and ratification precedents, while remaining within the doctrinal confines of the much-invoked *Wennall* Note, inventive American lawyers posited that the circumstances of a case could raise the implication of a previous request. This suggestion appeared in a 1798 English reporter's note, and it was soon adopted in an 1803 English case and in a string of early nineteenth century New York cases. These developments were the genesis of the modern American principle that a promise made in recognition of a previously received material benefit should be binding in the absence of consideration.[2]

The instigating suggestion that a defendant's previous request could be implied appeared in Serjeant-at-law Williams' 1798 Reporter's Note to *Osborne v. Rogers.*[3] Sjt. Williams suggested a way around the past consideration rule when a defendant "derives a benefit from the consideration it is sufficient, because equivalent to a previous request." He continued that once the defendant receives a benefit and then promises, this is "evidence of prior request" and a request can be deemed "implied."[4] Williams stretched for authority in citing dictum in *Hayes v. Warren* (1731),[5] wherein that court held for the defendant in reversing a default judgment but suggested that perhaps a request of the plaintiff by the defendant could have been implied, had there been circumstances taken into account by a jury in arriving at a verdict.[6]

Five years later in *Cooper v. Martin* (1803), the English court stated that when a stepson promised to pay his stepfather for necessaries provided during minority, it was a "good consideration" since "the law will imply a request."[7] Perhaps unwilling to cite a mere reporters' note, the court claimed *Southerton v. Whitlock* (1726)[8] as a precedent; however, this non-necessaries case made no reference to implied request but instead inaccurately announced there had been a ratification in line with Holt's decision in *Ball v. Hesketh.*[9]

The first American decision recognizing the possibility of implying a defendant's request previous to receipt of a material benefit appeared the next year in Justice Kent's[10] opinion in the New York case of *Livingston v. Rogers* (1804).[11] Without citing Williams' Note, Kent declared: "In many cases a request may be implied from the beneficial nature of the consideration, and the circumstances of the transaction."[12] He cited pre-republican precedents *Hayes v. Warren* and Wilmot, J.'s dictum in the famous decision *Pillans v. Van Mierop* (1765). Wilmot did not employ implied request logic, but he did announce that the previous request requirement's "strictness has been relaxed; as, for instance, burying a son, or curing a son, the considerations were both past, and yet holden good." Paraphrasing the plaintiff's attorney in *Hayes v. Warren*, Wilmot added: "It has been melting down into common sense, of late times."[13] Just as Sjt. Williams had written six years before, Kent pointed out that the circumstances of a promise made on account of a material benefit received obviated the past consideration rule's concern over an officious volunteer.[14] Kent's comments were dictum since the ruling concerned whether mutual promises were concurrent. Reporter Caine's doctrinaire note to *Livingston v. Rogers* stated that Kent's implied request dictum was in "very great doubt" and that it was "very questionable whether, on a moral obligation, a request or consideration can be implied," citing the "very able note" in *Wennall v. Adney*.[15]

After Kent became Chief Justice of the New York Court, that court rendered a *per curiam* opinion in *Comstock v. Smith* (1810),[16] which accepted the implied request dictum in *Livingston v. Rogers* as law, though the court did deny relief on a quibbling pleading defect.[17] The opinion read: "It does not seem requisite in every case of a past consideration to lay an express request in the declaration, though the cases in which it is not required are rather exceptions to the general rule. They are such in which a beneficial consideration and a request are necessarily implied from the moral obligation under which the party was placed."[18] In the continuing battle of the reporters, Reporter William Johnson's footnote stated: "A jury may infer a request from the circumstances of case."[19] Although the court allowed the defendant off on a quibble, the *Comstock v. Smith* opinion was cited as giving guidance to later courts on how an implied request case could be pleaded.[20]

A year before Kent, C. J. left the New York common law court, his court published a *per curiam* opinion in *Hicks v. Burhans* (1813),[21] which actually held for the first time in New York that a defendant's promise subsequent to receipt of a benefit was enforceable because of an implied previous request. In *Hicks v. Burhans*, a defendant promised to pay a plaintiff for his earlier efforts in pursuing the defendant's defaulting debtors. In the spirit of the dictum in *Hayes v. Warren*, the court stated: "A request, in this case, may have been implied; and we ought to intend it to have been proved upon the trial" and further that "a request may be implied from the beneficial nature of the consideration and the circumstances of the transaction."[22] The previous request requirement seemed close to being converted into a fiction.

Once the New York court signaled its willingness to arrive at a common sense solution by employing implied request, the defendant's lawyer in *Edwards v. Davis* (1819)[23] forced a determination of whether the material benefit could be received by someone other than the promisor, as for example, a relative or loved one. In this case, a widow promised to pay for maintenance that had been provided to her indigent parents. Spencer, C. J. noted that the maintenance provided the plaintiff's parents did not benefit her because she had only a moral duty to provide for her parents and thus "the circumstances negate the idea that any request was made by her"[24] to support her parents. Earlier, Sjt. Williams had likewise conditioned the implied request solution on the promisor's receipt of a benefit.[25] Those earlier cases not requiring a benefit directly to the promisor tended to involve a familial context, as a father promising to pay for medical care given his adult son or maintenance provided his bastard in his absence;[26] but the New York court was unwilling to go that far, perhaps in order to design a consistent rule applicable to market and non-market transactions.

In a footnote to *Edwards v. Davis,* Reporter Johnson added that all precedents involved a benefit to the promisor.[27] This was not in fact the case,[28] but, just as the *Wennall* Reporters' Note had ignored cases not falling under their construct, Johnson declared that the *Wennall* Note was absolutely correct that a subsequent promise could be binding only when, one, the benefit flowed to the promisor, and two, a prior legal obligation was barred by some positive rule of law.[29] This latter point was retrogressive in failing to recognize that the facts of recent New York cases like *Hicks v. Burhans* did not require a prior legal obligation. However, on the point that the promisor must receive the benefit, this remains the American rule to this day, in most instances.[30]

The *Wennall* Note should, however, be given its due in that a liberal reading of it can extract the elements of the notion that a previous request can be implied when there is a promise on a past material benefit received by the promisor. A close reading of the *Wennall* Note shows that it likewise used the technique of implying a request in order to bring old precedents not otherwise seeming to fall under the paradigm the Note announced. Thus, in rationalizing *Church v. Church,*[31] where the defendant promised to reimburse the plaintiff for paying for his son's funeral, the Reporters employed the same logic as the dictum in *Hayes v. Warren*[32] in declaring "that possibly after the verdict the Court presumed a request proved."[33] And, in explaining why in *Style v. Smith*[34] a father was held to his promise to pay a physician for care given a son in the father's absence, the Reporters cavalierly intoned that a request could "fairly [be] inferred from the circumstances."[35]

The New York position that a promise on a past benefit was enforceable via an implied previous request was followed in some jurisdictions[36] but remained a minority position in the nineteenth century in opposition to the Massachusetts majority rule supporting a conservative reading of the *Wennall* Note.[37] Nevertheless, some mid-nineteenth century treatise writers were supportive of the New York position. After retirement, Chancellor Kent acknowledged in his Commentaries that it was an "unsettled point, whether a moral obligation be, of itself, a sufficient consideration for a promise, except in those cases in which a prior legal obligation had once existed," but he added that a request may be "necessarily implied, from the moral obligation under which the party was placed."[38] By around 1840, the contract law commentator Theron Metcalf actively encouraged pleaders to utilize the implied request technique by writing: "A request is frequently implied from the circumstances of the transaction. Where a party derives a benefit from the consideration, it is often tantamount to a request; and a jury will infer one, for the purpose of enforcing a meritorious claim."[39]

CONSIDERATION FOUND WITHOUT IMPLIED REQUEST

Within a couple of decades, some nineteenth century courts began to move away from the finding of an implied request, while continuing to rationalize that promises made on account of the prior receipt of a material benefit were supported by consideration. This transition came in two stages: first, a promise subsequent to receipt of a benefit was declared to be "the equivalent of a previous request," thus in conformity with *Hunt v. Bate*;[40] and then some courts glided from there to boldly declare that consideration existed to support the subsequent promise without any reference to previous request.

An explanation is needed for the comparative ease with which nineteenth century American courts reformed the old past consideration rule to permit the step-by-step recognition of the three facilitating techniques of implied previous request, treatment of a subsequent promise as equivalent to a previous request and finding consideration present without concern for a previous request. The timing of the reforms can be substantially explained by the movement away from technical pleading, the advent of the consensual theory and the fusion of law and equity. Mansfield began the simplification of pleading in attempting to hear evidence of the parties' common consent.[41] The departure from arcane pleading was furthered by the urging of Bentham[42] and others and culminated in the abolition of the ancient forms of action by the mid-nineteenth century.[43] The simplification of pleading rules permitted juries to hear cases otherwise barred them. Juries could now inject their own sense of equity as they weighed the overall factual circumstances in inferring the consent of the parties.[44] Courts were now forced to fill in the gaps created in substantive doctrine by the abolition of the formulary structure.[45] As judges sought structure to replace the formulae of the forms of action, they gained inspiration from the civilian consensual theory in emphasizing the voluntary consent of the parties.[46] Furthermore, the fusion of law and equity accelerated the practices started by Mansfield of introducing equitable principles into the common law.[47] Common law courts now had to provide the equitable relief formerly dispensed by chancery.[48] Expansion of the moral obligation principle afforded fair results for plaintiffs supplying material benefits to defendants who later promised to pay for value received.

Subsequent Promise Equivalent to Previous Request

The proposition that a subsequent promise was the equivalent of a previous request also emanated from Sjt. Williams' 1798 Reporter's Note, which, as discussed earlier, was the stimulus for the notion that a previous request could be implied.[49] The 1817 New York decision *Doty v. Wilson* included both of Sjt. Williams' suggestions for rationalizing the presence of consideration: one, that a previous request could be implied from the circumstances, and two, "where a party derives a benefit from the consideration, it is sufficient, because equivalent to a previous request."[50] By viewing the defendant's subsequent promise as an analogue of *Hunt v. Bate's* previous request, the previous request requirement was effectively transmogrified into a fiction in these cases of a prior receipt of a material benefit. This approach overcame the pleading and proof problems of establishing the existence of a previous request, implied or express. Sjt. Williams' equivalency idea was not pursued by other courts, however, until there had been a period of experimentation with Williams' more conservative suggestion that juries be permitted to determine whether there was sufficient evidence to imply a previous request.

A spate of cases did begin to recognize the subsequent promise as the equivalent of a previous request in the 1830s. In South Carolina, the *McMorris v. Herndon* decision invoked Sjt. Williams' Note for this proposition in 1830.[51] New York returned to the analogy idea in the 1850s.[52] In 1864, in the influential Vermont leading case *Boothe v. Fitzpatrick*, the court ruled that: "a subsequent promise is equivalent to a previous request, and creates a legal liability where none existed before for want of a request. . . . The promise of the defendant obviates this obligation, it being equivalent to a previous request."[53] Decisions into the twentieth century continued to employ this logic.[54] The previous request requirement was now a fiction in these material benefit cases.

Boothe v. Fitzpatrick did make a technical pleading departure from Sjt. Williams and *Doty v. Wilson* in that Williams and the *Doty* court, both operating under the strictures of the common money count pleading formulae, made oblique reference to the technical need to plead an implied previous request. In contrast, the *Boothe* decision, rendered subsequent to the abolition of the common counts, could more flexibly rely solely on the logic that the subsequent promise was the equivalent of a previous request, while making no reference to the need to plead an implied request. Williams and the *Doty v. Wilson* court did not have the procedural flexibility to focus solely on the consent of the parties.

Once reforming jurisdictions began converting the previous request requirement into a mere fiction, it wasn't long before courts began discarding the fiction entirely and simply declaring that the moral obligation to pay for the unrequested benefit received constituted consideration (sometimes called "moral consideration") to support the freely given subsequent promise. Fictions had been employed during the period governed by the forms of action in order to realize fair results within the confined structure of the forms, but once the abolition of the formulary system shifted the emphasis from the ritual of the archaic forms to factual questions regarding intent, false assertions in the pleadings appeared absurd and unacceptable.[55]

Consideration Found without Reference to Previous Request

In the New York case *Bentley v. Morse* (1817),[56] a debtor had paid off a debt but had to pay a second time when the creditor later obtained a judgment against the debtor. When the creditor was informed of the debtor's claim that he had paid twice, the creditor promised to refund one payment if the debtor could produce a receipt; and the debtor in fact produced the receipt. The *Bentley v. Morse* court enforced the creditor's refund promise on the basis that "[t]here was such a moral obligation on the part of the [creditor] to refund the money, as would be a good consideration to support an assumpsit. . . . The moral obligation is as strong as any in the cases in which it has been held sufficient to revive a debt barred by a statute or some positive rule of law."[57] In finding consideration present, this modern sounding *per curiam* opinion employed no artifices, such as implied request or the promise being equivalent to a request. In its broadest reading, it smacked of Mansfield's moral obligation principle enunciated in *Hawkes v. Saunders*,[58] that a moral obligation constituted sufficient consideration. In its narrowest reading, it appeared the creation of another Holt-like exception, applicable only to such double payment cases. In a note to the opinion, Reporter Johnson questioned the decision in stating: "This doctrine is not fully sustained by the authorities. The better doctrine seems to be that the moral obligation must have a prior legal or equitable claim connected with it."[59] Johnson's Note then cited with approval his earlier mentioned Reporter's Note to *Edward v. Davis,*[60] which had more or less adopted the Reporters' Note to *Wennall v. Adney.*[61] New York left this straightforward innovation dangling as an aberration during the first half of the nineteenth century while it took the more conservative route of rationalizing recovery within the confines of the implied request bargain construct. However, throughout the nineteenth century, Pennsylvania courts found consideration without resorting to fictions, as *Bentley* had done. Pennsylvania's approach will be addressed in the next chapter; it was an aberration during the first half of the nineteenth century since their courts of law and equity had been fused since colonial days and hence were full of restrictive aspects of common law precedent, procedures and forms.

As jurisdictions began to find consideration without reference to a previous request during the second half of the nineteenth century, the emphasis shifted from the fiction of a previous request to modern restitutionary focus on the promisor's prior receipt of a benefit. In the 1868 Vermont decision, *Seymour v. Town of Marlboro,*[62] a resident discovered the town's offer of a $300 bounty to local military volunteers only after he had reenlisted in the Union Army. He applied for the bounty, and since the town obtained the benefit of being able to credit him against their mandated quota for that presidential call, the town voted to grant him the bounty. The Vermont court ordered the town to pay the bounty to the plaintiff, despite the objection of past consideration, because the court stated: "The consideration upon which it was made, moved from the plaintiff, was meritorious and beneficial."[63] The court cited as precedent the above-discussed 1864 Vermont case *Boothe v. Fitzpatrick,* but unlike *Boothe,* the *Seymour* court did not declare the town's subsequent promise to be the equivalent of a previous request. No concern was expressed over the lack of a previous request. This line of thinking was not immediately pursued in Vermont, however, due to the influence of the leading Vermont case *Boothe v. Fitzpatrick.*

The first widely recognized leading decision finding a moral obligation to be good consideration, without reference to the need for a previous request, was the 1899 New York decision *Drake v. Bell.*[64] *Drake v. Bell* involved a contractor who repaired the wrong vacant house; when the owner of the wrong house discovered the benefit, he promised to pay for the repairs. The *Drake v. Bell* court leveled a cogent, head-on assault upon the reasoning of the principal nineteenth century writers and judges who opposed extensions of Holt's precedents. First, Justice Gaynor distinguished the 1825 Massachusetts case *Mills v. Wyman,*[65] the leading American case opposing growth in the moral obligation principle past Holt's waiver and ratification exceptions. The difference was that the defendant-promisor in *Drake v. Bell* received a benefit to his property but there was no direct benefit received by the defendant-father in *Mills,* who promised to pay for care given his adult son while ill among strangers.[66] Gaynor stated that the *Drake* case "is not one of mere moral obligation resting on no consideration received. . . . The case is one of moral obligation created by a past valuable consideration derived from another."[67]

Second, Justice Gaynor distinguished *Eastwood v. Kenyon* (1840),[68] the decision stopping Mansfield's moral obligation ideas in their tracks in England.[69] While distinguishing *Eastwood v. Kenyon*, Gaynor made a statement critical of the absolutism of Denman's opinion, much as Denman had criticized Mansfield's broad verbiage. Gaynor said: "The language of the opinion in Eastwood v. Kenyon . . . is very large, but the point decided does not seem controlling of cases like the present one."[70] (The *Eastwood* facts related to technical nineteenth century rules regarding a husband's individual obligation for his wife's debt and were not germane here.) Six years prior to *Drake v. Bell*, a South Carolina court made a more direct attack on Denman's concern stated in *Eastwood v. Kenyon* that Mansfield's moral obligation ideas would "annihilate the necessity for any consideration at all"[71] by declaring that Denman's logic was "more specious than sound" for ignoring the distinction between a promise made under no obligation, either moral or legal, and a promise made on account of the moral obligation created by receipt of a material benefit.[72]

The third rebuttal in *Drake v. Bell* took on the Reporters' Note to *Wennall v. Adney*,[73] which had been closely followed by the Reporter Johnson's Note to the 1819 New York case *Edwards v. Davis*[74] and approved of by *Mills v. Wyman*.[75] Justice Gaynor pointed out that the *Wennall v. Adney* Note violated its own claimed statement of black letter doctrine that a subsequent promise could only revive a formerly enforceable legal obligation, now barred by positive law, by approving of precedents enforcing ratifications of moral obligations based on promises made during infancy and coverture, where no prior legal obligation had ever existed.[76] *Drake v. Bell* was by no means the only American court to criticize the *Wennall v. Adney* Note on this point during the century or so after the Note's publication.[77]

Justice Gaynor then proceeded to summarize the two grounds for enforcement of promises on moral obligations under New York law:

> The actual decisions most worthy of attention (not feeling bound by mere general remarks of judges and their citation) make two classes. In one of them the promise is held binding because based on a former obligation enforceable at law or in equity, which obligation it revives; in the other because the promisor though never under such obligation nevertheless received an antecedent valuable consideration.[78]

Justice Gaynor followed with a summary statement, which, standing alone, could arguably be interpreted as suggesting the modern view that enforcement would be possible in the absence of consideration: "Hence the rule seems to be that a subsequent promise founded on a former enforceable obligation, or on value previously had from the promisee, is binding."[79] The *Drake v. Bell* opinion, written after the fusion of New York's chancery and common law courts, concluded by declaring that the general principle enunciated fulfilled the demands of justice. As to the facts in *Drake*, a just result was obtained by enforcement of the subsequent promise because the promisor received the twin benefit of the house being immediately rented after the repairs and it also becoming salable.[80] In a larger sense, Gaynor's lack of obeisance to traditional English doctrine reflected a tendency gaining ascendancy among American judges of more extensive adaptation of common law principles to the demands of the American environment.

Despite the growing number of jurisdictions ruling that a moral obligation, created by receipt of a benefit, could act as an independent form of consideration to support a subsequent promise,[81] the final draft of the first Restatement of Contracts, completed in 1928 and published in 1932, did not recognize that a promise made in recognition of the prior receipt of a benefit could be supported by consideration, unless an enforceable legal obligation had formerly existed.[82] Williston, the Restatement's Reporter, had not altered his views since his 1893 editing of Parsons' eighth edition.[83] The first Restatement's drafters assumed the law to have remained static at Holt's waiver and ratification exceptions of more than three hundred years before, which had been effectively codified by the *Wennell v. Adney* Note of 1802. Nevertheless, the caselaw in support of an expanded role for the moral obligation principle continued to grow.[84]

Chapter 11

American Promissory Restitution Supported by Moral Obligation Alone

The continued judicial manipulation of consideration doctrine into the twentieth century in order to enforce promises made on account of the felt moral obligation generated by the prior receipt of a material benefit made a patent absurdity of the proposition that all enforceable promises must comply with the *Hunt v. Bate* bargain paradigm. As a consequence, prior to the middle of the twentieth century, a handful of American courts began enforcing such restitutionary promises as an open exception to the consideration construct. For one of the first times in the history of common law contract, some jurisdictions were beginning to say overtly that certain promises could be binding as contract obligations despite the absence of consideration. Legal realists supported this open refutation of the claim that the bargain paradigm encompassed the full gamut of definable consensual transactions which ought, in fairness, to be enforced.

INDEPENDENT GROUND OF MORAL OBLIGATION

In the face of the continuing opposition of conservative commentators like Williston,[1] the drafters of the Restatement Second of Contracts followed the lead of those few courts that had departed from the consideration model and abandoned the charade of rationalizing a bargain present by stating in Section 86(1): "A promise made in recognition of a benefit previously received by the promisor from the promisee is binding to the extent necessary to prevent injustice."[2] The restaters incorporated the parameters found in the caselaw regarding which types of promises, grounded on moral obligation, should be enforceable. Section 86 constitutes an open recognition that these restitutionary promises do not fit the consideration construct but nevertheless are enforceable based on the independent substantive ground of moral obligation.[3] Eight of the eleven decisions cited by the restaters as illustrative of enforceable restitutionary promises were in fact cases rationalized within the confines of consideration doctrine; of the remaining five, three Wisconsin opinions supplied alternative rationales of consideration and moral obligation[4] and only two rested their decisions solely on the independent ground of moral obligation.[5] The restaters were urging growth in the law based on a smattering of precedent, much as the drafters of the first Restatement had done earlier in positing Section 90.

In the remainder of this section, an analysis will be provided of the caselaw developments available to the restaters in the 1960s in preparing their drafts of what became Section 86. The focus will be on those cases supporting an independent ground of moral obligation either as an alternative to manipulation of consideration doctrine or as the exclusive basis of support. A fair number of cases decided prior to 1960 can be found stating the alternative grounds for enforcing a restitutionary promise of consideration and moral obligation.[6] As to the consideration logic in these cases, the courts finding consideration present were clearly basing their logic on a moral obligation to make restitution rather than on feigned bargain logic. Thus, opinions in the 1948 Oregon case *Marnon v. Vaughan Motor Co.* and the 1955 Oklahoma case *Kaiser v. Fadem* state that although the material benefit received was not moved by a previous request, it was conferred under such circumstances as to create a moral obligation to support a subsequent promise.[7] Since this solution of moral obligation constituting sufficient consideration was analyzed above, attention is turned to the focus of this section, namely, moral obligation acting as an independent ground for enforcement of a subsequent promise.

Prior to the initial drafts of Section 86 in the mid-1960s,[8] there had only been several decisions enforcing subsequent promises on the ground of moral obligation alone;[9] and, even as to those, applicable statutory law could arguably have made the difference. In *Muir v. Kane* (1909),[10] a broker rendered services for a buyer but failed to comply with the writing requirements of a Washington statute, which rendered such an oral contract void. The court enforced the buyer's subsequent written promise to pay the broker for his services because "the better rule is with the cases holding the moral obligation alone sufficient to sustain the promise."[11] The 1927 California case *Coulter v. Howard* cited and agreed with the logic in *Muir v. Kane* on substantially the same facts. In both cases the opinions equated a waiver of a statute of limitations with overcoming a writing deficiency without acknowledgment that a prior enforceable agreement had never existed in the oral brokerage transactions in contrast to a former contract barred by a statute of limitations.[12] Both opinions seemed to be preoccupied with disposing of the formality question and made no reference to the doctrine of consideration one way or the other.[13]

In *Old American Life Ins. Co. v. Biggers*,[14] a 1949 federal case decided under Oklahoma law, the appellate court said the trend was to enforce a promise made on account of a non-gratuitous conferment of a material benefit because "a moral obligation arises which will support a subsequent executory promise where there was originally no contract, perfect or imperfect, obligating the promisor."[15] In this case, the plaintiff promoted the revival of a nearly moribund insurance company by infusing his own funds into the operation. The later resuscitated company agreed to reimburse the plaintiff's advances. Since, unlike *Muir v. Kane*, there was no prior void or voidable obligation, this portion of the *Old American Life Insurance* rationale was a stronger statement than *Muir v. Kane* in support of moral obligation as an independent ground outside the bounds of the waiver and ratification precedents. The potency of the support for the moral obligation principle in the rationale in *Old American Life Ins. Co. v. Biggers* was diluted, however, by a secondary justification for the holding based upon an Oklahoma statute, which attempted to reform the rule along the lines of a few other state statutes by declaring that a moral obligation originating in a benefit conferred was good consideration for a subsequent promise.[16] These several decisions constituted the sum total of the precedents available to the restaters where there was anything approaching unequivocal judicial support for the moral obligation principle as an independent ground. Having said that, the restaters also relied on the logic found in other decisions that supplied support, in the alternative to consideration, for moral obligation as an independent ground for liability.

REASONS JUSTIFYING MORAL OBLIGATION AS AN INDEPENDENT GROUND

American judicial opinions have articulated a variety of reasons to justify the law shifting to afford support for moral obligation as an independent ground for enforcing promises. The reasoning can be found in the few cases basing their decisions solely on the moral obligation principle and in the more numerous cases supplying the alternative grounds of moral obligation and consideration. These reasons also reflect to a degree the parameters for actionability under the moral obligation principle. These reasons include: one, the moral obligation generated by receipt of a benefit should be treated as an exception to the consideration construct; two, the conferment of the benefit must not have been intended as a gift; three, the *Wennall v. Adney* Note requirement of a prior legal obligation is simply too narrow; four, the moral obligations in the traditional exceptions are of no higher force than a variety of other moral obligations; and five, one ought to honor promises to pay for non-gratuitous, non-officious benefits received.

Under the first factor above, modern courts began to point out that Holt's waiver and ratification precedents were really exceptions to the bargain paradigm and had been enforced on account of the moral obligation generated by receipt of a benefit rather than due to compliance with the reciprocity requirements of the doctrine of consideration.[17] The Wisconsin court in *Park Falls State Bank v. Fordyce* (1931) asserted that in none of the cases refusing enforcement of a subsequent promise, under the *Wennall* Note's strict rule, did the promisor originally receive something of value.[18] The moral obligation engendered by receipt of the benefit was the *sine qua non* for actionability of the subsequent promise, irrespective of notions of inducement and bargain. Indeed, if you strip away the traditional, but inconsistently applied, requirement of a prior legal obligation, the *Wennall* Note itself recognized the compelling force of receipt of a benefit when the Reporters stated that in all earlier cases enforcing subsequent promises, "[t]he party bound by the promise had received a benefit previous to the promise."[19]

Second, decisions recognizing the applicability of the moral obligation principle often emphasize that the plaintiff did not intend a gift when he or she conferred the benefit. When the benefit is provided in a business setting, the stronger language that "the promisee expected to be compensated"[20] is usually used. When the benefit is provided by a friend or relative, the plaintiff has more of a challenge in overcoming the presumption of a gift. Nevertheless, courts have regularly enforced the subsequent promise despite the fact that a gift may have at first glance seemed intended, so long as clear donative intent is not proven. In *In re Hatten's Estate* (1939),[21] the plaintiff provided extraordinary hospitality to a lonely millionaire bachelor friend over an extended period, and the Wisconsin court found no gift was intended. The cases involving relatives have to be considered some of the more liberal applications of the moral obligation principle when they enforce such promises. In *In re Schoenkerman's Estate* (1940),[22] the court rejected the defendant's argument that a gift was intended when the mother-in-law and a sister-in-law cared for the promisor's house and his children over a ten-year period before he made the promise. A 1902 Pennsylvania decision found no gift intended when a son and daughter provided services for their father and mother over a fifteen-year period; the father executed a $4,000 promissory note to each child when they later told him that he ought to pay them.[23] However, some judges are inclined to find a gift from the friend or relative and refuse enforcement of the promise. In the above-discussed case *In re Hatten's Estate*, a dissenting opinion characterized the long term hospitality as a gift or a courtesy to a friend and opposed enforcement.[24] And in *Jensen v. Anderson* (1970),[25] a Utah court ruled that the services provided around the promisor's property by the promisee-bachelor friend were intended as a gift and refused to enforce the subsequent promise.

Under the third and fourth factors listed above, courts began to question the traditional logic of limiting the range of enforceable moral obligations to Holt's waiver and ratification exceptions. As to the third factor listed above, modern courts began rejecting the fundamental precept in the *Wennall* Note that a subsequent promise could only revive a prior enforceable legal obligation now barred by a positive rule of law.[26] A number of earlier-discussed nineteenth century cases effectively rejected this proposition by enforcing promises ratifying prior transactions which were void because of usury or coverture.[27] In the twentieth century some courts began rejecting *in toto* the narrowness of the general proposition that a legal obligation must have originally existed. Judges pointed to the hole in the logic of the *Wennall* Note itself because the Note approved of Holt's enforcement of an adult ratification despite the fact that the minor's original promise was not binding.[28] If the prior legal obligation requirement did not apply to adult ratifications, why should it apply to other promises made in recognition of a moral obligation to pay for a benefit received?

Fourth, courts began to question why the moral obligation in the traditional exceptions to the past consideration rule, such as in statute of limitations waiver cases, should be considered of a higher force than promises prompted by other moral obligations. Just as with other moral obligations recognized by modern courts, at the time of a statute of limitations waiver or an adult ratification, only a moral obligation exists. The Wisconsin court in *In re Estate of Gerke* (1955) saw no valid distinction between a subsequent promise related to an original obligation, now barred by a statute of limitations, and a subsequent promise to pay for a benefit received when there was no legal obligation originally.[29] There seemed no logical justification for elevating the waiver to a higher moral plane. Along the same line, in *Muir v. Kane* (1909) the original contract was unenforceable because of a writing deficiency; the Washington court declared that the moral obligation to pay for services under an oral contract, which was required to be written, is just as binding as the moral obligation to pay for services now barred by a statute of limitations.[30] The preference given waivers and ratifications over other promises made on account of the receipt of benefits made no sense to these twentieth century courts.

Fifth, a theme found in judicial opinions supportive of the moral obligation principle, either expressly or impliedly, was that one who promised to pay for a non-officious benefit accepted is only doing what an honest man ought to do and thus he should be bound. This notion has long constituted an underlying justification for enforcing promises to make restitution; it is an adaptation of Mansfield's oft-quoted statement in *Hawkes v. Saunders* that: "[t]he promise is only to do what an honest man ought to do, the ties of conscience upon an upright man are a sufficient consideration."[31] Enforcement of restitutionary promises permits enforcement of obligations of honor arising in circumstances otherwise possibly falling short of qualifying for pure restitutionary relief in the absence of a promise.

Although it may have been possible to rationalize the presence of some form of benefit in *Hawkes v. Saunders*, Mansfield didn't limit his announced moral obligation principle to cases of promises that an honest man ought to make for past benefits received. Mansfield's failure to delimit boundaries for his moral obligation ideas by restricting it to promises made on account of the receipt of a non-gratuitous, non-officious conferment of a benefit meant that it was incumbent on modern courts to place parameters on Mansfield's idea in order for this field of obligation to be administrable. Nonetheless, Mansfield's proposition that promissory liability be grounded in conscience and morality has long been a part of the justification cited in support of fashioning a workable American moral obligation principle.

In the 1809 decision *Greeves v. McAllister*, the fused Pennsylvania court of law and equity found relevant the "morality and honesty of the promise on the part of the defendant."[32] Three years later, in the curious republican Pennsylvania case *Clark v. Herring*, the court paid obeisance to Mansfield's moral obligation ideas and declared that it was not bound by the House of Lords's 1778 repudiation of Mansfield's broad moral obligation principle because the House of Lords's repudiation in *Rann v. Hughes* came after July 4, 1776; in Pennsylvania, British decisions dated subsequent were denied the status of precedent by a Pennsylvania statute.[33] Other jurisdictions did not catch up with the equitable approach of Pennsylvania's early republican fused court of law and equity until their courts were fused later in the nineteenth century. Twentieth century American restitutionary promise cases have continued Pennsylvania's premature modern approach to support their decisions by employing Mansfield's verbiage regarding what an honest man ought to do.[34]

An honest man was not bound under Mansfield's principle, however, if he made no promise. In *Atkins v. Hill* (1775), Mansfield said that the promise on the past obligation was "made upon a good and valuable consideration. . . . It is so in cases of obligation which, without such promise, he could not be compelled to pay."[35] Thus, under the facts of *Boothe v. Fitzpatrick* (1864),[36] had the owner of a stray bull not promised to pay the farmer who found, protected and fed the bull until the owner located it, the owner would not have been bound on a moral obligation implied-in-law. There is no Roman or civil law doctrine of *negotiorum gestio*[37] in the common law binding a defendant for receipt of a benefit short of restitution, in the absence of a promise. Additionally, any promise made is binding only to the extent that it is proportionate to the value of the benefit received;[38] this limitation favors the restitution interest over the consent and expectation interests and underlines the restitutionary nature of liability on a promise for the value of the unrequested benefits received. Yet, there is a consensual side to liability in that recovery is limited to the extent of the promise if the value of the benefit exceeds it.

CONCLUSION: MORAL OBLIGATION PRINCIPLE

Had Mansfield not used such a broad brush in stating his moral obligation ideas, conservative English and American judges and writers would possibly have been more receptive to his reforms. In limiting Mansfield's controversial notions to the scope of Holt's waiver and ratification precedents, these guardians of common law doctrine disingenuously denied other long standing caselaw support for moral obligation by asserting that the bargain standard of *Hunt v. Bate* (1568) represented the sole test for determining when a promise was binding.

It was left to reform-minded American jurisdictions to fashion boundaries for actionable restitutionary promises falling under Mansfield's open-ended equitable theory. The initial American decisions rebutting the reactionary response of the Reporters' Note in *Wennall v. Adney* (1802) to Mansfield employed the same doctrinal means of manipulating the doctrine of consideration as the Reporters had done, in order to obtain the opposite result of rationalizing enforcement of promises grounded upon the felt moral obligation to pay for non-gratuitous benefits received. Once influential minority jurisdictions like New York and Pennsylvania had consolidated these gains, they glided to the equitable declaration that such a promise could be supported by a "moral consideration." A few twentieth century jurisdictions would later abandon the sham of bargain consideration being present and openly declare moral obligation to be an independent ground for relief on restitutionary promises. The moral obligation principle provided the grounds for creation of a new cause of action independent of the need for consideration. English precedent was being adjusted consistent with republican natural law notions of fairness and morality.

The onset of these American reforms in the nineteenth century was facilitated and encouraged by changes in procedural law and by a borrowing from civilian ideas promoted by some commentators. The procedural law reforms commenced at mid-century with the abolition of the ancient forms of action and the fusion of courts of law and equity. The end of the common contract counts empowered courts to shift their focus from the intricacies of the formulary system to the terms of freely-made agreements. A fused court of law and equity now had the necessary flexibility and discretion to fashion a category of black letter exceptions to the past consideration rule, permitting the enforcement of promises made in recognition of moral obligations generated by the receipt of non–officiously bestowed benefits.

In the wake of the abolition of the forms of action, reform-minded jurisdictions utilized the civilian consensual theory to replace the structure lost with the end of the forms. The consensual theory provided a theoretical construct to effectuate their goal of enforcing voluntary promises on moral obligations; this European idea buttressed American courts' perspective that freely consented-to promises made for good reasons, besides bargained-for promises, were deemed worthy of enforcement. When the reciprocal nature of the doctrine of consideration did not mesh with consensual theory support for certain promises motivated by moral obligations, the inclination of some nascent courts of law and equity was to craft equitable exceptions to the past consideration rule.

The elements of benefit, moral obligation and a subsequent promise became the parameters for enforcement of a consensual restitutionary promise by a growing number of modern courts of law and equity, despite the absence of bargain consideration. This moral obligation principle provided a balance between traditional concerns for reciprocity and predictability on the one side and notions of consent and the unfairness of unjust enrichment on the other. A majority of nineteenth century American courts opposed this exercise of equitable prerogative; nevertheless, the federal system afforded experimentation by pioneering state jurisdictions in developing extensions of the limited notion of moral obligation found in Holt's precedents. Other jurisdictions would follow in the twentieth century.

By incorporating the moral obligation principle in Restatement Second of Contracts Section 86, the restaters encouraged restitutionary relief in a more flexible manner than most courts had previously done, much as earlier restaters had done in encouraging reliance relief in the original Section 90. (Today, virtually all promises enforceable without consideration at common law are binding on account of either the reliance or the restitutionary interest.) The recognition of a defendant's binding restitutionary promise in Section 86 was a natural complement to actionable reliance relief under Section 90; together they provide exceptional equitable relief outside the consideration construct both on promises generated by a felt moral obligation to pay for a non-officious benefit previously received and on promises generating foreseeable reliance.

The justification for modern judicial enforcement of restitutionary promises resides in the joining of two interests deemed meritorious of relief, namely, free consent and receipt of a benefit hovering on the margins of restitution. Restitution is denied when there is a fear that the benefit was thrust on the recipient, but that fear of imposition is assuaged by the subsequent promise. A consensual promise is not binding unless the promise is made for a good reason that the community perceives to be worthy of support. Sporadically, over the centuries, a subsequent promise on a felt moral obligation to pay for a non-officious, non-gratuitous enrichment received has been deemed worthy of support if an injustice would otherwise occur. When there exists a coalescence of the receipt of an unrequested enrichment with a subsequent promise to pay, modern courts of law and equity have been inclined to find community support for enforcement of such a voluntary promise. Courts and restaters of the law have drawn on scattered precedents in the centuries of caselaw to articulate a rationale for an organized theory of recovery on restitution promises; reforms instituted, and others yet to be realized, must still be rationalized within the bounds of the common law construct.

In corralling Mansfield's ideas into a structured moral obligation principle, American courts noted the common theme in the moral obligation precedents since the sixteenth century of a promise made on account of a felt moral obligation to pay for the prior receipt of a benefit. These factors became the elements of the American moral obligation principle. The existence of a voluntary promise permitted contract enforcement of unjust enrichment that fell short of qualifying as a ground for restitution relief; now, in order to prevent injustice, such a promise would not fall through the cracks between the rules related to a contract supported by bargain consideration and to restitution. This gap-filling principle has not proven to be a threat to unseating the general consideration test for contract liability, as Denman had feared, since in performing its interstitial role to avert injustice the moral obligation principle acts as an exception to the principal contract formation ground of bargain and thus does not constitute a general competing basis of contract actionability. The fair results and reasonably predictable outcomes achievable by application of this restitutionary promise principle should eventually prove attractive to common law jurisdictions that have yet to significantly reform their traditional past consideration rule.

Notes

CHAPTER 2

1. The judicial discussions in *Foakes v. Beer* consolidated a variety of types of preexisting duty cases, involving increases and decreases in obligations, under the accord rule in Pinnel's Case (a/k/a Pynnell v. Cole), 5 Co. Rep. 117a (1602). Foakes v. Beer, 9 App. Cas. 605, 609, 615 (H.L. 1884). After *Foakes v. Beer,* the accord rule thus spread to preexisting duty cases generally. *See* JOHN DAWSON, GIFTS AND PROMISES 210 (New Haven: 1980); SAMUEL STOLJAR, A HISTORY OF CONTRACT AT COMMON LAW 130, 132 (Canberra: 1975).

2. Y.B. Mich. 33 Hen. VI, f. 48, pl. 32 (1455); Y.B. Mich. 10 Hen. VII, f. 4, pl. 4 (1495).

3. Y.B. Mich. 10 Hen. VII, f. 4, pl. 4 (1495) (Brian, C.J. added that a novelty would make the accord enforceable.).

4. In same 1495 case that Brian stated his view, Fyneux, J. said that he thought part-payment or a novelty, as a horse, would discharge the original liability: "I think there is no difference between accord and satisfaction in money and in a horse." In an earlier-cited case, Danvers, J. thought that payment of a lesser amount might be a good *quid pro quo,* but Moyle, J. had a view similar to what was to be Brian's later. Y.B. Mich. 33 Hen. VI, f. 48, pl. 32 (1455).

5. *Anon.,* Dal. 49, pl. 13 (1563) (Common Pleas held that £20 plus sealed acquittance was enough to discharge a £100 obligation.). Not many questions were raised about the law here because legal issues were hidden behind wager of law and the general issue in trial by jury. In *Anon.,* 4 Leon. 81 (C.P. 1588), a rare discussion about an accord occurred as an offshoot of the court's inquiry into whether an indigent should be permitted to wage his law. The raising of the novelty of early payment also opened the legal discussions about accords in the above 1563 case and in *Pinnel's Case. See* STROUD MILSOM, HISTORICAL FOUNDATIONS OF THE COMMON LAW 256 (London: 2d ed. 1981).

6. Pinnel's Case, 5 Co. Rep. 117a, 77 Eng. Rep. 237 (1602) (resolved by whole of Court of Common Pleas). Action was in debt on a bond. Defense based on subsequent agreement for £5, in-hand-paid, to satisfy £8 obligation.

7. An accord to discharge an unliquidated claim was not governed by *Pinnel's* debt rule since it did not qualify as a sum certain for *quid pro quo.* Hence the amount could be less than what the plaintiff might have recovered in damages. Adams v. Tapling, 4 Mod. 88, 89, 87 Eng. Rep. 278, 279 (1692). But here also the accord must be executed. Andrew v. Boughey, 1 Dy. 75a, 73 Eng. Rep. 160 (1552).

8. *See* CECIL FIFOOT, HISTORY AND SOURCES OF THE COMMON LAW: TORT AND CONTRACT 413 (London: 1949).

9. *See* STROUD MILSOM, *supra* note 5, at 260. Debt was based on a duty to pay for a property interest that had already passed. The defendant would in effect be ordered to disgorge the plaintiff's property.

10. Pinnel's Case, 5 Co. Rep. 117a, 77 Eng. Rep. 237 (1602). *See* CECIL FIFOOT, ENGLISH LAW AND ITS BACKGROUND 103 (London: 1932) (Absurd that if creditor takes horse or canary there is an accord and satisfaction but if he takes less money it's *nudum pactum.*). It's all the more absurd if the novelty would be a manufactured good in the modern era of interchangeable mass-produced goods.

11. The rule in *Pinnel's Case* was dictum since the defendant lost on a rule of pleading by failing to aver early payment, but Anderson, C. J. thought it a good plea. Reporter Coke seemed to be trying to settle the law himself by claiming that *Pinnel's Case* "was resolved by the whole court." Coke made no reference to Anderson's qualifying opinion. For Anderson's opinion, and two other justices who partially concede Anderson's point, *see* Pinnel's Case, LI MS. Maynard 66, fo. 56, *reprinted in* JOHN BAKER and STROUD MILSOM, SOURCES IN ENGLISH LEGAL HISTORY 262–263 (London: 1986). *And see* JOHN BAKER, AN INTRODUCTION TO ENGLISH LEGAL HISTORY 210 (London: 3d ed. 1990) (Coke would fail to distinguish his own views from those he was reporting; still he wrote the most influential named reports ever.).

12. Richards v. Bartlett, 1 Leon. 19, 74 Eng. Rep. 17 (1584). The rule in *Pinnel's Case* should be called the rule in *Richards v. Bartlett* since *Richards* is the instigating assumpsit case applying this principle; however, the influential Coke authored the debt case *Pinnel,* which added authority to the assumpsit rule being identified with *Pinnel's Case.*

13. Richards v. Bartlett, 1 Leon. 19, 74 Eng. Rep. 17 (1584). Translating it into consideration's two sides: the debtor incurred no detriment by paying part and the creditor received no benefit.

14. Ames wrote: "The rule is older than the doctrine of consideration and is simply a bit of formal logic of medieval lawyers." JAMES B. AMES, LECTURES ON LEGAL HISTORY 329 (Cambridge, Mass.: 1913). *Contra* CECIL FIFOOT, *supra* note 8, at 412–413 (Brian's argument in 1495 was logical. Also debt's accord rule in mid-sixteenth century was likewise influenced by contemporaneous development of bargain and benefit.); *cf.* SAMUEL STOLJAR, *supra* note 1, at 120–121 (The rule contains element of bargain also present in logic of consideration).

15. Fourteen years after *Pinnel's Case,* Coke, now Chief Justice of King's Bench, said 500 pounds wouldn't satisfy 1,000 pound bond but a promise to do that and payment would under assumpsit: "[for debt, it] is no satisfaction . . . but yet this is good and sufficient to make a promise, and upon a good consideration, because

he hath paid money. . . .'' Bagge v. Slade, 3 Bulst. 162, 81 Eng. Rep. 137 (1616). *See* SAMUEL THORNE, SIR EDWARD COKE 5 (SELDEN SOCIETY LECTURE: 1952) (Coke's writings dogmatized the results of the middle ages).

Furthermore, whereas *Pinnel's Case* involved satisfaction of a conditional bond under the action of debt *sur obligation*, assumpsit concerned enforcement of a promise. The rules for performance of a condition on a bond were inapplicable to a promise to pay money. *See* Alfred Simpson, *The Penal Bond with Conditional Defeasance*, 82 L.Q.R. 392, 405 (1966).

16. *See* CECIL FIFOOT, *supra* note 8, at 414. However, even before consideration was established doctrine, defendants raising the accord defense mentioned the ''consideration'' for the accord, *e.g.*, Hewton v. Forster, 27/1099, m. 76 (K.B. 1536).

17. *See* SAMUEL STOLJAR, *supra* note 1, at 121.

18. Reynolds v. Pinhowe, Cro. Eliz. 429, 78 Eng. Rep. 669 (1595) (prompt payment avoids cost of suit); Hubbard v. Farrer, 1 Vin. Abr. 306, pl. 17 (1635) (good consideration for creditor to have money in his purse). Lord Blackburn agreed, all but dissenting in Foakes v. Beer, 9 App. Cas. 605, 622 (H.L. 1884). *Cf.* (ENGLISH) LAW REVISION COMMITTEE, SIXTH INTERIM REPORT, CMND. No. 5449, at para. 33–35, 50 (1937) (may be more beneficial to creditor to accept prompt payment of part).

19. Pinnel's Case, 5 Co. Rep. 117a, 77 Eng. Rep. 237 (1602).

20. If there was a disputed amount, an account stated was enforceable. Milward v. Ingram, 1 Mod. 205, 2 Mod. 43, 86 Eng. Rep. 831, 930 (1675).

21. Peytoe's Case, 9 Co. Rep. 77b, 77 Eng. Rep. 847 (1611). *Cf.* 8 WILLIAM HOLDSWORTH, A HISTORY OF ENGLISH LAW 85 (London: 1926) (Cited Y.B. Pas. 11 Hen. VI, pl. 30 (1432), where a novation was unenforceable since creditor could not recover from new debtor who had not received *quid pro quo* from creditor.).

22. Richards v. Bartlett, 1 Leon. 19, 74 Eng. Rep. 17 (1584) (If there had been sufficient consideration, accord would have been unenforceable since defendant's promise had not been performed.).

23. Strangborough v. Warner, 4 Leon. 3, 75 Eng. Rep. 686 (1589) is landmark case recognizing enforceability of mutual promises.

24. *See* 8 WILLIAM HOLDSWORTH, *supra* note 21, at 83; CECIL FIFOOT, *supra* note 8, at 414. *See also* Arthur Corbin, *New Contract by a Debtor to Pay His Pre-existing Debt*, 27 YALE L.J. 535, 538 (1917) (If there is sufficient consideration, then an executory accord should be enforceable.). *See* Allen v. Harris, 1 Ld. Raym., 91 Eng. Rep. 978 (1696) (Defendant's attorney said that the recognition of mutual promises made an executory accord enforceable).

25. Goring v. Goring, Yelv. 11, 80 Eng. Rep. 8 (1601) (Accord to pay £150 in seven installments instead of original £205 was enforceable.); Case v. Barber, Sir T. Raym. 450, 83 Eng. Rep. 235 (1682) (Dictum that an executory accord was ''of late'' enforceable. Dictum because there was only part-payment without a novelty and it didn't comply with Statute of Frauds). *Cp.* RESTATEMENT (SECOND) OF CONTRACTS sect. 279 (1981) (If intent for ''substituted'' contract, original obligation is discharged whether or not substituted contract is performed).

26. *See* Allen v. Harris, 1 Ld. Raym. 122, 19 Eng. Rep. 978 (1696) (''And the books are so numerous, that an accord ought to be executed, that it is now im-

possible to overthrow all the books. But if it had been a new point it might be worthy of consideration." *Id.*). *And see* Cumber v. Wane, 1 Stra. 426, 93 Eng. Rep. 613 (1721).

27. Lynn v. Bruce, 2 H. Bl. 317, 126 Eng. Rep. 571 (1794); *accord* Foakes v. Beer, 9 App. Cas. 605 (1884); Warren v. Hodge, 121 Mass. 106 (1876).

28. *See* SAMUEL STOLJAR, *supra* note 1, at 124.

29. *See* 2 THOMAS STREET, THE FOUNDATIONS OF LEGAL LIABILITY 93 (Long Island: 1906).

30. *Cp.* (ENGLISH) LAW REVISION COMMITTEE, SIXTH INTERIM REPORT, CMND. No. 5449, at para. 33–35, 50 (1937) (Recommended abolition of *Pinnel* rule, with the proviso that the original obligation revives if the accord is not performed.).

31. Foakes v. Beer, 9 App. Cas. 605 (H.L. 1884) (written accord giving Dr. Foakes more time to pay). Lord Blackburn acknowledged that, though the rule in *Pinnel's Case* was dictum, it was the rule of law since cases had "on the whole" followed it since then.

32. New York took the lead in abolishing the formulary system by passing David Dudley Field's Code of Civil Procedure in 1848. England followed suit, a half century after Jeremy Bentham (1748–1832) urged it, by enacting the Common Law Procedure Acts of 1852 and 1854. Stat. 15 & 16 Vic., c. 76 (1852); Stat. 17 & 18 Vic., c. 125 (1854). Law and equity were fused in New York, and partially in England, in the process.

33. *See* Charles Hepburn, *The Historical Development of Code Pleading in America and England* in 2 SELECT ESSAYS IN ANGLO-AMERICAN LEGAL HISTORY 643, 681 (1909); CECIL FIFOOT, *supra* note 8, at 370–371; Mitchell Williams, *Pleading Reform in Nineteenth Century America: The Joinder of Actions at Common Law and Under the Codes*, 6 J. LEG. HIST. 299, 313–315 (1985).

34. England now emphasized the detriment side of consideration. Tweddle v. Atkinson, 1 B & S. 393, 121 Eng. Rep. 762 (1861). American jurisdictions emphasized the bargain aspects of the doctrine. *See* Wisconsin & Michigan Ry. v. Powers, 191 U.S. 379, 386 (1903) (per Holmes); OLIVER HOLMES, JR., THE COMMON LAW 292–294 (Boston: 1881) ("reciprocal conventional inducement"); RESTATEMENT (FIRST) OF CONTRACTS sect. 75(1) and cmt. (b) (1932) ("bargained for").

35. *Pinnel's Case* involved a debt action, and debt required actual receipt of the benefit (a part performance would not discharge a duty to pay the whole), but assumpsit was based on a promise. *See* CECIL FIFOOT, *supra* note 8, at 413; *cp.* James B. Ames, *Two Theories of Consideration* (pt. 1), 13 HARV. L. REV. 515, 521 (1899) (misconception to think of part-payment rule as corollary of consideration).

36. *See* CECIL FIFOOT, *supra* note 8, at 414; *and see* JOHN DAWSON, GIFTS AND PROMISES 207 (New Haven: 1980) (Consideration has to do with formation but has been confused with discharge and irrevocable offers.).

37. The rule, called the "doctrine of *Cumber v. Wane*," had been seriously challenged by Sibree v. Tripp, 153 Eng. Rep. 745 (1846), *infra*. *See* Cumber v. Wane, 1 Stra. 426, 93 Eng. Rep. 613 (1721).

38. James B. Ames, *supra* note 35, at 523 (Cited cases finding consideration for part-payment: Bagge v. Slade, 3 Bulst. 162, 81 Eng. Rep. 137 (1616) (per Coke himself) and Rawlins v. Lockey, 1 Vin. Abr. 308, pl. 24 (1639). Ames deplored the

fact that these cases were not brought to *Foakes*' court's attention. *Contra* CECIL FIFOOT, *supra* note 8, at 414n. (Ames' two cited cases weren't accord cases since defendants promised to pay part in exchange for plaintiffs performing new acts.). *And see* SAMUEL STOLJAR, *supra* note 1, at 120–121 (Accord arose in assumpsit before Pinnel's Case). As to where Coke ultimately stood, it seems clear that he preferred the rule that a preexisting duty could not act as consideration since he included *Pinnel's Case* in EDWARD COKE, COMMENTARY ON LITTLETON 212b (London: 1628).

39. Stock v. Mason, 1 B. & P. 286, 290 (1798) (per Buller, J.).

40. Every creditor undertakes to accept the composition in consideration of the like undertaking by the other creditors, as well as the debtor's promise to pay it. Creditors' compositions stood up against the later objection of a single creditor in order to bar one creditor from committing a fraud on the others. Butler v. Rhodes, 1 Esp. 236, 170 Eng. Rep. 341 (1794); Good v. Cheesman, 2 B. & Ad. 328, 109 Eng. Rep. 1165 (1831); Bartlett v. Woodsworth Co., 41 A. 264 (N.H. 1898).

41. Sibree v. Tripp, 15 M. & W. 22, 153 Eng. Rep. 745 (1846). *Sibree* partially overruled *Cumber v. Wane* since negotiable paper for less could now satisfy. *See* Cumber v. Wane, 1 Stra. 426, 93 Eng. Rep. 613 (1721) (Promise to take £5 note to satisfy £15 debt was no satisfaction.). *Cumber* merely cited *Pinnel's Case* by volume and page, didn't name the case and buried it amidst other citations. *See* 1 JOHN SMITH, SELECTION OF LEADING CASES 357, 359 (Philadelphia 8th ed. 1879) (*Cumber* followed *Pinnel*, which never seems to have been questioned.). *But cf.* D. & C. Builders Ltd. v. Rees, 3 All Eng. Rep. (1965), 2 Q. B. 617 (1966) (Judge Denning rejected *Sibree* since a negotiable check is the same as cash.). A smaller sum in a different currency was enforceable. City of San Juan v. St. John's Gas Co., 195 U.S. 510 (1904).

42. Foakes v. Beer, 9 App. Cas. 605, 622 (1884) (Per Blackburn: Coke was mistaken since merchants can find part-payment more beneficial.). Coke, C. J. later admitted in Bagge v. Slade, 3 Bulst. 162, 81 Eng. Rep. 137 (1616) that actual part-payment pursuant to an agreement between sureties was good consideration. A better case yet is Reynolds v. Pinhowe, Cro. Eliz. 429, 78 Eng. Rep. 669 (1595), where court held part-payment was good consideration "for it is a benefit unto him to have it without suit or charge."

43. The unified approach taken by the law lords, under Blackburn's leadership, reflected support for the push afoot to unify (and codify) the complexity and inconsistencies of common law contract rules buried in the scattered caselaw. This was further supported by Blackburn's referencing John Smiths's LEADING CASES' annotation of a so-called leading case like *Cumber v. Wane*; treatise writers were contributing to the unification and clarification process by their organizing work and their emphasis on first principles found in landmark cases.

Bentham's earlier codification push saw partial fruition during the second half of the nineteenth century. *Foakes v. Beer* was published two years after the English Bill of Exchange Act (Stat. 45 & 46 Vic., c. 61 (1882)) and nine years before the English Sales of Goods Act of 1893 retained the rule in *Foakes v. Beer*. *See* Samuel Williston, *The Law of Sales in Proposed Uniform Commercial Code*, 63 HARV. L. REV. 561, 564 (1950) (English Sales Act formulated in treatises by *Blackburn* and Benjamin.). The American Uniform Sales Act of 1906, drafted by Williston, followed on the heels of the English Sales Act.

44. *See* GEOFFREY CHESHIRE, CECIL FIFOOT and MICHAEL FURMSTON, LAW OF CONTRACT 88–90 (London: 11th ed. 1986); RESTATEMENT (SECOND) OF CONTRACTS sect. 73 (1981); 15 SAMUEL WILLISTON, A TREATISE ON THE LAW OF CONTRACTS, sect. 1837–1847 (New York: 3d ed. 1974 & Supp. 1986). *See also* JOHN DAWSON, *supra* note 36, at 209–210; FREDERICK POLLOCK, PRINCIPLES OF CONTRACT 187–188 (London: 10th ed. 1936). *And see* Levine v. Blumenthal, 117 N.J.L. 23, 186 A. 457 (1936) (Attempted modification of lease lacked consideration, citing *Pinnel* and *Foakes* as precedents.). Some types of obligations, earlier considered outside the scope of *Pinnel's Case,* were later precluded by the Statute of Frauds writing requirements. *See* SAMUEL STOLJAR, *supra* note 1, at 131–132 (citing examples of types of waivers, modifications and surrenders). Willistons's Uniform Sales Act of 1906 did not attempt to reform the preexisting duty rule; the Act was adopted by 37 jurisdictions.

45. *See* JAMES B. AMES (pt. 1), *supra* note 35, at 531; *see also* PATRICK ATIYAH, THE RISE AND FALL OF FREEDOM OF CONTRACT 440 (Oxford: 1979); *and see* ALLAN FARNSWORTH, CONTRACTS 280 (Boston: 1982) (frustrated the justified expectations of parties). Was freedom of contract merely a weapon of business to dispense with when it didn't benefit them as creditors? *See* LAWRENCE FREIDMAN, CONTRACT LAW IN AMERICA 189 (Madison: 1965).

46. Richards v. Bartlett, 1 Leon. 19, 74 Eng. Rep. 17 (1584).

47. *E.g.,* Vanderbilt v. Schreyer, 91 N.Y. 392 (1883) (Performance of preexisting duty is neither a benefit to promisor nor a detriment to promisee.); Warren v. Hodge, 121 Mass. 106 (1876).

48. *See* Edwin Patterson, *An Apology for Consideration,* 58 COLUM. L. REV. 929, 937 (1958).

49. *See* Harold Havighurst, *Consideration, Ethics and Administration,* 42 COLUM. L. REV. 1, 27–31 (1942).

50. Many of these cases involve law enforcement officers bargaining to obtain private advantage for performing their duties and are usually refused on public policy grounds, e.g., Somerset Bank v. Edmund, 76 Ohio St. 396, 81 N.E. 641 (1907) (reward refused); *but cf.* Board of Commissioners of Montgomery County v. Johnson, 126 Kans. 36, 266 P. 749 (1928) (Reward allowed since constables had no duty to arrest fugitive from another state.). There are constitutional bars to agreeing to pay extra money to government contractors. *See* McGovern v. New York, 234 N.Y. 377, 138 N.E. 26 (1923); Kizior v. City of St. Joseph, 329 S.W. 2d 605 (Mo. 1959).

51. The law lords in *Foakes v. Beer* casually cited accord precedents and the seamen's wage increase cases as fitting under the rule in *Pinnel's Case.* This influenced consolidation of modifications for increased and decreased duties under *Pinnel's* preexisting duty rule.

52. Harris v. Watson, Peake 102, 170 Eng. Rep. 94 (1791). From an equitable perspective, this plaintiff is in a weaker position than the plaintiffs in the next two seamen's cases since he was holding up the captain when in dire straits. It could be harmful to the morale of the remainder of the crew were the court to hold otherwise here.

53. Stilk v. Myrick, 2 Camp. 317, 319, 170 Eng. Rep. 1168, 1169 (1809) (2 deserters). *Accord* Alaska Packers' Assn. v. Domenico, 117 F. 99, 102 (1902) (No consideration found in similar promise made in remote place to pay seamen and

workers more.). *Cf.* GRANT GILMORE, THE DEATH OF CONTRACT 23–28 (Columbus, Ohio: 1974) (criticizes use of consideration logic in this case). In Yates v. Hall, 1 T.R. 73, 99 Eng. Rep. 979 (1785), a British sailor was induced by promise of payment by the captain to become a hostage (for nearly four years) as security for ransom in an incident during the American Revolutionary War. Lord Mansfield relied on policy to grant the plaintiff his extra wages, which were in excess of the value of the ship's cargo, because the agreement was a benefit to the owner, was a "just contract" and he added, "I would be loth to say, that this sailor, who was the means of obtaining the liberty of the rest of the crew, should not receive his wages; and I have not been able to bring myself to say that upon principle he shall not recover." Policy seems a better way of handling these cases. *See* ANTHONY KRONMAN and RICHARD POSNER, THE ECONOMICS OF CONTRACT LAW 57 (Boston: 1979) (If modifications of seamen's wages were enforced by courts, seamen could not expect to be able to negotiate a high wage thereafter in their original contracts because employer would know that seamen need not honor their original contracts and could extort.).

54. Harris v. Carter, 3 El. & Bl. 559, 118 Eng. Rep. 1251 (1854). The accepted practice was that seamen were expected to perform whatever duties were necessary during a voyage.

55. This dictum would be exploited in some American courts under the fiction of a rescission of the original contract and a later substitution of a new contract, thus disingenuously averting the preexisting duty rule.

56. *See* JAMES B. AMES, *supra* note 35, at 527–528 (Given the rule in *Pinnel's Case*, it follows that a promise in consideration of a duty owed would be invalid, but Ames could only find the seamen's cases on point.). Attorney for the debtor in *Foakes v. Beer* argued that the seamen's wages cases were decided on public policy rather than consideration. Foakes v. Beer, 9 App. Cas. 605, 609 (1884). This was true of two of the three seamen's wages cases.

CHAPTER 3

1. *E.g.*, Johnson v. Brannan, 5 Johns. 268 (N.Y. 1809); Kellogg v. Richards, 14 Wend. 116 (N.Y. 1837); Brooks v. White, 2 Met. 283 (Mass. 1840); Harper v. Graham, 20 Ohio 105 (1851); Engbretson v. Seiberling, 122 Ia. 522, 98 N.W. 319 (1904).

2. Brooks v. White, 2 Met. 283 (Mass. 1840).

3. Foakes v. Beer, 9 App. Cas. 605, 628 (H.L. 1884).

4. Brown v. Kern, 21 Wash. 211, 57 P. 798, 799 (1899) (cited Kellogg v. Richards, 14 Wend. 116 (N.Y. 1837), where transfer to creditor of a note for a lesser sum from a third person was good accord and satisfaction.). *Accord* Chicago, M. & St. P. Ry. Co. v. Clark, 178 U.S. 353 (1900) (Disputed claim found. Rule is considered with disfavor and should be strictly confined.).

5. *See* CHRISTOPHER LANGDELL, A SELECTION OF CASES ON THE LAW OF CONTRACTS (Boston: 1871); JOHN SMITH, SELECTION OF LEADING CASES (Philadelphia: 8th ed. 1879). *See also* KERMIT HALL, WILLIAM WIECEK and PAUL FINKELMAN, AMERICAN LEGAL HISTORY 316–325 (New York: 1991) (codification movement).

6. Cumber v. Wane, 1 Stra. 426, 93 Eng. Rep. 613 (1721).

7. Foakes v. Beer, 9 App. Cas. 605, 622 (1884); 1 JOHN SMITH, *supra* note 5, at 357, 359.

8. 1 JOHN SMITH, *supra* note 5, at 359.

9. Cumber v. Wane, 1 Stra. 426, 93 Eng. Rep. 613 (1721).

10. Sibree v. Tripp, 15 M. & W. 22, 31, 36, 153 Eng. Rep. 745, 749, 751 (1846).

11. Sibree v. Tripp, 15 M. & W. 22, 34, 153 Eng. Rep. 745, 750 (1846).

12. Sibree v. Tripp, 15 M. & W. 22, 31, 153 Eng. Rep. 745, 749 (1846).

13. Sibree v. Tripp, 15 M. & W. 22, 31, 153 Eng. Rep. 745, 749 (1846). Holt, C. J. had not required that consideration be proved for promissory notes well before *Cumber v. Wane.* Meredith v. Chute, 2 Ld. Raym. 759, 760, 92 Eng. Rep. 7 (1702). Commercial paper was a widely used mercantile method of transferring the equivalent of cash and had been recognized by Parliament during Holt's tenure on the bench. Stat. 3 & 4 Anne, c. 9 (1705).

14. Foakes v. Beer, 9 App. Cas. 605, 621 (1884).

15. *Fitch v. Sutton* was the other. Fitch v. Sutton, 5 East. 230, 232, 102 Eng. Rep. 1058 (1804) was one of three relevant composition of creditors cases that Lord Ellenborough participated in as lawyer or judge. He supported *Pinnel's Case* and *Cumber v. Wane* in *Fitch v. Sutton,* as a judge, after having argued earlier as an attorney, with Buller, J.'s support, that "[Cumber v. Wane] has since been repeatedly denied by this Court to be law." Heathcote v. Crookshanks, 2 T. R. 24, 26, 100 Eng. Rep. 14, 16 (1787). But then Ellenborough, C. J. seemed to hedge his support for *Cumber v. Wane* in Steinman v. Magnus, 11 East. 390, 394, 103 Eng. Rep. 1055, 1056 (1809) ("[i]f the evidence had gone but a little further, it would have altered our decision.").

16. Foakes v. Beer, 9 App. Cas. 605, 621–622 (1884).

17. Foakes v. Beer, 9 App. Cas. 605, 622 (1884); 1 JOHN SMITH, *supra* note 5, at 357, 363.

18. Foakes v. Beer, 9 App. Cas. 605, 607 (1884).

19. 1 JOHN SMITH, *supra* note 5, at 367. J. W. Smith's note was retained by his subsequent editors.

20. James B. Ames, *Two Theories of Consideration* (pt. 1), 13 HARV. L. REV. 515, 531 (1899) (Definition supports freedom of contract and business practices. *Id.* at 518, 520–1, 530, 531.).

21. Lord Mansfield (C. J. K. B. 1756–1788) urged enforcement of promises generally based on moral obligation, especially if commercial. *See* Pillans v. Van Mierop, 3 Burr. 1663, 97 Eng. Rep. 1035 (1765); Atkins v. Hill, 1 Cowp. 284, 98 Eng. Rep. 1088 (1775); Hawkes v. Saunders, 1 Cowp. 289, 98 Eng. Rep. 1091 (1782). The promises in these three cases were based on past consideration. *Cf.* James B. Ames, *supra* note 20, at 531 (Any act given in exchange for a promise should be a basis for enforcement.).

22. *See* James B. Ames, *supra* note 20, at 531 (Rule "is repugnant alike to judges and men of business."); Lon Fuller, *Consideration and Form,* 41 COLUM. L. REV. 799, 818 (1941) (Channeling function of expression of intent satisfied by agreed-to contract modification.). *And see* Wright, *Ought the Doctrine of Consideration Be Abolished from the Common Law?* 49 HARV. L. REV. 1225, 1229 (1936) (defeats legitimate interests of parties in ordinary business transactions). Lord Selbourne, in 1884 Foakes v. Beer, 9 App. Cas. 605, at 613, said: "The courts might very well have held the contrary and left the matter to the agreement of the parties." *See also*

Langdon v. Langdon, 4 Gray (70 Mass.) 186, 189 (1855) (Shaw, C. J. said the rule is "somewhat harsh, contrary to the apparent intention of the parties in making a compromise settlement, and not in harmony with the dictates of natural justice, it is to be strictly construed."); Milliken v. Brown, 1 Rawle (16 Pa.) 391, 397, 398 (1829) ("Universally the law is, or ought to be, that the meaning or intention of the parties is, if it can be distinctly known, to have effect unless the intention contravenes some well-established principle of law." *Id.* at 397.).

23. *See* PATRICK ATIYAH, THE RISE AND FALL OF FREEDOM OF CONTRACT 388 (Oxford: 1979); MORTON HORWITZ, THE TRANSFORMATION OF AMERICAN LAW (1780–1860) 263–264 (Cambridge, Mass. 1977); *see also* MAX WEBER, ON LAW IN ECONOMY AND SOCIETY 301–321 (M. Rheinstein ed. Cambridge, Mass.: 1954).

24. Common Law Procedure Acts of 1852 & 1854, 15 & 16 Vic., c. 76 (1852), 17 & 18 Vic., c. 125 (1854); Judicature Act, 38 & 39 Vic., c. 77 (1875); *see* Charles Hepburn, *The Historical Development of Code Pleading in America and England* in 2 SELECT ESSAYS IN ANGLO-AMERICAN LEGAL HISTORY 643 (1909); *see also* CECIL FIFOOT, HISTORY AND SOURCES OF THE COMMON LAW: TORT AND CONTRACT 232–241 (London: 1949).

25. *See* 1A ARTHUR CORBIN, CORBIN ON CONTRACTS sect. 174 (St. Paul: 1950); Alfred Denning, *Recent Developments in the Doctrine of Consideration*, 15 MOD. L. REV. 1, 3–5 (1952). *And see* 1 JOHN SMITH, *supra* note 5, at 372 (Since 1873 Judicature Act, 36 & 37 Vic., c. 66, s. 24, sub. 2, court will give equitable defense to contract the same effect as chancery would.).

26. Brooks v. White, 2 Met. 283, 285 (Mass. 1840). *Cf.* Ebert v. Johns, 206 Pa. 395, 55 A. 1064 (1903) (Once the creditor decides to take less, "justice and common honesty ought to hold him to his agreement.").

27. *E.g.*, Harper v. Graham, 20 Ohio 105 (1851) (no rational difference between the rule and exceptions).

28. *See* Herman v. Schesinger, 114 Wis. 382, 90 N.W. 460 (1902) (Any little benefit to creditor is enough.).

29. Couldery v. Bartrum, 19 Ch. Div. 394, 399 (1881) (composition). *See* Ebert v. Johns, 206 Pa. 395, 55 A. 1064 (1903) (Questions "scholastic logic" that agreement to pay less on debt not due is enforceable but agreement for part after due date is unenforceable.).

30. *See* Edwin Patterson, *An Apology for Consideration*, 58 COLUM. L. REV. 929, 936 (1958); Wright, *supra* note 22, at 1229–1231, 1247. *And see* James B. Ames, *supra* note 20, 521–531.

31. Harold Havighurst, *Consideration, Ethics and Administration*, 42 COLUM. L. REV. 1, 25n. (1942) (92 of 183 instances found in West's Northeast and Northwest Reporters.).

32. Reynolds v. Pinhowe, Cro. Eliz. 429, 78 Eng. Rep. 669 (1594). The fact that payment was made early was probably relevant. *See* ALFRED SIMPSON, A HISTORY OF THE COMMON LAW OF CONTRACT 474–475 (Oxford: 1975).

33. Rawlins v. Lockey, 1 Vin. Abr. 308, pl. 24 (1639), cited and quoted in James B. Ames, *supra* note 20, at 523. *See also* Johnson v. Astell, 1 Lev. 198 (1667) ("Payment without suit or trouble is good consideration.").

34. Foakes v. Beer, 9 App. Cas. 605, 622 (1884); *see also* Melroy v. Kemmerer, 218 Pa. 381, 67 A. 699 (1907) (There is a beneficial "practical importance of the

difference between the [creditor's] right of the thing and the actual possession of it.'').

35. Curtiss v. Martin, 20 Ill. 557, 577 (1858) (exception when failing debtor pays less); Brown v. Kern, 21 Wash. 211, 57 P. 798 (1899).

36. Brown v. Kern, 21 Wash. 211, 57 P. 798, 800 (1899). There was no concern about whether the paper was negotiable.

37. Bagge v. Slade, 3 Bulst. 162, 81 Eng. Rep. 137 (1616).

38. Wadsworth v. Thompson, 8 Ill. 423 (1846) (Debtor didn't make original deadline because of reliance on promise made before deadline giving more time.). In the twentieth century, this dispute might be resolved under promissory estoppel rather than needing to manipulate the doctrine of consideration.

39. *See* Frye v. Hubbell, 74 N.H. 358, 68 A. 325 (1907).

40. 1A ARTHUR CORBIN, *supra* note 25, at sect. 172.

41. *See* Edwin Patterson, *supra* note 30, at 936–938 (Coercion would seem to be the commonest ground for avoiding second bargain.). *See* also Alaska Packers Ass'n v. Domenico, 117 Fed. 99 (9th Cir. 1902).

42. Of the three seamen's wages cases discussed above, Harris v. Watson, Peake 72, 170 Eng. Rep. 94 (1791) especially comes to mind since the plaintiff-seaman exacted the captain's promise of higher wages in the midst of a storm.

43. *See* CECIL FIFOOT, *supra* note 24, at 414 (An element essential to formation is irrelevant to discharge.); Alfred Denning, *supra* note 25, at 1: *cf.* SAMUEL STOLJAR, A HISTORY OF CONTRACT AT COMMON LAW 120–121 (Canberra: 1975). U.C.C. sect. 2–209(1) follows from this.

44. *See* Lon Fuller, *supra* note 22, at 805–806, 818. *Cp.* RESTATEMENT (SECOND) OF CONTRACTS sect. 74 (1981).

45. *See* Merton Ferson, *The Rule in Foakes v. Beer*, 31 YALE L.J. 15, 23 (1921). *And see* SAMUEL STOLJAR, *supra* note 43, at 120–1 (Bargain is essential basis of accord, though it might have been preferred policy to enforced freely consented-to agreement.).

46. Wentz v. Dehaven, 1 Serg. & R. (40 Pa.) 311, 315 (1815).

47. *See, e.g.*, Frye v. Hubbell, 74 N.H. 358, 68 A. 325, 334 (1907).

48. Some of the parallel modern common law contract doctrines which did develop to accommodate change include: (1) the use of good faith to police open-ended language in long term contracts, (2) excuse for impossibility, frustration and impracticability, (3) liberal application of the parol evidence rule, (4) easy incorporation of trade usage, (5) limitations on remote damages, (6) enforceability of futures contracts and (7) broad judicial support for arbitration of disputes over adjustments to contracts.

49. *See* Harold Havighurst, *Consideration, Ethics and Administration*, 42 COLUM. L. REV. 1, 25n. (1942) (survey of N.E. and N.W. West reporter systems).

50. Pinnel's Case, 5 Co. Rep. 117a (1602). Adequacy of the novelty was of course irrelevant and it was supposed to also be irrelevant to a part-payment in cash, but a court would occasionally slip and use inadequacy logic. *See* Cumber v. Wane, 93 Eng. Rep. 613 (1721) (per Pratt).

51. Lynn v. Bruce, 2 H. Bl. 317, 126 Eng. Rep. 571 (1794).

52. Sibree v. Tripp, 15 M. & W. 22, 153 Eng. Rep. 745 (1846); *see* Baker v. Walker, 14 M. & W. 465, 468, 22 Eng. Rep. 252, 259 (1845) (negotiable instrument ''resembles a specialty'' sealed).

53. *See* Henderson v. Stobart, 5 Exch. 99, 155 Eng. Rep. 43 (1850); Kellogg v. Richards, 14 Wend. 116 (N.Y. 1837).

54. *See* Fuller v. Kemp, 138 N.Y. 231, 33 N.E. 1034 (1893) (dispute); Wilkinson v. Byers, 1 A. & E. 106 (1834) (unliquidated claim).

55. *See* Stoudenmeier v. Williamson, 29 Ala. 558, 568 (1857); Evans v. Oregon & W.R. Co., 58 Wash. 429, 108 P. 1095 (1910) (abandonment of old and creation of new). Restatement Second rejects this fiction both because rescission and substitution are simultaneous and because it opens door to unfair modifications. RESTATEMENT (SECOND) OF CONTRACTS sect. 89 cmt. b (1981).

56. Pillans v. Van Mierop, 3 Burr. 1663, 97 Eng. Rep. 1035 (1765). *See* Lon Fuller, *supra* note 22, at 799, 800.

57. *See* Jaffray v. Davis, 124 N.Y. 164, 26 N.E. 351 (1891) (accord). England retains the seal today.

58. *See* Aborn v. Rathbone, 54 Conn. 44, 8 A. 677 (1886) (controversy over whether receipt was on account or in discharge of obligation).

59. *See* Dreyfus v. Roberts, 75 Ark. 354, 87 S.W. 641 (1905) (Court expressly didn't rule on whether a fully satisfied oral accord was sufficient. Also court said: "Commercial affairs adjust themselves along practical, and not technical lines."); Marysville Development Co. v. Hargis, 41 Idaho 257, 239 P. 522 (1925) (Consideration said to be immaterial at discharge.).

60. *See* Linz v. Schuck, 106 Md. 220, 232–3, 67 A. 286, 289 (1907) (Swamp-like conditions found under excavation site.); King v. Louisville & N.R. Co., 131 Ky. 46, 114 S.W. 308 (1908) (Since both parties expected loose earth rather than rock, there was a "sufficient consideration upon which to base a subsequent agreement with respect to the changed circumstances." *Id.* at 310.); Blakeslee v. Water Commissioners, 106 Conn. 642, 139 A. 106 (1927); Liebreich v. Tyler State Bank & Trust Co., 100 S.W. 2d 152 (Tex. 1936) (Unexpected depression was consideration for modification.).

61. *See* King v. Duluth, 61 Minn. 482 (1895) (dictum).

62. *See* Butler v. Rhodes, 1 Esp. 236, 170 Eng. Rep. 341 (1794); Good v. Cheesman, 2 B. & Ad. 328, 109 Eng. Rep. 1165 (1831).

63. *See* Gray v. Barton, 55 N.Y. 68 (1873); McKenzie v. Harrison, 120 N.Y. 260, 24 N.E. 458 (1890) (Gift logic makes it unnecessary to approve or disapprove of *Foakes v. Beer.*).

64. *See* Meech v. City of Buffalo, 29 N.Y. 198, 218 (1864); Watkins & Son, Inc. v. Carrig, 91 N.H. 459, 464 21 A. 2d 591, 594 (1941).

65. *See* Milward v. Ingram, 1 Mod. 205, 86 Eng. Rep. 831 (1686); Egles v. Vale, Cro. Jac. 70, 79 Eng. Rep. 59 (1606).

66. Harper v. Graham, 20 Ohio 105, 115 (1851) (payment at different place).

67. Clayton v. Clark, 74 Miss. 499, 21 So. 565 (1896).

68. Clayton v. Clark, 74 Miss. 499, 21 So. 565, 567 (1896). Sibree v. Tripp, 15 M. & W. 22, 153 Eng. Rep. 745 (1846) came closest to overturning the rule earlier.

69. Clayton v. Clark, 74 Miss. 499, 21 So. 565, 568 (1896). This phraseology was apt for the Reconstruction period.

70. Clayton v. Clark, 74 Miss. 499, 21 So. 565, 569 (1896).

71. Frye v. Hubbell, 74 N.H. 358, 68 A. 325 (1907).

72. Frye v. Hubbell, 74 N.H. 358, 68 A. 325, 334 (1907) ("[t]he greater principle [is] that reason is the life of the law.").

73. Rye v. Phillips, 203 Minn. 567, 282 N.W. 459 (1938).

74. Winter-Wolff & Co. v. Co-Op Lead & Chem. Co., 261 Minn. 199, 111 N.W. 2d 461 (1961). Case had a dissenting opinion because debtor's use of a part-payment check in full satisfaction shouldn't constitute an accord just because creditor retained the check; dissent stated there needed to be a negotiated settlement agreement before the check could answer as satisfaction.

75. Rye v. Phillips, 203 Minn. 567, 282 N.W. 459, 460 (1938) (cited critical dictum in Oien v. St. Paul City Ry. Co., 198 Minn. 363, 373, 270 N.W. 1, 6 (1936)). The *Oien* case (at 270 N.W. 6), along with Herman v. Schlesinger, 90 N.W. 460, 466 (Wis. 1902), incorrectly claimed that Connecticut had abandoned preexisting duty rule, but Ford v. Hubinger, 64 Conn. 129, 29 A. 129 (1894) had involved a compromise of a dispute.

76. Rye v. Phillips, 203 Minn. 567, 282 N.W. 459, 460 (1938) (accord on non-negotiable note). *But cf.* Frye v. Hubbell, 74 N.H. 358, 68 A. 325, 333 (1907) (Confusion arises over failure to distinguish between legal and moral obligation.).

77. Brown v. Everhard, 52 Wis. 205, 8 N.W. 725 (1881) (consideration and Statute of Frauds issues intertwined); *accord* Wisconsin Sulphite Fibre Co. v. Jeffries Lumber Co., 111 N.W. 237 (1907) (involved Statute of Frauds and consideration issues). What seemed to begin as a rule for contract changes raising a potential Statute of Frauds problem was converted by the 1930s into a general rule that consideration from the original contract was "imported" into the contract modification in order to overcome the preexisting duty rule. In 1902, Wisconsin courts still recognized that an accord required consideration, but by 1935, Wisconsin courts weren't mentioning the preexisting duty rule in contract modification cases generally, even where there was no direct Statute of Frauds issue, and were "importing" consideration into the modification. *See* Herman v. Schlesinger, 90 N.W. 460, 466 (Wis. 1902) (accord needs consideration); Holly v. First Nat. Bank of Kenosha, 260 N.W. 429, 430 (Wis. 1935) (Change of pledge agreement needs no new consideration since consideration imported.).

78. Stead v. Dawber, 10 Ad. & El. 57, 66, 113 Eng. Rep. 22, 26 (1839). The issue in the case concerned whether modification complied with Statute of Frauds; Denman's dictum that consideration of first contract was imported to second one was merely intended to keep the focus on the writing issue. *See Id.* at 25–26. No English decision subsequent to *Stead v. Dawber* misinterpreted it as the Wisconsin court did.

79. *See* SAMUEL THORNE, SIR EDWARD COKE (1552–1952) 7, 13 (Selden Society Lecture, 1952) (When Coke wrote "for it is an ancient maxim" or listed an inordinate number of authorities, be prepared for Coke's enunciation of a new rule.) The language in some of the cases using the fiction of a rescission sounds very much like Wisconsin's import fiction. *See* Awe v. Gadd, 179 Ia. 520, 161 N.W. 671, 673 (1971) ("In such case the old agreement would be the consideration for the new.").

80. Moore v. Williamson, 213 Ala. 274, 104 So. 645, 646–647 (1925) (Modification allowed "without any new, independent, or distinct consideration for the change, other than that of mutual assent." *Id.* at 646.). Since the old precedent Strangborough v. Warner, 4 Leo. 3, 74 Eng. Rep. 686 (1589), reciprocal promises could be consideration for each other. The court in Moore v. Williamson, 104 So. 645, 647 (Ala. 1925) claimed that Hembree v. Glover, 93 Ala. 622, 8 So. 660, 661

(1890) specifically said that no consideration was required other than the parties' mutual assent, but in fact *Hembree v. Glover* only declared a modification binding without giving a reason. *Cf.* Clark v. Jones, 85 Ala. 127, 4 So. 771, 773 (1888) ("Parties, before a breach, may rescind at pleasure and their mutual assent is a sufficient consideration."). American appellate courts played fast and loose with precedent in order to enforce common consent.

81. George v. Roberts, 186 Ala. 521, 65 So. 345 (1914) (Executory contract may be modified "without any new or independent consideration."). *And see* Cooper v. McIlwain, 58 Ala. 296 (1877) ("There can be no doubt that the parties to a contract may rescind or modify it, at pleasure; and their mutual assent is all that is necessary to support the modification or rescission." *Id.* at 300.).

82. Industrial Development Board of the Town of Section v. Fuqua Ind., Inc., 523 F. 2d 1226, 1241 (1975) (construction project).

83. Harris v. Watson, Peake 72, 170 Eng. Rep. 94 (1791) (per Lord Kenyon).

84. Stilk v. Myrick, 2 Camp. 317, 170 Eng. Rep. 1168 (1809) (per Lord Ellenborough).

85. Foakes v. Beer, 9 App. Cas. 605 (H.L. 1884). *Foakes v. Beer* promoted the uniting of a variety of preexisting duties categories under the head of the rule in *Pinnel's Case.* The seamen's wage increase cases were cited, as precedent, though the *Foakes* case involved a *Pinnel*—like accord to pay less than originally agreed. The *Pinnel* rule prevailed despite the support Campbell, C.J. gave for Kenyon's policy logic in 1854. Harris v. Carter, 3 El. & Bl. 559, 118 Eng. Rep. 1251 (1854). For an extended discussion criticizing the role of the preexisting duty rule as a policing mechanism, *see* Mark Wessman, *Retraining the Gatekeeper: Further Reflections on the Doctrine of Consideration,* 29 LOYOLA L.A. LAW REV. 713, 745–771 (1996).

86. Munroe v. Perkins, 26 Mass. 303, 9 Pick. 298, 20 Am. Dec. 475 (1830); Parrot v. Mexican Cent. Ry. Co., 207 Mass. 184, 194, 93 N.E. 590, 594 (1911); *see* Wescott v. Mitchell, 95 Me. 377, 50 A. 21 (1901) (followed "Massachusetts rule").

87. Parrot v. Mexican Cent. Ry. Co., 207 Mass. 184, 93 N.E. 590, 594 (1911) (If defendant desires to secure the work rather than damages, his promise to pay more is enforceable.); Swartz v. Lieberman, 323 Mass. 109, 80 N.E. 2d 5, 6 (1948) (Defendant refused to do more work unless paid more.).

88. *E.g.*, King v. Duluth, M. & N. Ry. Co., 61 Minn. 482, 63 N.W. 1105, 1106 (1895).

89. Munroe v. Perkins, 26 Mass. 303, 9 Pick. 298, 20 Am. Dec. 475 (1830) (First contract "waived" by plaintiff electing to breach and thereby subjecting self to damages. Defendant accepted waiver and promised higher pay for new contract, to keep job going. Plaintiff continued in reliance on defendant's promise.); Parrot v. Mexican Cent. Ry. Co., 207 Mass. 184, 93 N.E. 590, 594 (1911); Swartz v. Lieberman, 323 Mass. 109, 80 N.E. 2d 5, 6 (1948). The technique of rescission and substitution is sometimes used in Massachusetts cases. Some courts have applied the Massachusetts consideration logic when there was an unanticipated circumstance prompting a modification. *See* Michaud v. McGregor, 61 Minn. 198, 63 N.W. 479, 480 (1895) (Rule not coercive because of circumstances and fact that contractor agreed to do something more.); Curry v. Boeckeler Lumber Co., 27 S.W. 2d 473, 475 (Mo. 1930) (Gave up right to breach and no coercion).

90. *See* Blakeslee v. Board of Water Com'rs of City of Hartford, 139 A. 106, 110 (Conn. 1927).

91. *See* Willard Barbour, *The "Right" to Break a Contract,* 16 MICH. L. REV. 106, 107–109 (1917) (Promisor has duty to perform since time of Bracton.); 1A ARTHUR CORBIN, *supra* note 25, at sect. 182 (There's no right to breach but rather a primary duty to perform and a secondary duty to pay damages). Holmes had promoted the Massachusetts view: "The duty to keep a contract at common law means a prediction that you must pay damages if you do not keep it,—and nothing else." Oliver Holmes Jr., *The Path of the Law,* 10 HARV. L. REV. 457, 462 (1897) ("Nowhere is the confusion between legal and moral ideas more manifest than in the law of contract." *Id.*). In the ongoing Transatlantic correspondence between Holmes and Pollock, Pollock continually chided Holmes for his view on contract breach. Pollock subtly questioned the proposition's morality and preferred instead the law's protection of the promisee's reasonable expectations. *See* 1 HOLMES-POLLOCK LETTERS 80 (ed. Mark Howe, Cambridge: 1946) and 2 *Id.* at 233.

92. HENRY DE BRACTON, DE LEGIBUS, fo. 16b–17 (d. 1268); *but cf.* Y. B. 20 Edw. III (Lib. Ass.) 72, pl. 14 (1346) (release ineffective since made under pressure of seizure of signer's lifestock).

93. EDWARD COKE, SECOND INSTITUTES 482–483 (London: 1642); *accord* 1 WILLIAM BLACKSTONE, COMMENTARIES ON THE LAWS OF ENGLAND 131 (Oxford: 1765) ("but no suitable atonement can be made for loss of life or limb.").

94. Astley v. Reynolds, 2 Stra. 915, 93 Eng. Rep. 939 (K.B. 1732). *See* Summer v. Ferry, 11 Mod. 201, 88 Eng. Rep. 989 (K.B. 1709) (Defense lawyer alleged duress of goods had been upheld in earlier case, but Holt, J. rejected it.).

95. *See* John Dawson, *Economic Duress—An Essay in Perspective,* 45 MICH. L. REV. 253, 268–282 (1947).

96. Ashmole v. Wainwright, 2 Q.B. 837, 114 Eng. Rep. 325 (1842); Parker v. Great Western Ry., 7 Man. & G. 253, 135 Eng. Rep. 107 (C.P. 1844); Newland v. Buncombe Turnpike Co., 26 N.C. 372 (1844).

97. *See* MORTON HORWITZ, *supra* note 23, at 261–263; *cf.* John Dawson, *supra* note 95, at 277–278, 287–288 (Equitable concern for equivalency sometimes made analysis of free will incidental.).

98. Skeate v. Beale, 11 Ad. & E1. 983, 113 Eng. Rep. 688 (1840). There was an alternative remedy here of suing on the excessive distraint. It is also arguable that *Skeate* differs from cases of duress of goods and of utilities exacting overcharges in that they were restitutional actions but *Skeate* involved a defense to a common law damages action.

99. Restitution was available under *Astley v. Reynolds* for any unlawful payment, but *Skeate v. Beale* held that the modification agreement itself was valid. The *Skeate v. Beale* court didn't seem to consider the effect of the preexisting duty rule since the agreement at issue involved removal of the creditor's possessory lien.

100. *See* Cobb v. Charter, 32 Conn. 358 (1865) (duress of goods); Brumagin v. Tillinghast, 18 Cal. 265, 272 (1861) (Dictum that it was duress to exert power over person or property to exact payment when no alternative for victim.); *accord* Radich v. Hutchins, 95 U.S. 210, 213 (1877) (Per Field, J., who also wrote *Brumagin* opinion.); *and see* RESTATEMENT OF CONTRACTS sect. 493(d) (1932).

101. For the recent recognition of economic duress in England, *see* GUENTER TREITEL, THE LAW OF CONTRACT 363–365 (London: 1991). A modern version of a seamen's wage dispute was resolved, as Lord Kenyon had approached the

problem in Harris v. Watson, 170 Eng. Rep. 94 (1791), on the grounds of economic duress. The Universe Sentinel, 1 A.C. 366, 383 (1983) (Agreement of shipowner to pay more to crew was found unenforceable in England.).

102. Hackley v. Headley, 45 Mich. 569, 8 N.W. 511 (1881).

103. The alleged economic duress related to refusal to pay at due date.

104. A later remand of the case concluded that in fact there was no dispute. Headley v. Hackley, 50 Mich. 43, 14 N.W. 693 (1883), *infra.*

105. Hackley v. Headley, 45 Mich. 569, 8 N.W. 511, 513 (1881).

106. Hackley v. Headley, 45 Mich. 569, 8 N.W. 511, 514 (1881).

107. Goebel v. Linn, 47 Mich. 489, 11 N.W. 284 (1882).

108. Goebel v. Linn, 47 Mich. 489, 11 N.W. 284, 286 (1882).

109. Goebel v. Linn, 47 Mich. 489, 11 N.W. 284, 286 (1882).

110. Cooley's enforcement of the modification agreement due to the "very extraordinary circumstances of the entire failure of the local ice crop" may be considered one of the harbingers of Restatement (Second) of Contracts sections 89(a), *infra.* Cooley said: "Unexpected and extraordinary circumstances had rendered the contract worthless; and they must either make a new arrangement, or, in insisting on holding the ice company to the existing contract, they would ruin the ice company and thereby at the same time ruin themselves. It would be very strange if under such a condition of things the existing contract, which unexpected events had rendered of no value, could stand in the way of a new arrangement." Goebel v. Linn, 47 Mich. 489, 11 N.W. 284, 285–286 (1882). *Cf.* Lingenfelder v. The Wainwright Brewing Co., 103 Mo. 578, 15 S.W. 844 (1891) (Criticized Cooley's enforcement of modification in *Goebel v. Linn* as "not in accord with the almost universally accepted doctrine" of the preexisting duty rule. *Id.* at 848.). Alternatively, Cooley may not have referred to the preexisting duty rule because he did not support what *Foakes v. Beer* did two years later in unifying price decreases (*Pinnel*) with price increases (*e.g., Stilk v. Myrick* seamen's wage case) under the single head of the preexisting duty rule. Assuming the absence of economic duress, Cooley's approach in *Goebel v. Linn* was a departure from the earlier seamen's wage cases' refusal to enforce modifications prompted by changed circumstances. *Goebel's* changed circumstances obviated fear of coercion.

111. *See* RESTATEMENT OF CONTRACTS sect. 493(d) (1932) (Duress of goods can preclude free will.); RESTATEMENT (SECOND) OF CONTRACTS sect. 176(d) and cmts. (a) and (e) (1981) (Modification induced by economic duress may be avoided.).

112. Headley v. Hackley, 50 Mich. 43, 14 N.W. 693 (1883).

113. Headley v. Hackley, 50 Mich. 43, 14 N.W. 693, 694 (1883). The first review of the case assumed there was a bona fide dispute. Once the second trial verdict included a finding of no dispute, a formalist court could have employed the preexisting duty rule to refuse to enforce the agreement rather than basing its ruling on bad faith; instead, this court adopted an equitable ground to support the second jury's insistence that the defendant was in the wrong. The decision came one year prior to the preexisting duty case *Foakes v. Beer.*

114. Headley v. Hackley, 50 Mich. 43, 14 N.W. 693, 695 (1883).

115. Lingenfelder v. The Wainwright Brewing Co., 103 Mo. 578, 15 S.W. 844 (1891).

116. Lingenfelder v. The Wainwright Brewing Co., 103 Mo. 578, 15 S.W. 844,

848 (1891). Effectively, the court merged the policy logic of the seamen's wage case, *Harris v. Watson*, with the consideration logic of the seamen's wage case, *Stilk v. Myrick*, to rule that consideration was lacking on policy grounds.

117. Lingenfelder v. The Wainwright Brewing Co., 103 Mo. 578, 15 S.W. 844, 848 (1891). For another case, where a finding of lack of consideration was a stalking horse for a finding of economic duress, *see* Alaska Packers' Assn' v. Domenico, 117 P. 99, 102 (1902) (Public policy notions used to find no consideration when sailors and workers at a remote location refused to work unless paid more.).

118. Fitzgerald v. Fitzgerald & Mallory Construction Co., 44 Neb. 463, 62 N.W. 899 (1895).

119. Fitzgerald v. Fitzgerald & Mallory Construction Co., 44 Neb. 463, 62 N.W. 899, 909 (1895). *See* Foote v. DePoy, 126 Iowa 366, 370–372, 102 N.W. 112, 114 (1905) (Duress found when elderly man in feeble condition signed contract with his ex-wife in order to obtain dismissal of lawsuit as a means of relieving himself of stress.).

120. Thomas & Cross v. Brown, 116 Va. 233, 81 S.E. 56 (1914).

121. Thomas & Cross v. Brown, 116 Va. 233, 81 S.E. 56, 57 (1914). *See* Virginia Code, sect. 2828 (1887).

122. *See* RESTATEMENT (SECOND) OF CONTRACTS sect. 176 (1981).

123. The remedy for economic duress is to obtain a ruling declaring the modification agreement unenforceable and to then recover for any benefits conferred under restitution. *See* RESTATEMENT OF THE LAW OF RESTITUTION sects. 47, 51, 150–152 (1937). Tort relief is normally unavailable for economic duress, in the absence of a traditional tort. *See* John Dawson, *supra* note 95, at 285.

124. *Cf.* Williams v. Roffey, 1 All Eng. Rep. 512, 526 (1990) (The presence of economic duress defense makes court more inclined in commercial cases "to look for mutual advantages which would amount to sufficient consideration to support the second agreement under which the extra money is paid."). The U.C.C. abandoned the preexisting duty rule for sales contracts roughly contemporaneously with economic duress becoming a majority rule. U.C.C. sect. 2–209(1) (1952).

125. By the fifteenth century, chancery was providing relief for weak parties dominated by the local strong man. *See* Willard Barbour, *The History of Contract in Early English Equity* in IV OXFORD STUDIES IN SOCIAL AND LEGAL HISTORY 78–80 (P. Vinogradoff ed., 1914). There was consistent relief from the penalty on the conditioned bond by the seventeenth century. *See* ALFRED SIMPSON, *supra* note 32, at 119–121. The fountainhead unconscionability decision in chancery, and which influenced the modern common law, was Earl of Chesterfield v. Janssen, 2 Ves. Sen. 125, 28 Eng. Rep. 82 (1750) (Chancellor Hardwicke rejected "unequitable and unconscientious bargains" which "no man in his senses . . . would make . . . and as no honest and fair man would accept."). American law provided equitable relief against "hard and unconscionable" bargains by the early nineteenth century. *See* 1 JOSEPH STORY, COMMENTARIES ON EQUITY JURISPRUDENCE sect. 258 (Boston: 1836); 2 JAMES KENT, COMMENTARIES ON EQUITY JURISPRUDENCE 490 (New York: 12th ed. 1873); *and see* Coles v. Trecothick, 9 Ves. Jr. 234, 236, 32 Eng. Rep. 592, 597 (1804) ("the inadequacy of price is such as shocks the conscience").

126. *See* cases between 1920s and 1950s cited in Comment 1 to U.C.C. sect. 2–302.

127. U.C.C. Reporter Karl Llewellyn's first drafts of an unconscionability section between 1941 and 1947 limited the applicability of unconscionability to the boiler plate language in standardized contracts. The 1948 draft, and succeeding ones leading to the final 1952 version, opened it up to any type of contract or contract provision. *See* KARL LLEWELLYN, THE COMMON LAW TRADITION: DECIDING APPEALS 370 (Boston: 1960); Leff, *Unconscionability and the Code—The Emperor's New Clause,* 115 U. PA. L. REV. 485, 489–495 (1967).

128. *See* Benjamin Boyer, *Promissory Estoppel: Principle from Precedents,* 50 MICH. L. REV. 639, 644 (1952); 1 SAMUEL WILLISTON, TREATISE ON THE LAW OF CONTRACTS 307–308 (New York: 1921).

129. *E.g.,* James Baird Co. v. Gimbel Bros., 64 F. 2d 344, 346 (2d Cir. 1933) (per Learned Hand, J.).

130. *See* Northwestern Engineering Co. v. Ellerman, 69 S.D. 397, 10 N.W. 2d 879 (1943); Drennan v. Star Paving Co., 51 Cal. 2d 409, 333 P. 2d 757 (1958) (per Traynor, J.).

131. Wadsworth v. Thompson, 8 Ill. 423 (1846). *See* Munroe v. Perkins, 26 Mass. 303, 9 Pick. 298, 20 Am. Dec. 475, 479 (1830). While the *Munroe* decision employed logic akin to a rescission fiction to answer call for consideration for the modification, the court also emphasized that, once the promise of more pay was given, "he afterward went upon the faith of the new promise, and finished the work."

132. Maxwell v. Graves, 59 Ia. 613, 13 N.W. 758 (1882).

133. Maxwell v. Graves, 59 Ind. 613, 13 N.W. 758, 759 (1882). The return delivery of the cows to the defendant seemed a very modest reliance.

134. McKenzie v. Harrison, 120 N.Y. 260, 24 N.E. 458 (1890).

135. McKenzie v. Harrison, 120 N.Y. 260, 24 N.E. 458, 460 (1890).

136. McKenzie v. Harrison, 120 N.Y. 260, 24 N.E. 458, 459 (1890).

137. McKenzie v. Harrison, 120 N.Y. 260, 24 N.E. 458, 459–460 (1890).

138. Brown v. Kern, 21 Wash. 211, 57 P. 798 (1899).

139. Brown v. Kern, 21 Wash. 211, 57 P. 798, 799 (1899); *but cf.* King v. Duluth, M. & N. Ry. Co., 61 Minn. 482, 63 N.W. 1105, 1107 (1895) (Modification, in violation of preexisting duty rule, is unenforceable even if reliance.).

140. Brown v. Kern, 21 Wash. 211, 57 P. 798, 799 (1899). Nonetheless, allowing the partial payment to stand as consideration was effectively rejection of the rule. For other cases around the turn of the century enforcing modifications because of reliance disguised as consideration, *see* Arbogast v. Mylius, 55 W. Va. 101, 46 S.E. 809 (1904) ("The contract having been rescinded by mutual consent, and [seller] having in good faith" resold, the buyer is "estopped" from objecting. Two-pronged rationale of estoppel and consideration used.); Blaess v. Nichols & Shepard Co., 115 Ia. 373, 88 N.W. 829 (1902) (Where one party under modification has performed, the other can't object that there was no consideration.); American Food Co. v. Halstead, 165 Ind. 633, 76 N.E. 251 (1905).

141. *See* Meech v. City of Buffalo, 29 N.Y. 198 (1864) (Contractor proceeded with work on the faith of the promise of extra compensation.); King v. Duluth, M. & N. Ry. Co., 61 Minn. 482, 63 N.W. 1105 (1895) (Construction work done in reliance on promise.); Michaud v. McGregor, 61 Minn. 198, 63 N.W. 479 (1895) (Promisee did work in reliance on waiver.); Schwartzreich v. Bauman-Basch, 231

N.Y. 196, 131 N.E. 887 (1921) (Employee relied on employer's promise of more salary and didn't change jobs.); Blakeslee v. Board of Water Com'rs of City of Hartford, 139 A. 106, 110, 112 (Conn. 1927) (Inducing promisee to perform was indicator of consideration.). *See* RESTATEMENT (SECOND) CONTRACTS sect. 89(c). Cases of unanticipated circumstances will be more fully developed in Chapter 5.

142. RESTATEMENT OF CONTRACTS sect. 90 (1932); *and see* RESTATEMENT OF CONTRACTS sect. 88(2) (1932) (Retraction of waiver of condition permitted but only before relied on.).

143. Sheehan v. Commercial Travelers, 186 N.E. 627, 630 (Mass. 1933).

144. This case could be viewed as applying equitable estoppel since the company was estopped from proving a fact contrary to their misrepresentation relied upon. But it can also be rationalized as promissory estoppel because the misstatement constituted an implied promise about how long the insurance contract would run in the future before it lapsed.

145. Hetchler v. American Life Ins. Co., 266 Mich. 608, 254 N.W. 221 (1934).

146. Fried v. Fisher, 328 Pa. 497, 196 A. 39 (1938).

147. Central London Property Trust Ltd. v. High Trees House Ltd., K.B. 130 (1947). Denning extended the rule in Hughes v. Metropolitan Ry., 2 App. Cas. 439 (1877), where a promise by a contracting party (but not a creditor) to not enforce his legal rights had a limited effect in equity without consideration.

148. *E.g.*, RESTATEMENT (SECOND) OF CONTRACTS sect. 89(c) (1981) (Illustration number 7 and Reporter's Note to Comment (d) reference *High Trees*.).

149. Ironically, rule in *Pinnel's Case* was not assumed to prevent rent reductions until *High Trees* case. *See* SAMUEL STOLJAR, *supra* note 43, at 132. In this respect Denning actually extended the impact of the preexisting duty rule.

150. Alfred T. Denning (b. 1899). Subsequent to serving as a law lord in the House of Lords, he served from 1962–1982 as Master of the Rolls, the appellate judicial position affording the greatest opportunity to influence the English common law.

151. Denning's rationale was based on promissory estoppel logic rather than equitable estoppel logic because it was based on the landlord's promise about future rent obligations. Denning made it clear he wasn't basing his decision on equitable estoppel because of Jorden v. Money, 5 H.L.C. 185 (1854), which ruled that a representation as to the future had to be in a contract or it was unenforceable.

152. The reliance found in *High Trees* has been questioned since it is difficult to see how the tenant's act of simply paying less rent constituted detrimental reliance. *See* E. ALLAN FARNSWORTH, CONTRACTS 280n. (Boston: 1982). Denning effectively held in *High Trees* that the preexisting duty rule is no bar once the terms of the modification are performed. An alternative solution might have been to rationalize the ruling of enforcing the modification under the doctrine of consideration by pointing to the bargained-for detriment of the obligor actually applying his funds to satisfy the modification agreement rather than using the funds for some other purpose; this reasoning answers the consideration requirement that consideration must move from the promisee in reliance on the promisor's request.

153. Central London Property Trust Ltd. v. High Trees House Ltd., K.B. 130, 135 (1947).

154. Denning said, "I prefer to apply the principle that a promise intended to

be binding, intended to be acted on and in fact acted on is binding so far as its terms properly apply." Central London Property Trust Ltd v. High Trees House Ltd, K.B. 130, 136 (1947).

155. In Combe v. Combe, 2 K.B. 215, 219–220 (1951), Denning said: "Much as I am inclined to favour the principle stated in the *High Trees* case, it is important that it should not be stretched too far, lest it should be endangered." This fear about pushing conservative wing of the judiciary too far is a paraphrase of Mansfield's expression of concern about pushing the doctrine of quasi-contract too much. *See* Weston v. Downes, 1 Doug. 23, 24, 99 Eng. Rep. 19 (1778). *Cf.* Brikom Investments Ltd. v. Carr, Q.B. 467, 486 (1979) ("It would be wrong to extend the doctrine of promissory estoppel, whatever its precise limits at the present day, to the extent of abolishing in this back-handed way the doctrine of consideration.").

156. Combe v. Combe, 2 K.B. 215, 219, All Eng. Rep. 767 (1951); *contra* ENGLISH LAW REVISION COMMITTEE, SIXTH INTERIM REPORT, 1937, CMND. No. 5449, at pp. 24–25 (Promise should be enforced without consideration if detrimental reliance.). Denning's interpretation of *High Trees* in *Combe v. Combe* is analogous to the approach taken by Holt and Mansfield in the moral obligation cases of waivers of bankruptcy and statute of limitations in that moral obligation was not declared a general ground for creating contract obligations but was rather a narrow exception to a strict application of the law related to bankruptcy and statute of limitations which would not have achieved a just and moral result in those cases. *And see* JOHN CARTER and DAVID HARLAND, CONTRACT LAW IN AUSTRALIA 372–376 (Sydney: 2d ed. 1991) (Australia applied promissory estoppel to a preexisting duty case in 1983 and since 1988 has recognized that the doctrine can be the ground for creating liability where none existed before.).

157. *Cf.* CECIL FIFOOT, *supra* note 24 at 414. This comment harks back to the earlier comment herein that consideration applies to contract formation but not to discharge or modification.

158. *See* GUENTER TREITEL, THE LAW OF CONTRACT 67 (London: 1991) (Consideration may be "invented" in England, as finding a prejudice to promisee to be a detriment even though not in fact suffered.). England's detriment side of consideration, not necessarily bargained-for, provides greater flexibility in treating reliance as consideration than is possible under American bargain consideration. To a degree, this may explain why there has been greater pressure in the United States to reform the preexisting duty rule and to expand the scope of promissory estoppel generally.

159. *See* Stroud Milsom, *A Pageant in Modern Dress*, 84 YALE L.J. 1585, 1587–1588 (1975). However, in the single legal jurisdiction of England and Wales, there is no lack of uniform legal rules to be used as an excuse to restate the law in order to reform it.

160. RESTATEMENT (SECOND) OF CONTRACTS sect. 89(c) (1981). Section 89 adapted reliance ideas found in Section 90 and U.C.C. sect. 2–209(5) (reliance on a waiver). Tentative drafts of the Restatement (Second) of Contracts were published periodically from 1964 onward.

161. *See* Billman v. V.I. Equities Corp., 743 F. 2d 1021 (3rd Cir. 1984) (Waiver is more akin to promissory estoppel than equitable estoppel.); U.C.C. sect. 2-209(5).

162. *See* Loper v. O'Rourke, 86 Misc. 2d 441, 382 N.Y.S. 2d 663 (1976) (cited

first Restatement sect. 88(2)); Canada v. Allstate Insurance Co., 411 F. 2d 517 (1969) (cited tentative draft of Restatement (Second) of Contracts).

163. *See* Wachovia Bank and Trust Co. v. Rubish, 306 N.C. 417, 293 S.E. 2d 749, 757 (1982) (promise implied from informal waiver of written notice requirement).

164. Reliance relief for actions subsequent to the signing of the original contract is in line with the modern tendency in the law toward less reverence for written contracts in order to realize intent, e.g., liberalization of parol evidence rule and modern exceptions to the Statute of Frauds found in the U.C.C. and in the restatements of contracts. *See* U.C.C. sect. 2–209(4) (Failure to rescind or modify due to writing requirement may still act as waiver.); U.C.C. sect. 2–209(5) (Retraction of waiver is permitted unless relied on.). Reliance performs a function of form in place of the technical written requirements.

CHAPTER 4

1. Statute of Frauds, 29 Chas. II, c. 3 (1677). The Statute of Frauds actually aggravated the dilemma of how to modify a contract since some types of contract, not seen as falling under *Pinnel's Case* until the nineteenth century, could not be modified orally after 1677 if they fell under the Statute.

2. Ala. Code, Sect. 2774 (1898); Cal. Civ. Code, sect. 1524 (1872); Dak. Comp. Laws, sect. 3486; Ga. Code, sect. 3735 (1890); Maine Rev. St., c. 82, sect. 45 (1895); N.C. Code, sect. 574 (1898); N.D. Rev. Code, sect. 3827 (1895); Hill, Ann. Laws of Oregon, sect. 755 (1890); Tenn. Code (1884), sect. 4539; Va. Code (1887), sect. 2828.

3. The shifts generated by the Great Depression increased the incidence of contracts modifications as ongoing contracts needed to be adjusted for the dislocations created.

4. STATE OF NEW YORK REPORT OF THE LAW REVISION COMMISSION 67, 172 (Second Annual: 1936) (Documents 65 C & D). Commission thought a signed writing adequate to fulfill the cautionary functions as well as the evidentiary function of consideration, much as Mansfield had promoted in Pillans v. Van Mierop, 3 Burr. 1663, 97 Eng. Rep. 1035 (1765).

5. ENGLISH LAW REVISION COMMITTEE, SIXTH INTERIM REPORT, CMND. NO. 5449 at pp. 19–21 (1937). The Committee also recommended abolishing both the Statute of Frauds and consideration when there was a written contract. England abolished the Statute of Frauds in 1954.

6. Indian Contract Act, sect. 63 (1872) ("Every promisee may dispense with . . . the performance of the promise made to him . . . or may accept instead of it any satisfaction which he thinks fit."). *See* 1 ATUL PATRA, THE INDIAN CONTRACT ACT 1872, 834–847 (Bombay: 1966). The Indian Contract Act influenced the development of contract law in the legal systems of other developing Asian countries of the British Commonwealth, e.g., Malaysia, Singapore and Hong Kong.

7. In 1872, California permitted written accord and satisfaction without consideration. Cal. Code sect. 1524 (1872). The Statute of Wales, 12 Edw. I (1284) covered more than contract since it was an attempted restatement of the common law for use in administering Wales; a similar purpose was achieved in India in 1872. A parallel example is found in the U.S. Virgin Islands where the American

Law Institute's restatements of the law have been adopted as *statutes*, assuming no prior inconsistent local rules. V.I. Code Ann. tit.1, s.4 (1990).

8. *See* M. P. JAIN, OUTLINES OF INDIAN LEGAL HISTORY 675 (Bombay: 2d ed. 1966) (Henry Maine drafted first proposal and James Stephen revised it.). Although David Dudley Field's procedural code was passed in New York in 1848, he failed in convincing New York to adopt his substantive codes in 1885, in part due to the opposition of the commercial bar. *See* Reimann, *The Historical School Against Codification: Savigny, Carter and the Defeat of the New York Civil Code*, 37 AM. J. COMP. LAW 95, 98–99, 103–14, 114–116 (1989). Field's substantive codes fared better in California, Georgia, Montana, Idaho, the Dakota Territory and in India. With the exception of Georgia, at the time these jurisdictions adopted codes on substantive law, they had not developed a significant corpus of their own common law.

9. Virginia Code, sect. 2828 (1887). The modern Virginia code reads verbatim. Virginia Code, sect. 11–12 (1950). Since Virginia's statute focuses on "acceptance by creditor" of "part performance" "in satisfaction," it would appear to not cover the seamen's wage-type agreement for the debtor to pay more; however, the New York and Michigan exceptions for written modifications would cover either increase or decrease in the amount owed.

10. Georgia Code, sect. 20–1204 (1960); Maine Rev. Stat. Ann. tit. 14, sect. 155 (1955); North Carolina Gen. Stat., 1953, sect. 1–540. Government contractors are often barred by state statute or constitution from receiving extra compensation. *See* McGovern v. New York, 234 N.Y. 377, 138 N.E. 26 (1923).

11. Arizona Code Ann. §1–111 (1939); Indiana Stat. Ann., sects. 2–1601-[492], 2–1602 [493], 2–1603 [494] (Burns, 1933); Mississippi Code Ann., sects. 3302, 3303, 3304 (1930); New Mexico Stat., sect. 45–608 (Courtright, 1929); Wyoming Rev. Stat., §97–123 (Courtright, 1931) ("every writing not sealed shall have the same force and effect that it would have if sealed."). *Cp.* U.C.C. sect. 2–203 (seals inoperative).

12. Massachusetts G.L.A. c. 4, sect 9A (1973). French law recognizes a gift promise of property so long as there's a formal *donation* (agreement for gift) before a notary. *See* BARRY NICHOLAS, THE FRENCH LAW OF CONTRACT 146 (2d ed. Oxford: 1992).

13. *See* 1 SAMUEL WILLISTON, A TREATISE ON THE LAW OF CONTRACTS sect. 218 (3d ed. Jaeger. New York: 1957) (raises only a rebuttable presumption).

14. Samuel Williston's successful draft of the Uniform Sales Act in 1906 had not tinkered with the preexisting duty rule, but the 1925 Uniform Written Obligations Act tried to set the clock back to when the seal was in regular usage.

15. Pennsylvania Stat. Ann., tit. 33, sects. 6–8 (Purdon 1967).

16. Utah Laws, c. 62 (1929).

17. Penn National Bank v. Tinkler, 351 Pa. 123, 40 A. 2d 389 (1945).

18. *See* Comment, *Contracts—Proposals for Legislation Abrogating the Requirement of Consideration in Whole or in Part*, 46 MICH. L. REV. 58, 68 (1947). From the opposite perspective, the Act is awkward in requiring that, besides the promise, there be "an additional express statement . . . that the signer intends to be legally bound."

19. STATE OF NEW YORK REPORT OF THE LAW REVISION COMMISSION 67, 172 (Second Annual: 1936) (Documents 65 C & D).

20. New York Personal Property Law, sect. 33 and Real Property Law, sect. 282

were amended by N.Y. Laws, c. 281 (1936) ("agreement . . . to modify or to discharge . . . any contract, obligation, or lease, or any mortgage or other security interest.").

21. Michigan Compiled Laws Ann., sect. 566.1 (1941).

22. New York General Obligations Act, sect. 5–1103.

23. Calif. Code, sect. 1524 (1872); Montana Rev. Code Ann., sect. 28–1–1403 (1902); North Dakota Cent. Code, sect. 9–13–07; South Dakota Codified Laws Ann., sect. 20–7–4. California passed Field's Civil Code in 1872 and was followed by the Dakota Territory, Georgia, Idaho and Montana.

24. Tennessee Code, 1858, sect. 3789; Alabama Code, tit. 7, sect. 381.

25. *See* Grand Lodge Knights of Pythias v. Williams, 245 Ala. 220, 222, 16 So. 2d 497, 499 (1944) (Consideration was required under the old statute unlike the new one.). *Cf.* Note, *The Present Statutory Law of Consideration*, 47 COLUM. L. REV. 431, 443 (1947).

26. Tennessee Code Ann., sect. 24–7–107 (1930); Alabama Code, sects. 12–21–109, 8–1–23 (1935). The writing supplants the elements of seriousness and formality provided by consideration.

27. *See* Mermelstein v. Realty Associates Securities Corp., 272 App. Dir. 205, 69 N.Y.S. 2d 763 (1947) (agreement not found in letter signed by creditor).

28. Consideration is not required for formation of a commercial contract under any legal system other than the common law. Mercantile capitalism assumes by its very nature that obligations are expected to be kept. In the eighteenth century, Mansfield had tried to drop it as a requirement for commercial contracts, but the force of precedent surrounding this keystone common law doctrine was too much to overcome. Llewellyn found that in actual practice merchants of the 1930s treated modifications as binding and adopted the practice in U.C.C.

29. *See* Lon Fuller, *Consideration and Form*, 41 COLUM L. REV. 799, 806 (1941) (Requirement that parties' intention be expressed is in essence a requirement of form.). Without clear evidence of a modification agreement, a modification under 2–209 fails. Amerdyne Ind., Inc. v. POM, Inc., 760 F. 2d 875 (8th Cir. 1985) (Arkansas); U.S. for Use of Premix Concrete, Inc. v. Santa Fe Engineers, Inc., 515 F. Supp. 512 (1981) (Colorado); Hughes v. Jones, 206 Kans. 82, 476 P. 2d 588 (1970).

30. U.C.C. sect. 2–209 cmt. 1 (1952). *See* U.C.C. sect. 2–209 (2) and (3).

31. Rye v. Phillips, 203 Minn. 567, 282 N.W. 459, 460 (1938).

32. Frye v. Hubbell, 74 N.H. 358, 68 A. 325, 334 (1907). Nonetheless, the New Hampshire court manipulated the facts to find consideration for the accord.

33. Virginia Code, sec. 2828 (1887); Virginia Code, sec. 11–12 (1950).

34. New York General Obligations Act, sec. 5–1103 (1970).

35. The Virginia and New York statutes dropped consideration for contract modifications generally, not just for sales.

36. U.C.C. sect. 2–209 Official Comments acknowledged the contribution of the Uniform Written Obligation Act (1925).

37. Nor does the Code require the Act's element of "intent to be bound" in addition to the agreement.

38. *See* Fuller, *supra* note 29, at 800–801. The channeling function may be fulfilled by the expression of common intention in a modification related to an existing contract, as distinguished from mere exploratory discussions. *See Id.* at 818. The evidentiary function can be fulfilled by clear proof of an agreement, supplemented by a writing when necessary.

39. U.C.C. sect. 2–209(2) (Consumer must sign separately a clause barring an oral modification.); *and see* U.C.C. sect. 2–209 cmt. 3 (Provision addresses the situation where a merchant might orally assure a modification, which is, unbeknownst to the consumer, barred by the standardized language.).

40. U.C.C. sect. 2–209(2) & (3). Subsect. (2) permits the addition of the formality of a private statute of frauds, contrary to the Code's stated policy here of removing "technicalities which . . . hamper such adjustments." *See* U.C.C. sect. 2-209 cmt. 1. The U.C.C. Statute of Frauds provides the added safeguards of limits based on the part "received and accepted" and "the quantity of goods shown in such writing." U.C.C. sects. 2–201(1) & (3)(c). But there are problems regarding when the Statute of Frauds applies to a modification. If the original contract was under the Statute, must the modification be? Is a writing required only when the modification causes the original contract to exceed $500? Is a writing necessary only when the modification itself falls under the Statute? See JAMES WHITE and ROBERT SUMMERS, UNIFORM COMMERCIAL CODE 44–45 (St. Paul: 1980); *see also* Robert Hillman, *A Study of Uniform Commercial Code Methodology: Contract Modification Under Article Two*, 59 N.C.L. REV. 335, 356–363 (1981). Restatement (Second) of Contracts sect. 148 does not recognize the contractual right to bar an oral modification. The Restatement Second provides in Section 149 that the Statute of Frauds applies to the modification if the Statute applied to the original contract, but an oral rescission is possible under Section 148.

41. U.C.C. sect. 2–209 cmt. 3; *and see* U.C.C. sect. 2–209 cmt.1.

42. U.C.C. sect. 2–209 cmt. 3. The Code follows the dissent of Field, J. in Green v. Doniger, 300 N.Y. 238, 90 N.E. 2d 56, 60–61 (1949) (Written modification required under original contract, as allowed by N.Y. statute, and a contract provision could not be orally abandoned unilaterally. *Id.* at 60–61.).

43. U.C.C. sect. 2–209(4). *See* Robert Hillman, *supra* note 40, at 359–370 (Waiver and writing rules of 2–209 are defective.). The lack of clear definitions raises risk that a modification, intended to be barred without a writing, can slip in as a waiver. *And see* U.C.C. sect. 1–107, where a claim arising out of an alleged breach can be discharged without consideration by a written waiver; this provision is intended to fill a void left by end of the seal.

44. The Code provides that no consideration is required for a modification and for some waivers. *See* U.C.C. sect. 2–209(1); U.C.C. sect. 1–107. Rescission of a contract shall not be construed to discharge any damages claim for an antecedent breach. U.C.C. sect. 2–720. The requirement of consideration for mutual rescission depends upon whether the contract is executory or not. The writing requirements for a modification depend on the U.C.C. Statute of Frauds or the parties' original agreement. *See* U.C.C. sect. 2–209(2) & (3); U.C.C. sect. 2–201; *and see* sect. U.C.C. 2–316. The parties' original agreement can also dictate writing requirements for rescission. U.C.C. sect. 2–209(2). And the writing requirements for waiver vary, *e.g.*, U.C.C. sect. 2–209(4); U.C.C. sect. 1–107; U.C.C. sect. 2–605.

Terminology *not* used in U.C.C. sect. 2–209 in describing subsequent changes in the original contract relationship includes the widely used terms "accord" and "discharge." Discharge is a term used in parallel reform statutes, such as the New York–type statute, and the term accord is employed in California-type statutes; these two changes in the contract relationship are covered by the U.C.C. term "modification" in that an accord is a type of modification, and the satisfaction of the accord constitutes a discharge. *And see* the following sections of RESTATEMENT (SECOND) OF CONTRACTS: sect. 273 (assent to discharge requires consideration), but assent to discharge of duty of return performance needs no consideration, per sect. 275, nor does cancellation of a written obligation, per sect. 274; an agreement of "partial rescission," that discharges less than all the parties' remaining duties, is treated as a modification, per sect. 283 cmt. a; and, if each party agrees to discharge all the other parties' duties, called an "agreement of rescission," consideration is provided by each party's discharge of the duties of the other, per sect. 283 cmt. a.

45. *See* Fuller, *supra* note 29, at 820–821 (A release of a claim is made with deliberation rather than casually. *Id.* at 821.); *see also* 6 ARTHUR CORBIN, CORBIN ON CONTRACTS sect. 1289 (St. Paul: 1950) (Creditor's express assent to modification or discharge should be enforced without consideration because no new rights are created.); CECIL FIFOOT, HISTORY AND SOURCES OF THE COMMON LAW: TORT AND CONTRACT 414 (London: 1949). (An element essential to formation is irrelevant to contract discharge.). However, if the modification increases the obligation, as in the seamen's wage increase cases, the cautionary concern is as great as at original contract formation.

46. Lingenfelder v. The Wainwright Brewing Co., 103 Mo. 578, 15 S.W. 844 (1891) is a good example of how an obvious bad faith extortion of a modification was barred by the preexisting duty rule. An architect, angered by the landowner giving a separate contract to a competitor, took advantage of the landowner's timetable to force a price higher than originally agreed.

47. The parallel use of good faith in policing open-ended language in long term contracts appeared by the early twentieth century. *See* New York Cent. Iron Works Co. v. United States Radiator Co., 174 N.Y. 331, 66 N.E. 967 (1903). Soon New York courts began to declare that a general duty of good faith existed in *all* contracts. *See* Simon v. Etgen, 213 N.Y. 589, 107 N.E. 1066, 1067–1068 (1915); Wigand v. Bachmann-Bechtel Brewing Co., 222 N.Y. 272, 118 N.E. 618 (1918).

The traditional requirement of consideration can sometimes be seen to, in effect, be fulfilling the function of policing bad faith short of economic duress. In Recker v. Gustafson, 279 N.W. 2d 744, 747, 758 (Ia. 1979), the court was bothered by the pressure placed on the young buyer by the more experienced seller of land and his attorney and refused to allow the rescission fiction to avert the use of consideration to bar the pressured modification.

48. One of the traditional functions of consideration was to enforce the promise if there was an accepted reason or motivation (or *causa*) for the promise.

49. *Cf.* 1A ARTHUR CORBIN, *supra* note 45, at sect. 106 (Contract cannot be explained exclusively by a subjective or objective standard.). Corbin thought that if the "moral and economic elements" were right, courts should not apply the preexisting duty rule. *Id.* at sect. 171.

50. A general standard of good faith in all contracts was being applied in chancery by at least the seventeenth century, and it was urged by Mansfield in the following century. After the fusion of law and equity, it became the common law rule in the United States by the second decade of the twentieth century. *See* Simon v. Etgen, 213 N.Y. 589, 107 N.E. 1066, 1067–1068 (1915); Wigand v. Bachmann-Bechtel Brewing Co., 222 N.Y. 272, 118 N.E. 618 (1918).

51. In Brooks v. White, 2 Met. 283 (Mass. 1840), the court said the preexisting duty rule itself was often "urged in violation of good faith."

52. The developments in the area of undue pressure and advantage taken in contract formation by a party in a stronger position, in the form of economic duress and unconscionability, were also influences on the use of good faith negotiation of modifications.

53. Headley v. Hackley, 50 Mich. 43, 14 N.W. 693, 694 (1883).

54. Headley v. Hackley, 50 Mich. 43, 14 N.W. 693, 695 (1883).

55. Lingenfelder v. The Wainwright Brewing Co., 103 Mo. 578, 15 S.W. 844, 848 (1891).

56. De-Mars v. Musser-Sauntry Land, Log. & Mfg. Co., 37 Minn. 418, 419, 35 N.W. 1, 2 (1887) (no bona fide dispute found).

57. Berger v. Lane, 190 Cal. 443, 450–451, 213 P. 45, 48 (1923) (The statement "I will not pay it unless you sue me" can be considered coercive, or not, depending on the circumstances. *Id.* at 48.).

58. *See* Krell v. Henry, L.R. 2 K.B. 740 (Ct. App. 1903) (Rental of room for viewing coronation parade was frustrated by king's appendectomy.); RESTATEMENT OF CONTRACTS sect. 288 (1932).

59. *See* Mineral Park Land Co. v. Howard, 172 Cal. 289, 156 P. 458 (1916) (Cost of extracting gravel increased tenfold due to rise in water level.); RESTATEMENT OF CONTRACTS sect. 288 (1932).

60. This was the first Restatement's position. See commentary to illustration number 8 of Restatement Section 76 (If unforeseen difficulties justify rescinding the contract, there is sufficient consideration for a promise to pay more.).

61. *E.g.*, a market shift where performance would cause a loss. *See* U.C.C. sect. 2–209 cmt. 2.

62. *See* Simon v. Etgen, 213 N.Y. 589, 107 N.E. 1066, 1067–1068 (1915) ("Every contract implies good faith and fair dealing between the parties." *Id.* at 1067.); Wigand v. Bachman-Bechtel Brewing Co., 222 N.Y. 272, 118 N.E. 618, 619 (1918). The drafters of the Restatement of Contracts (1932) did not see enough of a general caselaw development to include this general standard. The U.C.C. announced it, however, for sales by mid-century. U.C.C. sect. 1–203. The Restatement Second then recognized it for all contracts in 1981. RESTATEMENT (SECOND) CONTRACTS sect. 205.

63. *E.g.*, Dodge v. Kimball, 203 Mass. 364, 89 N.E. 542 (1909) (Builder willfully failed to fully perform.); Brazil v. Maryland Cas. Co., 210 N.Y. 235, 104 N.E. 622 (1914) (Insurer refused reasonable settlement offer resulting in great expense to the insured.); Carns v. Bassick, 187 App. Div. 280, 175 N.Y. Supp. 670 (1st Dept. 1919) (Broker was hired but prevented from performing.).

64. *E.g.*, Obrecht v. Crawford, 175 Md. 385, 395, 2 A. 2d 1, 6–8 (1938). *See* Faxton v. Faxon, 28 Mich. 159, 161 (1873) (In estoppel case, where there was reliance on mortgagee's promise to not foreclose, the court said, "There is no rule more necessary to enforce good faith than that which compels a person to abstain from enforcing claims which he has induced others to suppose he would not rely on.").

65. *See* Headley v. Hackley, 50 Mich. 43, 14 N.W. 693, 695 (1893); Lingenfelder v. The Wainwright Brewing Co., 103 Mo. 578, 15 S.W. 844, 848 (1891).

66. U.C.C. sects. 1–203, 1–201 (19), 2–103.

67. U.C.C. sect. 2–209 cmt. 2 ("the extortion of a 'modification' without legitimate commercial reason is ineffective"); *see* RESTATEMENT (SECOND) OF CONTRACTS sect. 205 cmt. c.

68. Good faith *bargaining* has been required in this century in certain sensitive areas: for certain commercial disclosures to consumers; for contracts with a public interest, as utilities, insurance, collective bargaining and government bids; and in certain cases of reliance and estoppel, as in franchise negotiations.

69. This opens the debate to the argument that there is no authority for the application of a good faith standard during the negotiations of the modification. *Cf.* Robert Hillman, *Policing Contract Modifications Under the U.C.C.: Good Faith and the Doctrine of Economic Duress*, 64 IA. L. REV. 849, 859 (1979) (Text of U.C.C. sect. 2–103(1)(b) suggests it shouldn't be used unless specifically mentioned in text of Act.).

70. The following cases don't discuss the possibility of bad faith, even though the facts raise eyebrows. Barnwell & Hays, Inc. v. Sloan, 564 F. 2d 254 (1977) (Farmer said he couldn't complete contract because cotton burned but then it appeared he sold some cotton elsewhere.); Farmland Services Coop v. Jack, 196 Neb. 263, 242 N.W. 2d 624 (1976) (Farmer changed mind because price he agreed to sell for was now too cheap.).

71. *See* Roth Steel Products v. Sharon Steel Corp., 705 F. 2d 134, 146 (6th Cir. 1983) (Proponent of modification must establish good faith as a part of his burden of proof.).

72. *Cf.* Business Incentives, Inc. v. Sony Corp. of America, 397 F. Supp. 63, 69 (S.D. N.Y. 1975) (It's not coercion to insist on legal right which has coercive effect, here the right of termination.); *see* Roth Steel Products v. Sharon Steel Corp., 705 F. 2d 134, 146 (6th Cir. 1983) (Under honesty in fact, party must show that commercial reason for the modification wasn't just a pretext.); *and see* Skinner v. Tober Foreign Motors Inc., 187 N.E. 2d 669 (Mass. 1963) (Good business reason found for modification in buyer's difficulties caused by high and unexpected expenses of repairing purchased airplane.); *see also* RESTATEMENT (SECOND) OF CONTRACTS sect. 176 cmt. e.

73. *See* Roth Steel Products v. Sharon Steel Corp., 705 F. 2d 134, 146 (1983); U.C.C. sect. 2–209 cmt. 2; U.C.C. sect. 2–103.

74. *See* U.C.C. sect. 2–302 cmt. 1 ("The basic test is whether, in light of the general commercial background and the commercial needs of the particular trade or case, the clauses involved are so one-sided as to be unconscionable under the circumstances existing at the time of the making of the contract.").

75. *See* United States for Use of Crane Co. v. Progressive Enterprises, Inc., 418 F. Supp. 662 (1976) (Economic duress can be found in coerced modifications governed by Section 2–209, but buyer failed to raise protest, citing Sections 2–209 and 2–103(1)(b).); Pirrone v. Monarch Wine Co. of Georgia, 497 F. 2d 25 (5th Cir. 1974); *see* U.C.C. sect. 2–209 cmt. 2.

76. *See* RESTATEMENT (SECOND) OF CONTRACTS sect. 176(d) and cmts. a & e (Under developing notions of economic duress, breach of U.C.C.'s standard of good faith and fair dealing is improper threat and violates economic duress provisions of Sect. 176 and application of U.C.C. sect. 2–209.).

77. *See* United States for Use of Crane Co. v. Progressive Enterprises, Inc., 418 F. Supp. 662, 664 (1976) (The need for modifications in long term contracts is

common and is a fair business method to preserve the desirability of the business relationship.). *And see* U.C.C. sect. 2–209 cmt. 1 ("This section seeks to . . . make effective all *necessary*" modifications (emphasis added)).

CHAPTER 5

1. RESTATEMENT OF CONTRACTS sects. 76(a), 84(c) & (d) (1932).

2. The restaters were on untrod ground in attempting a restatement of contracts, and their credibility could have been compromised had courts refused to follow their deviation from the traditional rule. It was easier to suggest a new ground for relief based on reliance, which courts may or may not take up, than to announce as bad law an accepted principle that was regularly applied to uphold an existing original bargained-for contract.

3. Exceptional treatment of duress, reliance, formality and unjust enrichment were noted. RESTATEMENT (SECOND) OF CONTRACTS sect. 73 cmt. (b) (1981). The exceptional treatment of reliance, changed circumstances and statutory reforms are covered separately in RESTATEMENT (SECOND) OF CONTRACTS sect. 89. *And see* RESTATEMENT (SECOND) sect. 281 (Accords were still viewed as suspensory until satisfied.).

4. RESTATEMENT (SECOND) OF CONTRACTS sect. 73.

5. *Cf.* RESTATEMENT (SECOND) OF CONTRACTS sect. 89 cmt. b (1981) (Simultaneity could foment unfair modifications.); *accord* King v. Duluth Ry. Co., 61 Minn. 482, 63 N.W. 1105, 1106 (1895) (Legal presumption of voluntariness of rescission invites party to repudiate whenever he feels he can gain advantage.); Watkins v. Carrig, 21 A. 2d 591, 592 (1941); *but cf.* Martiniello v. Bamel, 255 Mass. 25, 150 N.E. 838 (1926) (parties rescinded pursuant to fair dealing once mistake regarding condition of land discovered). At least one jurisdiction has ceased using the rescission fiction in light of the doctrinal argument in Section 89's Comment (b) and has thereby actually broadened the scope of the preexisting duty rule in that jurisdiction. *See* Recker v. Gustafson, 279 N.W. 2d 744, 757–758 (Ia. 1979) (Court expressed concern about the pressure put on the young buyers by the experienced seller and his lawyer, which would not usually be evaluated if a rescission was automatically assumed binding.).

6. RESTATEMENT OF CONTRACTS sect. 76b. *See* Cohen v. Sabin, 452 Pa. 447, 307 A. 2d 845 (1973) (Disputed debt found under Tentative Draft No. 2, Restatement Second of Contracts sect. 76B (1965).) So the combined subjective and objective standard was reduced to a subjective one.

7. *See* RESTATEMENT (SECOND) OF CONTRACTS sect. 73 cmt. a.

8. When the novelty exception was announced in *Pinnel's Case* itself, the decision did not have in mind the benefit its accord rule could do to avert duress. Modern consensual theory views of the rule justify Coke's rule from the standpoint of avoiding duress; however, under this view, to allow a novelty to support a modification and thus permit the coercion would be absurd.

9. Williams v. Roffey Bros. & Nicholls (Contractors) Ltd., 1 All Eng. Rep. 512, 526 (1990) (per Purchase, L. J.).

10. Rexite Casting Co. v. Midwest Mower Corp., 267 S.W. 2d 327 (Mo. 1954).

11. Rexite Casting Co. v. Midwest Mower Corp., 267 S.W. 2d 327, 331 (Mo.

1954) (No consideration since defendant received nothing additional but instead had to pay more for same castings.). There had been an attempt to establish economic duress at the trial level but the trial court refused it.

12. An analogy to the treatment of adequacy of consideration at-law and in equity seems apt. At-law, adequacy of consideration is irrelevant (e.g., a novelty); but, if specific performance is requested in equity, the court will look to the relationship between the price and the property value in passing on questions of fraud, unfairness, duress, etc. *And see* George v. Schuman, 168 N.W. 486, 488 (1918).

13. Given enough time, the buyer found castings later from another supplier at near the original contract price, which raised questions about the legitimacy of the claim that the price increase modification in *Rexite v. Midwest* was necessary or reasonable.

14. *See* RESTATEMENT (SECOND) OF CONTRACTS sect. 89(a). But the court said there was no such exception to the requirement of consideration recognized in Missouri. Rexite Casting Co. v. Midwest Mower Corp., 267 S.W. 2d 327, 331 (Mo. 1954).

15. RESTATEMENT (SECOND) OF CONTRACTS sect. 73 cmt. c (The Comment expressed frustrated solicitude for "when an impecunious debtor has paid part of his debt in satisfaction of the whole.").

16. Williams v. Roffey Bros. & Nicholls (Contractors) Ltd., 1 All Eng. Rep. 512, 524 (1990) (per Russell, L. J.).

17. RESTATEMENT (SECOND) OF CONTRACTS sect. 73 cmt. c.

18. Williams v. Roffey Bros. & Nicholls (Contractors) Ltd., 1 All Eng. Rep. 512 (1990).

19. Williams v. Roffey Bros. & Nicholls (Contractors) Ltd., 1 All Eng. Rep. 512, 527 (1990) (per Purchas, L. J.).

20. Williams v. Roffey Bros. & Nicholls (Contractors) Ltd., 1 All Eng. Rep. 512, 522, 525–526 (1990) (Seamen's wage cases based on strong public policy grounds.); Stilk v. Myrick, 2 Camp. 317, 170 Eng. Rep. 1168 (1809); Harris v. Watson, Peake 102, 170 Eng. Rep. 94 (1791); *cf.* Linz v. Schuck, 106 Md. 220, 67 A. 286 (1907) (Would've been different outcome in seamen's cases if risks that had arisen were not contemplated in the contract.).

21. Williams v. Roffey Bros. & Nicholls (Contractors) Ltd., 1 All Eng. Rep. 512, 525, 527 (1990). For a fact situation somewhat similar to *Williams v. Roffey* resolved without the need to show consideration, under U.C.C. sect. 2–209(1), *see* Skinner v. Tober Foreign Motors, Inc., 187 N.E. 2d 669 (Mass. 1963). In *Skinner v. Tober* the seller of an airplane offered to lower the price in light of buyer's unexpected airplane repair costs and the financial problems it created for the buyer. The court found a good business reason for the modification. This modification can be justified under the rule of Restatement (Second) Sections 73 or 89(a) or under U.C.C. Section 2–209(1): Under Section 73, it was more beneficial to seller to receive lower payments rather than repossession of a defective airplane but only if it was a resolution of an "honest dispute." Under Section 89(a), the unexpected costs of repair would be a ground for exceptional treatment. And under U.C.C. Section 2–209(1), a good faith modification needs no consideration.

22. Williams v. Roffey Bros. & Nicholls (Contractors) Ltd., 1 All Eng. Rep. 512, 522, 527 (1990) ("This arrangement was beneficial to both sides." *Id.* at 525.). *Cf.*

Ward v. Byham, 2 All Eng. Rep. 318, 319 (1956) (Denning, J. said he thought promise to perform preexisting duty was consideration since there was a benefit to the recipient of the promise.). This benefit-based consideration logic is a bit of a departure since detriment consideration has been the prevailing English consideration test for over a century; Glidewell and Purchas, L. J. J. acknowledged this but thought the consideration requirement could be equally satisfied when a promisee confers a benefit on a promisor without suffering a detriment himself. Williams v. Roffey Bros. & Nicholls (Contractors) Ltd., 1 All Eng. Rep. 512, 522, 527 (1990); *see* John Adams and Roger Brownsword, *Contract, Consideration and The Critical Path,* 53 MOD. L. REV. 536, 541 (1990) (Relaxation of consideration requirement increases importance of economic duress as a regulator of price modification. *Id.); cf.* GUENTER TREITEL, THE LAW OF CONTRACT 116 (London: 1991) (A benefit similar to the type in *High Trees* case was allowed as consideration for a promise in *Williams v. Roffey.*). On the detriment side, however, there was sub-contractor's forbearance from breaching.

Perhaps rather than redefining consideration under English law, *Williams v. Roffey* has simply devised a special consideration rule for modifications, much as English law recognizes promissory estoppel solely for contract modifications under Central London Property Trust Ltd. v. High Trees House Ltd., 1 K.B. 130 (1947).

23. Williams v. Roffey Bros. & Nicholls (Contractors) Ltd., 1 All Eng. Rep. 512, 525, 527 (1990) (general contractor admitted sub-contractor bid too low). In fact, sub-contractor only did about one-half of the performance under the modification agreement, but that lowered the penalty and put the project that much closer to completion; the court adjusted the damages recoverable by the sub-contractor accordingly.

24. Williams v. Roffey Bros. & Nicholls (Contractors) Ltd., 1 All Eng. Rep. 512, 524, 527 (1990). *See* Blakeslee v. Board of Water Com'rs of City of Hartford, 139 A. 106 (Conn. 1927) (Added compensation so party won't breach is a benefit in that business contract continues. *Id.* at 110.). *And see* Oken v. National Chain Co., 424 A. 2d 234, 237 (R.I. 1981) (Continuation of employment of employee-at-will was consideration for employer unilaterally lowering the commission rate.)

25. Musumeci v. Winadell Pty Ltd, 34 New So. Wales L. Rep. 723, 747 (1994) (Landlord agreed to reduce the rent).

26. *In Re* Selectmove Ltd., 1 W.L.R. 474 (1995) (Arguably dictum since agency law may have rendered the promise invalid.); *Re* C (A Debtor), Unreported English Court of Appeal decision of May 11, 1994, discussed in J. W. Carter, Andrew Phang, and Jill Poole, *Reactions to Williams v. Roffey,* 8 J. CONTRACT LAW 248, 257 (1995). In 1995 decision, the court was reluctant to overrule *Foakes v. Beer* when the *Williams v. Roffey* court hadn't broached that possibility, and the 1994 court emphasized that *Williams v. Roffey* had not even mentioned either *Pinnel's Case* or *Foakes v. Beer* nor had it discussed the distinction between a promise like the one in *Stilk v. Myrick* and the type of promise in *Pinnel's Case.* A Singaporean court seems to agree that *Williams v. Roffey* does not completely upend *Foakes v. Beer.* Sea-Land Services Inc. v. Cheong Fook Chee Vincent, 3 Singapore L. Rep. 631, 634, 635 (1994) (a "limited exception").

27. Eastwood v. Kenyon, 11 Ad. & El. 438, 713 Eng. Rep. 482 (1840). The unanticipated circumstances exception is a feature of the current American position. *See* RESTATEMENT SECOND OF CONTRACTS Sect. 89(a).

28. The first English case applying *Williams v. Roffey* to a *Stilk v. Myrick*-type promise involved unanticipated circumstances, though that decision did not limit the *Williams v. Roffey* approach to such circumstances. Anangel Atlas Compania Naviera SA v. Ishikawajima-Harima Heavy Ind. Co. Ltd. (No. 2), 2 Lloyd's Rep. 526 (1990).

29. This was the type of benefit Blackburn thought should qualify in the accord case *Foakes v. Beer*, and it was likewise wistfully alluded to in Restatement (Second) of Contracts sect. 73 comment c.

30. Since the origins of the rule in *Pinnel's Case* were intertwined with the action of debt's emphasis on the benefit of *quid pro quo*, an escape from the clutches of the rule is perhaps easier to rationalize on the benefit side of consideration. *Cf.* Pinnel's Case, 5 Co. Rep. 117a, 77 Eng. Rep. 237 (1602) (It "might be more beneficial to the plaintiff . . . or otherwise plaintiff would not have accepted it in satisfaction."). Indeed, in *Williams v. Roffey*, the court saw a benefit to both parties in fashioning a commercially workable modification so the project could continue. Williams v. Roffey Bros., 1 All Eng. Rep. 512, 527 (1990). Because the financial difficulties in *Williams*, brought on by the sub-contractor's poor job of bidding, were not a basis for an excuse from performance, the general contractor could have demanded performance under the original terms and sued upon breach, but the general contractor found more value in continued performance, and so he waived the breach action by agreeing to the modification. In Watkins & Son v. Carrig, 91 N.H. 459, 21 A. 2d 591 (1941), the court found no basis to excuse the risk of performance, but once a modification was found more valuable to the promisor, he was bound by the terms of the modification. *Id.* at 592, 594.

31. Munroe v. Perkins, 26 Mass. 303, 9 Pick. 298, 20 Am. Dec. 475 (1830) (construction of hotel). *Accord* Swartz v. Lieberman, 323 Mass. 109, 80 N.E. 2d 5, 6 (1948).

32. English judges operate within a single jurisdiction system, where *stare decisis* thrives best. They perceive that American common law courts play too fast and loose with precedent; it would therefore be near heresy to openly admit the persuasive influence of an American precedent. In Williams v. Roffey, 1 All Eng. Rep. 512, 526 (1990), the plaintiff urged the American case, Watkins v. Carrig, 91 N.H. 459, 21 A. 2d 591 (1941), which was inappropriate since key facts emphasized there were unanticipated circumstances. Furthermore, *Watkins v. Carrig* surely went further than any conservative English court would be willing to go in not requiring any rationalization of the presence of consideration.

33. Munroe v. Perkins, 26 Mass. 303, 9 Pick. 298, 20 Am. Dec. 475 (1830) ("having a losing bargain, and being unable and unwilling to go on with the work," owners' agents assured him that they would pay for every minute of work and that he wouldn't suffer. *Id.*). Even if English courts recognized the unanticipated circumstances exception to the preexisting duty rule, inadequacy of contract price by making too low a bid does not fall under the exception since each party bears the risk of a loss based on known facts. *See* King v. Duluth, M. & N. Ry. Co., 61 Minn. 482, 63 N.W. 1105, 1107 (1895) ("inadequacy of the contract price which is the result of an error in judgement, and not excusable mistake of fact is not sufficient."); *accord* Rexite Casting Co. v. Midwest Mower Corp., 267 S.W. 2d 327 (Mo. 1954); Western Litograph Co. v. Vanomar Producers, 185 Cal. 366, 197 P.

103 (1929); McGowan & Connolly Co. v. Kenny-Moran Co., 207 App. Div. 617 (1924).

34. Admittedly, some additional benefit to the promisor, past continuation of contract performance, can be found in the facts of both *Munroe v. Perkins* and *Williams v. Roffey*. In *Munroe* there were some changes in plans by the owner which placed a greater burden on the contractor, and in *Williams* timely performance would avoid the penalty provision in the general contractor's contract with the owner. So, even in these cases, the facts include something different or additional being received, but in most contracts of any complexity or time period, some extra bit can be found. *Cf.* Michaud v. McGregor, 61 Minn. 198, 63 N.W. 479 (1895) (The something extra provided was contractor's promise to keep a record of extent of unforeseen rocks unearthed in order to aid owner in documenting potential suit against third party wrongfully depositing the rock there.). For other cases where the courts have found a little bit additional consideration to take it out of the preexisting duty rule, *see* Simon v. Gray, 316 Ill. 488, 147 N.E. 459 (1925); D. L. Godbey & Sons Constr. Co. v. Deane, 39 Cal. 2d 429, 246 P. 2d 946 (1952); Gannon v. Emtman, 66 Wash. 2d 755, 405 P. 2d 254 (1965).

35. In Williams v. Roffey, 1 All Eng. Rep. 512, 527 (1990), Purchas, J. could have stuck to the detriment version of consideration followed in England by focusing on the promisee's forbearance from breaching and thus avoided the unconventional benefit-based logic he employed.

36. King v. Duluth, M. & N. Ry. Co., 61 Minn. 482, 63 N.W. 1105, 1106 (1895) (If there are "no exceptional circumstances," it "invites" coercion.). Purchas, J. said the new English approach could not be used if there was coercion. Williams v. Roffey, 1 All Eng. Rep. 512, 527 (1990).

37. Blakeslee v. Board of Water Com'rs of City of Hartford, 139 A. 106, 110 (Conn. 1927).

38. *See* Willard Barbour, *The "Right" to Breach a Contract*, 16 MICH. L. REV. 106, 107–109 (1917); 1A ARTHUR CORBIN, CORBIN ON CONTRACTS sect. 182 (St. Paul: 1950); RESTATEMENT (SECOND) OF CONTRACTS sect. 89 cmt. b (1981).

39. Williams v. Roffey, 1 All Eng. Rep. 512, 527 (1990).

40. There was no equivalent section in the first Restatement. The separation in the Restatement Second of the preexisting duty rule into two separate sections (Sections 73 and 89) is another modern example of a general rule breaking down into a number of separate sub-rules in order to take into account new factors, which have begun to cause an uneven application of the general rule. *Cf.* 1A ARTHUR CORBIN, *supra* note 38, at sect. 171.

41. A paradigmatic modification falling under Section 89 might involve a promise to pay more for construction work due to unanticipated circumstances, as an excavator unexpectedly running into granite. (These cases present a challenge to the precedents denying increases under the rulings in the earlier seamen's wage increase cases.) Not all the illustrations of the unanticipated circumstances exception listed under Section 89 were rationalized under the unanticipated circumstances exception to Section 73. For example, Schwartzreich v. Bauman-Basch, 231 N.Y. 196, 131 N.E. 887, 889–890 (1921), is the basis of Illustration number 3 but relief was granted under rescission and substitution logic in the absence of changed circumstances.

42. *See* Linz v. Schuck, 106 Md. 220, 67 A. 286, 288 (1907) (Contract made

upon supposed facts that turned out incorrect when it was discovered that cellar being dug was in swampy conditions over buried creek bed. Court said it would be a harsh rule if law did not allow modification.).

43. *See* Roth Steel Products v. Sharon Steel Corp., 705 F. 2d 134, 147 (1983) (Dictum in this U.C.C. decision: "[t]he single most important consideration in determining whether the decision to seek a modification is justified in this context is whether, because of changes in the market or other unforeseeable conditions, performance of the contract has come to involve a loss." *Id.*).

44. *See* King v. Duluth, M. & N. Ry. Co., 61 Minn. 482, 63 N.W. 1105, 1106 (1895); Linz v. Schuck, 106 Md. 220, 67 A. 286, 288–289 (1907); Pittsburgh Testing Laboratory v. Farnsworth & Chambers Co., 251 F. 2d 77, 79 (1958) (Extra compensation based on unforeseen difficulties provides protection against coercion.).

45. *Accord* Linz v. Schuck, 106 Md. 220, 67 A. 286, 290 (1907).

46. *See* ROBERT POTHIER, A TREATISE ON THE LAW OF OBLIGATIONS 4, 81 (William Evans ed., London: 1806); Alfred Simpson, *Innovation in Nineteenth Century Contract Law,* 91 L.Q. REV. 247, 265–277 (1975).

47. *See* ROBERT POTHIER, *supra* note 42, at 81; 2 JAMES KENT, COMMENTARIES ON AMERICAN LAW 480 (Boston: 4th ed. 1830); THEODORE SEDGWICK, A TREATISE ON THE MEASURE OF DAMAGES 64, 67 (New York: 1847).

48. Hadley v. Baxendale, 9 Ex. 341, 354, 156 Eng. Rep. 145, 151 (1854). Baron Parke cited the American writer Sedgwick's adoption of the French rule that: "The debtor is only liable for the damages foreseen, or which might have been foreseen." *Id.* at 147; *see* THEODORE SEDGWICK, *supra* note 47, at 64, 67. In searching for theories to accommodate unprecedented change fomented by an industrial economy, common law judges were turning, like never before, to treatise writers for inspiration—a practice commonplace in civil law countries.

49. Meech v. City of Buffalo, 29 N.Y. 198, 210 (1864).

50. King v. Duluth, M. & N. Ry. Co., 61 Minn. 482, 63 N.W. 1105, 1107 (1895) (Declared existence of exception but didn't apply it because other consideration found in extra work done due to railway's changing the route of the line.). *Accord* Blakeslee v. Board of Water Com'rs of City of Hartford, 139 A. 106, 112 (Conn. 1927) (circumstances not contemplated by parties); Curry v. Boeckeler, 27 S.W. 2d, 473, 475 (Mo. 1930) ("difficulty which was not known or anticipated by the parties when the contract was entered into."). *Cf.* Goebel v. Linn, 47 Mich. 489, 11 N.W. 284, 286 (1882) (Modification enforced because buyer "freely" and "independently" agreed to higher price due to unanticipated failure of ice crop. Preexisting duty rule not mentioned.).

51. Linz v. Schuck, 106 Md. 220, 67 A. 286, 288 (1907).

52. *Cf.* Richard Danzig, *Hadley v. Baxendale: A Study in the Industrialization of the Law,* 4 J. LEG. STUDIES 249, 282 (1975) (Potential breachor could calculate whether breach would be an efficient move.).

53. Paradine v. Jane, Aleyn 26, 82 Eng. Rep. 897 (1647) was touted in the nineteenth century to have declared the strict contract liability rule; in *Paradine v. Jane,* a lessee was bound to pay the rent even though he was physically ousted by an invader during the English civil war. Modern law has given relief from *Paradine's* strict contract liability rule when unanticipated circumstances arise under doctrine recognizing excuse and enforcement of a resultant contract modification. The court in *Paradine v. Jane* did say that the lessee could have protected himself by

stipulating against the risk in the language of the contract. Since the contingent risk might be hard to predict, there was a desire to use flexible, open-ended language to exclude highly unpredictable risk, but such indefinite language was unenforceable until good faith standard applied in the twentieth century.

54. Taylor v. Caldwell, 3 Best & S. 826, 833, 835, 122 Eng. Rep. 310, 312, 313 (1863) (Blackburn cited the civilian Pothier's ideas on consent. *Id.* at 313–314.).

55. Krell v. Henry, L.R. 2 K.B. 740 (Ct. App. 1903).

56. *See* Mineral Park Land Co. v. Howard, 172 Cal. 289, 156 P. 458, 460 (1916) (Water caused 1,000% increase in cost.); RESTATEMENT OF CONTRACTS sects. 288, 454 (1932). *Cf.* Moss v. Smith, 9 C.B. 94, 103, 137 Eng. Rep. 827, 831 (1850) ("[i]n matters of business, a thing is said to be impossible when it is not practicable; and a thing is impracticable when it can only be done at an excessive or unreasonable cost.").

57. King v. Duluth Ry. Co., 61 Minn. 482, 63 N.W. 1105, 1107 (1895). Despite the existence of decisions like *King v. Duluth,* Michaud v. McGregor, 63 N.W. 479, 480 (1895) and Blakeslee v. Bd. of Water Com'rs, 139 A. 106, 112 (Conn. 1927), which ruled that the facts need not be enough for an excuse discharge, in 1932 the drafters of the first Restatement sect. 76 commented in their illustration number 8 that a modification would not be binding unless the facts were enough for an excuse. However, by the mid-1960s, tentative drafts of what would become Restatement (Second) Sect. 89 cmt. (b) stated that a modification was binding even though there was foresight of a remote possibility of the contingency occurring, so long as it was not clearly covered in the contract.

58. This long standing exception to the preexisting duty rule was recognized in both Restatements. RESTATEMENT OF CONTRACTS sect. 76 (1932); RESTATEMENT (SECOND) OF CONTRACTS sects. 73 & 74 (1981).

59. *See* Burton Brody, *Performance of a Pre-Existing Contractual Duty as Consideration: The Actual Criteria for the Efficacy of an Agreement Altering Contractual Obligation,* 52 DENVER L.J. 433, 456–465 (1975) (Changed circumstance exception is grounded in bona fide dispute settlement.). The good faith belief might be in a contract defense or it might be the belief that the entire contract is excused due to impossibility.

60. Michaud v. McGregor, 61 Minn. 198, 63 N.W. 479 (1895).

61. Michaud v. McGregor, 61 Minn. 198, 63 N.W. 479, 481 (1895) ("These facts disclose a valid consideration to support the contract. The bona fide dispute was settled." *Id.*).

62. United Steel Co. v. Casey, 262 F. 889, 893 (1920).

63. Pittsburgh Testing Laboratory v. Farnsworth & Chambers Co., 251 F. 2d 77 (1958).

64. Pittsburgh Testing Laboratory v. Farnsworth & Chambers Co., 251 F. 2d 77, 79 (1958).

65. Watkins & Son v. Carrig, 91 N.H. 459, 21 A. 2d 591, 592 (1941).

66. Siebring Mfg. Co. v. Carlson Hybrid Corn Co., 246 Ia. 923, 70 N.W. 2d 149, 152 (1955) (Modification to pay more for steel corn crib due to steel strike. Court said it could be rescinded while executory.). Illustration number 4 to Section 89 is based on this case. But the principle in *Siebring* has been overruled in Iowa as it relates to modifications. Recker v. Gustafson, 379 N.W. 2d 744 (Iowa 1979)

(Consideration is required for a modification in Iowa, though not for a true rescission. *Id.* at 756–758.).

67. RESTATEMENT (SECOND) OF CONTRACTS sect. 89, cmt. b (1981) (Rescission fiction opposed on doctrinal and fairness grounds.).

68. King v. Duluth, M. & N. Ry. Co., 61 Minn. 482, 63 N.W. 1105, 1107 (1895). This influential detriment consideration rule was in fact dictum because the modified agreement required the contractor to perform something extra, so that consideration was found. Nevertheless, the case's dictum became influential because of its thorough and logical airing of the relevant ingredients of the emerging exception. Thus, the dictum in *King* partially toppled the dictum in *Pinnel*!

69. King v. Duluth, M. & N. Ry. Co., 61 Minn. 482, 63 N.W. 1105, 1107 (1895).

70. Nash v. St. Paul, 23 Minn. 132 (1876). This traditional view is in line with the strict contract liability principle in Paradine v. Jane, Aleyn 26, 82 Eng. Rep. 897 (1647).

71. The twentieth century view is in concert with the point that a changed circumstance short of excuse leaves the risk with the contractor, but, once the owner elects to waive a breach action because he finds more value in a modification, he is bound by that modification. *See* Watkins v. Carrig, 21 A. 2d 591, 592 (N.H. 1941).

72. Meech v. City of Buffalo, 29 N.Y. 198, 213 (1864) ("A cause unforeseen by the parties is about to lead to an abandonment of the work in its half-finished state, when the corporation agrees, with the view of insuring its completion, to increase the contract price and the work is accordingly completed." *Id.* at 216.). Reliance is implied element in rationale. *But cf.* New York Constitution, art. 3, sect. 28 (rendered invalid a promise to pay a contractor extra compensation on a state project). These state constitutional bars on enforcement of modified contracts with government employees are usually narrowly construed so that many of these contracts made for a good reason are enforceable, as in *Meech.*

73. *E.g.*, Linz v. Schuck, 106 Md. 220, 67 A. 286, 289 (1907); Curry v. Boeckeler Lumber Co., 27 S.W. 2d 473, 475 (Mo. 1930).

74. Goebel v. Linn, 47 Mich. 489, 11 N.W. 284, 285–286 (1882).

75. Blakeslee v. Board of Water Com'rs of City of Hartford, 139 A. 106, 112, 113 (Conn. 1927).

76. The "Massachusetts rule" found the benefit to the promisor in the promisee forbearing from exercising his "right" to breach. Several cases included in the Reporter's Note to Section 89 cited this analysis with approval. *See* Michaud v. McGregor, 61 Minn. 198, 63 N.W. 479, 480 (1895); Curry v. Boeckeler Lumber Co., 27 S.W. 2d 473, 475 (Mo. 1930). *Contra* King v. Duluth, M. & N. Ry. Co., 61 Minn. 482, 63 N.W. 1105, 1106 (1895); 1A CORBIN, *supra* note 45, at sect. 182.

77. Pittsburgh Testing Co. v. Farnsworth & Chambers Co., 251 F. 2d 77, 79 (1958) (based on fairness).

78. RESTATEMENT (SECOND) OF CONTRACTS sect. 89 cmt. c. (1981) (acknowledges that written evidence is sometimes required by statutes).

79. Watkins & Son v. Carrig, 91 N.H. 459, 21 A. 2d 591 (1941).

80. Watkins & Son v. Carrig, 91 N.H. 459, 21 A. 2d 591, 592–593 (1941). Although Comment (b) to Section 89 rejects the fiction, other cases cited with approval in the Section's Reporter's Note also employ the fiction. *See* Schwartzreich v. Bauman-Basch, Inc., 231 N.Y. 196, 131 N.E. 887 (1921); Siebring Mfg. Co. v.

Carlson Hybrid Corn Co., 246 Ia. 923, 70 N.W. 2d 149, 152 (1955). Massachusetts' cases regularly utilize the rescission technique. The above-cited case, *Schwartzreich*, is the basis for Illustration number 3 to Section 89, which seems more to do with reliance than with an unanticipated circumstance.

81. *See* Frye v. Hubbell, 74 N.H. 358, 68 A. 325 (1907). *Frye v. Hubbell* was discussed in *Watkins v. Carrig*, the latter noting the ready means available to find consideration for a modification in New Hampshire but doubting whether consideration should even be required in that type of case. Watkins v. Carrig, 21 A. 2d 591, 593, 594 (N.H. 1941).

82. Watkins v. Carrig, 91 N.H. 459, 21 A. 2d 591, 593 (1941).

83. Watkins v. Carrig, 91 N.H. 459, 21 A. 2d 591, 594 (1941).

84. Watkins v. Carrig, 91 N.H. 459, 21 A. 2d 591, 594 (1941) (The court pointed out that the owner didn't have to agree to the modification because there was no basis for excuse, and thus the risk under the original contract was with the contractor. *Id.* 592.).

85. Watkins v. Carrig, 91 N.H. 459, 21 A. 2d 591, 594 (1941). An analogy was drawn to moral obligation found in past consideration cases of waivers of bankruptcy and of statute of limitations. This analogy was not apt because the facts were found insufficient to afford the contractor an excuse defense in *Watkins*; and so, absent the modification, the defendant had the right to demand performance under the original contract, a demand unavailable to the creditors in the past consideration waiver cases.

86. Watkins v. Carrig, 91 N.H. 459, 21 A. 2d 591, 594 (1941).

87. Watkins v. Carrig, 91 N.H. 459, 21 A. 2d 591, 593 (1941).

88. *See* Pittsburgh Testing Laboratory v. Farnsworth & Chambers Co., 251 F. 2d 77, 79 (Unforeseen difficulties constituted consideration and provided protection against coercion.); Liebreich v. Tyler State Bank & Trust Co., 100 S.W. 2d 152 (Tex. 1936) (Economic depression was a sufficient consideration.). *See also* Commercial Car Line v. Anderson, 224 Ill. App. 187 (1922); 1A ARTHUR CORBIN, *supra* note 38, at sect. 184. The occurrence of the unexpected event in and of itself provides evidence of the need for an adjustment in the contractual relationship.

89. *See* RESTATEMENT (SECOND) OF CONTRACTS sect. 89 cmt. a (1981). *See also* Lon Fuller, *Consideration and Form*, 41 COLUM. L. REV. 799, 805 (1941) (Need for formality may be rendered superfluous by "forces native to the situation, including the habits of the parties.").

90. Witness how the court in *Watkins v. Carrig* assured itself that the promise to pay more was voluntary, without protest and perceived by the promisor to be beneficial. Watkins v. Carrig, 91 N.H. 459, 21 A. 2d 591, 594 (1941). The absence of economic duress must not be automatically assumed, however, as exemplified by Recker v. Gustafson, 279 N.W. 2d 744, 747, 757–758 (Ia. 1979). The *Recker* court could well have found that the dramatic drop in Iowa land prices in the 1980s qualified for the changed circumstances exception, but instead judicial comments alluded to pressure put on the young buyer by the experienced seller and his attorney. The Iowa court neither recognized the exception nor found duress but instead declared consideration was lacking. The court also rejected the rescission fiction, which if blindly applied, could likewise overlook the duress issue. *And see*

RESTATEMENT (SECOND) OF CONTRACTS sects. 205 & 208 for recognition of the doctrines of good faith and unconscionability being applicable to all contracts.

91. *See* Lon Fuller, *supra* note 89, 810–812, 814, 817 (Channeling function then decreases. *Id.* at 814.). The form functions performed by a writing are also deemed relevant in Comments (b) and (c) to Section 89. Under Restatement (Second) Section 74(2), a written surrender of a claim or defense, by one who does not believe it is valid, constitutes consideration, but if a similar surrender is oral, it fails as consideration under Section 74(1)(b).

92. *See* Meech v. City of Buffalo, 29 N.Y. 198 (1864) (Contractor proceeded with work on the faith of the additional compensation.); King v. Duluth, M. & N. Ry. Co., 61 Minn. 482, 63 N.W. 1105 (1895) (Construction work done in reliance on promise.); Michaud v. McGregor, 61 Minn. 198, 63 N.W. 479 (1895) (Promisee did work in reliance on waiver.); Schwartzreich v. Bauman-Basch, 231 N.Y. 196, 131 N.E. 887 (1921) (Employee relied on employer's promise of more salary by not changing jobs.); Blakeslee v. Board of Water Com'rs of City of Hartford, 139 A. 106, 110, 112 (Conn. 1927) (Inducement of promisee's performance was indicator of consideration.). *Cf.* RESTATEMENT (SECOND) OF CONTRACTS sect. 89 cmts. a & b (1981).

93. *See* Sheehan v. Commercial Travelers, 186 N.E. 627, 630 (Mass. 1933); Hetchler v. American Life Ins. Co., 266 Mich. 608, 254 N.W. 221 (1934); Fried v. Fisher, 328 Pa. 497, 196 A. 39 (1938); Central London Property Trust Ltd. v. High Trees House Ltd., K.B. 130 (1947).

94. *See* RESTATEMENT (SECOND) OF CONTRACTS sect. 89(c). If the modification is not performed, the promisee may fail to recover because the terms of the modification may well require satisfaction. *See* RESTATEMENT (SECOND) OF CONTRACTS sect. 281 (1981).

95. Watkins v. Carrig, 91 N.H. 459, 21 A. 2d 591, 592 (1941).

96. *E.g.*, Curry v. Boeckeler Lumber Co., 27 S.W. 2d 473, 475 (Mo. 1930); Linz v. Schuck, 106 Md. 220, 67 A. 286, 290 (1907). *Cf.* RESTATEMENT (SECOND) OF CONTRACTS sect. 283 cmt. a (1981) (Consideration for rescission of partly performed contract is provided by each parties' discharge of the duties of the other.).

97. *See* Lon Fuller, *supra* note 89, at 816 (The reason for judicial intervention diminishes when wholly executory.).

98. *See* Linz v. Schuck, 106 Md. 220, 67 A. 286, 290 (1907) ("While the contract is *executory* on both sides, the parties are at liberty to rescind it." (emphasis added)).

99. *See* James Gordon, *Consideration and the Commercial-Gift Dichotomy*, 44 VAND. L. REV. 283, 289–290 (1991).

100. *See* Hayes v. Plantations Steel Co., 438 A. 2d 1091, 1094 (R.I. 1982) (It is required for a modification, as a type of bargain, that the consideration *not* have been delivered earlier without reference to the promise.). The promise of extra pay may be prompted by other dealings, contemporaneous or yet to come, between the parties. The moral obligation principle is relevant to promises to pay more for overcoming unforeseen difficulties.

101. King v. Duluth, M. & N. Ry. Co., 61 Minn. 482, 63 N.W. 1105, 1107 (1895). *Accord* Linz v. Schuck, 106 Md. 220, 67 A. 286, 289 (1907).

102. King v. Duluth, M. & N. Ry. Co., 61 Minn. 482, 63 N.W. 1105, 1107 (1895).

See, e.g., Linz v. Schuck, 106 Md. 220, 67 A. 286 (1907) (swampy conditions from covered-over creek bed); Watkins v. Carrig, 91 N.H. 459, 21 A. 2d 591 (1941) (solid rock encountered); Angel v. Murray, 322 A. 2d 630 (R.I. 1974) (unprecedented growth of houses to collect garbage from); Quigley v. Wilson, 474 N.W. 2d 277 (Ia. App. 1991) (drastic decrease in land value). The English rent reduction case *High Trees* could have been resolved under this exception because of wartime conditions, even without the reliance found. Central London Property Trust Ltd. v. High Trees House Ltd., 1 K.B. 130 (1947). The unanticipated circumstances doesn't necessarily mean there has to be a change in circumstances; it can simply be that matters turned out differently than expected, as finding solid rock during earth excavation. *And see* RESTATEMENT (SECOND) OF CONTRACTS sect. 89 cmt. a (1981) (Failure of a material contract condition, due to unanticipated circumstances, can be a basis for waiver of a condition under this section, and if it's not material, then under Section 84(1).).

103. King v. Duluth, M. & N. Ry. Co., 61 Minn. 482, 63 N.W. 1105, 1107 (1895); *and see* RESTATEMENT (SECOND) OF CONTRACTS sect. 89 (In Illustration number 2, a modification made, because of a mistake in bidding on a contract, is binding based on ruling in Lange v. United States, 120 F. 2d 886 (1941).).

104. *Accord* Linz v. Schuck, 106 Md. 220, 67 A. 286, 289 (1907); Recker v. Gustafson, 279 N.W. 2d 744, 758 (Iowa 1979); Western Litograph Co. v. Vanomar Producers, 185 Cal. 366, 197 P. 103 (1929); Rexite Casting Co. v. Midwest Mower Corp., 267 S.W. 2d 327 (Mo. App. 1954); McGowan & Connolly Co. v. Kenny-Moran Co., 202 N.Y.S. 513, 207 App. Div. 617 (1924). There is, however, a strain of consideration-based modification cases where a modification has been enforced because a party who was losing on a contract resumed work in exchange for higher payments. *See* Skinner v. Tober Foreign Motors, Inc., 187 N.E. 2d 669 (Mass. 1963); Williams v. Roffey, 1 All Eng. Rep. 512, 527 (1990).

105. Rexite Casting Co. v. Midwest Mower Corp., 267 S.W. 327 (Mo. App. 1954).

106. Seller wanted 50% increase in contract price. The fact that, once the buyer had reasonable time to search, he was able to buy the product elsewhere for near the original contract price reinforced the court's suspicions. The court ruled there was no consideration, thereby denying the coerced modification. Rexite Casting Co. v. Midwest Mower Corp., 267 S.W. 327, 331 (Mo. App. 1954). *Cf.* Roth Steel Products v. Sharon Steel Corp., 705 F. 2d 134, 146–147 (1983) (Changed circumstances can cause substantial loss and inefficiency.).

107. RESTATEMENT OF CONTRACTS sect. 76 (1932) (Commentary on Illustration number 8: "If unforeseen difficulties justifying [a party] in rescinding the contract exist, there is sufficient consideration for a promise of additional payment.").

108. *E.g.*, King v. Duluth, M. & N. Ry. Co., 61 Minn. 482, 63 N.W. 1105, 1107 (1895); Blakeslee v. Board of Water Com'rs of City of Hartford, 139 A. 106, 111 (Conn. 1927); Watkins v. Carrig, 91 N.H. 459, 21 A. 2d 591, 592 (1941).

109. King v. Duluth, M. & N. Ry. Co., 61 Minn. 482, 63 N.W. 1105, 1107 (1895).

110. Watkins v. Carrig, 91 N.H. 459, 21 A. 2d 591, 592 (1941).

111. Michaud v. McGregor, 61 Minn. 198, 63 N.W. 479, 480–481 (1895).

112. RESTATEMENT (SECOND) OF CONTRACTS sect. 89 cmt. b (1981) (It can be unanticipated even if it was foreseen as a remote possibility.).

113. RESTATEMENT (SECOND) OF CONTRACTS sect. 89(a) (1981).

114. Meech v. City of Buffalo, 29 N.Y. 198, 218–219 (1864).

115. Linz v. Schuck, 106 Md. 220, 67 A. 286, 289 (1907).

116. *See* King v. Duluth, M. & N. Ry. Co., 61 Minn. 482, 63 N.W. 1105, 1107 (1895) (Changed circumstances can show whether demand for more money is "manifestly fair." *Id.*); Linz v. Schuck, 106 Md. 220, 67 A. 286, 289 (1907) (A "just and equitable" principle for exception to the preexisting duty rule. *Id.* at 287. When changed circumstances, the fair course is either let party out of deal or pay more. *Id.* at 288.).

117. *See* RESTATEMENT (SECOND) OF CONTRACTS sect. 89 cmt. b (1981). If it does not involve an unanticipated circumstance, the formation process and terms of the modification would still be subject to the doctrines of unconscionability and good faith. *See* RESTATEMENT (SECOND) OF CONTRACTS sects. 205 & 208.

118. From the equity side, courts over the last century have characterized a modification as "inequitable" if the presence of coercion would be grounds for equity granting a rescission. *See* King v. Duluth, M. & N. Ry. Co., 61 Minn. 482, 63 N.W. 1105, 1107 (1895). It was also said that unforeseen substantial difficulties could be the reason or basis for an equitable refusal to comply with the original contract terms. *See Id.* at 1107; *see also* Linz v. Schuck, 106 Md. 220, 67 A. 286, 289 (1907) (Refusal to perform could be "equitable and fair."); *cf.* RESTATEMENT (SECOND) OF CONTRACTS sect. 89 cmt. b (1981) (" 'fair and equitable' goes beyond absence of coercion and requires an objectively demonstrable reason for seeking a modification.").

119. Watkins v. Carrig, 91 N.H. 459, 21 A. 2d 591, 594 (1941) (If promisor agrees without protest, then in fairness he should honor it. *Id.*); *see* Pittsburgh Testing Laboratory v. Farnsworth & Chambers Co., 251 F. 2d 77, 79 (1958) ("[t]he courts generally sustain the consideration for the new promise, based upon standards of fair dealing and affording adequate protection against unjust or coercive exactions." *Id.*).

120. RESTATEMENT (SECOND) OF CONTRACTS sect. 89 cmt. (b) draws from and roughly parallels U.C.C. sect. 2–209 cmt. 2; but the Restatement Comments make no mention of fair dealing, and the U.C.C. Comments only say the showing of an objectively demonstrable reason "may" be required.

CHAPTER 6

1. *E.g.*, Angel v. Murray, 322 A. 2d 630 (R.I. 1974); Quigley v. Wilson, 474 N.W. 2d 277, 280–281 (Ia. App. 1991).

2. *See* Barnwell & Hays, Inc. v. Sloan, 564 F. 2d 254 (1977); Farmland Services Coop v. Jack, 196 Neb. 263, 242 N.W. 2d 624 (1976); Skinner v. Tober Foreign Motors, Inc., 187 N.E. 2d 669 (Mass. 1963). Some courts do require the proponent of the modification to establish good faith as a part of his burden of proof, though the suggestion of abuse in the surrounding circumstances may be the cause for this judicial position in a given case. *See* Roth Steel Products v. Sharon Steel Corp., 705 F. 2d 134, 146 (1983). The affirmative duty of the plaintiff in *Roth* and under Section 89(a) is unique under common law contract in requiring the plaintiff to go past proving the agreement to also establish good faith before the burden shifts to the defendant; contract law normally places the burden on the defendant to

raise the issues of bad faith and coercion as a part of rebutting the plaintiff's prima facie case.

3. *E.g.*, Barnwell & Hays Inc. v. Sloan, 564 F. 2d 254 (1977) (The farmer's claim that he couldn't complete the contract because of a fire destroying his cotton crop appeared shaky since he was later found selling cotton to another buyer. The good faith issue was not even mentioned.); Farmland Services Coop v. Jack, 196 Neb. 263, 242 N.W. 2d 624 (1976) (Farmer changed his mind about selling to the grain elevator operation both because the price was too cheap and because he received bad advice from the elevator agent. Good faith was not discussed.). In most states the status of a farmer, when he only sells his crop at harvest, is usually deemed that of a non-merchant. The leniency of these decisions may be explainable on the basis of the courts treating them as an economic underdog in their dealings with grain elevators over price.

4. *See generally* CHRISTOPHER LANGDELL, A SELECTION OF CASES OF SALES OF PERSONAL PROPERTY (Boston: 1871); SAMUEL WILLISTON, THE LAW GOVERNING SALES OF GOODS AT COMMON LAW AND UNDER THE UNIFORM SALES ACT (New York: 1909); *see also* Karl Llewellyn, *Across Sales on Horseback*, 52 HARV. L. REV. 725, 740–745 (1939); Lawrence Friedman, *Formative Elements in the Law of Sales: The Eighteenth Century*, 44 MINN. L. REV. 411, 435–450 (1960). Lord Holt's ruling that consideration could be presumed present to support a promissory note according to mercantile usage, at a time when transfer of notes was still considered a contract assignment at common law, was a progenitor of using trade practices to determine whether a commercial promise was binding. *See* Meredith v. Chute, 2 Ld. Raym. 759, 760, 92 Eng. Rep. 7 (1702) ("[i]t was not necessary for the plaintiff to prove, upon what consideration the note of (the maker) was given, the defendant having admitted it to have been given upon good consideration by his promise.").

5. *Cf.* 1A ARTHUR CORBIN, CORBIN ON CONTRACTS sect 183 (St. Paul: 1950) (Preexisting duty rule makes sense when coercion, but if no coercion, the finding of consideration ought to mean it's in conformity with mores and practices.).

6. Pinnel's Case, 5 Co. Rep. 117a, 77 Eng. Rep. 237 (1602) (debt on a bond).

7. Stilk v. Myrick, 2 Camp. 317, 170 Eng. Rep. 1168 (1809) (ship captain's promise to pay rest of crew more after two sailors deserted).

8. Foakes v. Beer, 9 App. Cas. 605 (H.L. 1884) (modification of amount due on judgment debt).

9. Central London Property Trust Ltd. v. High Trees House Ltd., K.B. 130 (1947) (wartime reduction of rent relied upon).

10. Farmland Services Coop v. Jack, 196 Neb. 263, 242 N.W. 2d 624 (1976) (sale of grain).

11. Williams v. Roffey Bros. & Nicholls (Contractors) Ltd., 1 All Eng. Rep. 512 (1990) (construction services).

12. *See* E. Allan Farnsworth, *Ingredients in the Redaction of The Restatement (Second) of Contracts*, 81 COLUM. L. REV. 1, 10–12 (1981) (Restatement Second Reporter highlighted Code's treatment of good faith, trade usage and written waiver without consideration.); Robert Braucher, *Interpretation and Legal Effect in the Second Restatement of Contracts*, 81 COLUM. L. REV. 13, 15–17 (1981).

13. Excluding states which employ a fiction or rationalize the presence of con-

sideration, only Minnesota has flatly rejected the requirement of consideration for modifications generally. Rye v. Phillips, 282 N.W. 459 (Minn. 1938) (dictum); Winter Wolff & Co. v. Co-Op Lead & Chem. Co., 261 Minn. 199, 111 N.W. 2d 461 (1961). Watkins v. Carrig, 91 N.H. 459, 21 A. 2d 591, 593–594 (1941) dropped the consideration requirement for modifications made because of unanticipated circumstances.

14. Angel v. Murray, 322 A. 2d 630 (R.I. 1974) (unexpected growth in number of units that garbage company had to collect from). The *Angel v. Murray* decision stated a view in line with the philosophy of U.C.C. Sect. 2–209(1): It "fulfills society's expectations that agreements (entered) into voluntarily will be enforced by the courts." *Id.* at 636. But, ultimately, the court latched onto the Section 89 exception to the requirement of consideration.

15. *E.g.*, Quigley v. Wilson, 474 N.W. 2d 277, 281 (Ia. App. 1991) (unanticipated circumstances found); Fondedile v. Maquire, 610 A. 2d 87, 92 (R.I. 1992) (consideration is required for modification); McCallum Highlands Ltd. v. Washington Capital Dus, Inc., 66 F. 3d 89 (5th Cir. 1995) (Preexisting duty rule barred modification under Texas law.); Thermoglaze, Inc. v. Morningside Gardens Co., 583 A. 2d 1331 (Conn. App. Ct. 1991) (modification unenforceable due to lack of consideration); Metro Communications Co. v. Ameritech Mobile Communications, Inc., 984 F. 2d 739 (6th Cir. 1993) (modification lacked consideration); Tierney v. Capricorn Investors, L.P., 592 N.Y.S. 2d 700 (App. Div. 1993) (increase lacked consideration); DeCecchis v. Evers, 54 Del. 99, 174 A. 2d 463 (Super. Ct. Dela. 1961) (consideration needed for bailment); Rexite v. Midwest Mower, 267 S.W. 2d 327 (Mo. 1954) (no consideration to support the modification); Recker v. Gustafson, 279 N.W. 2d 744, 758–759 (Ia. 1979) (modification found unenforceable since consideration lacking); Mainland v. Alfred Brown Co., 85 Nev. 654, 461 P. 2d 862, 864 (1969) (modification needed consideration despite assurances after fire); Walden v. Backus, 81 Nev. 634, 408 P. 2d 712 (1965) (no consideration found for accord); Heckman & Shell v. Wilson, 158 Mont. 47, 487 P. 2d 1141, 1147 (1971) (no consideration found); Mountain Shadows of Indine v. Kopsho, 555 P. 2d 841, 842 (Nev. 1977) (the need for meeting of minds and consideration absent for accord); Tri-City Concrete Co. v. A.L.A. Constr. Co., 343 Mass. 425, 179 N.E. 2d 319, 320–321 (1962) (construction contract); Green v. Millman Bros., Inc., 7 Mich. App. 450, 151 N.W. 2d 860, 865 (1967) (lease); Block v. Drucker, 212 So. 2d 890 (Fla. Dist Ct. App. 1968) (brokerage account); Massey-Ferguson Credit Corp. v. Peterson, 626 P. 2d 767, 775–776 (Idaho 1981); Matter of Estate of Easterbrook, 319 N.W. 2d 655, 659 (Mich. App. 1982); Sambo's Restaurant, Inc. v. City of Ann Arbor, 663 F. 2d 686, 690 (1981) (Performance of existing obligation doesn't constitute consideration.); Bucker v. Nat'l Mgt. Corp., 16 Mass. App. 36, 448 N.E. 2d 1299, 1303 (1983); Rickett v. Doze, 603 P. 2d 679, 680–681 (Mont. 1979) (consideration found to take it outside rule); Sergeant v. Leonard, 312 N.W. 2d 541, 545 (Ia. 1981) (consideration found to go outside rule).

16. *See* Recker v. Gustafson, 279 N.W. 2d 744, 757–759 (Ia. 1979) (Rescission fiction may no longer be used to avoid consideration requirement for modification, citing tentative draft predecessor of Restatement Second sect. 89 cmt. b.); *and see* Robert Hillman, *Contract Modification in Iowa—Recker v. Gustafson and the Resurrection of the Preexisting Duty Doctrine*, 65 IA. L. REV. 343, 353 (1980) (In process of averting harm of rescission theory, *Recker* bars voluntary modifications formerly

enforced under now improper rescission theory.). *Recker* is a good example of why automatic judicial allowance of the rescission fiction can result in enforcement of a coerced modification. Although coercion was not established in *Recker*, the court expressed concern over pressure put on the young buyer by the experienced seller and his lawyer. Recker v. Gustafson, 279 N.W. 2d 744, 747, 758.

17. RESTATEMENT (SECOND) OF CONTRACTS sect. 73 cmts. a, b & c, and sect. 89 cmt. b (1981).

18. *See* BARRY NICHOLAS, THE FRENCH LAW OF CONTRACT 145 (2d ed. Oxford: 1992); JOHN DAWSON, GIFTS AND PROMISES 211 (New Haven: 1980) (German and French law).

19. *See* Watkins v. Carrig, 91 N.H. 459, 21 A. 2d 591 (1941) (Business practice is to modify contracts due to change. *Id.* at 593. In fairness, party should honor voluntary modification promise. *Id.* at 594.); Brooks v. White, 2 Met. 283 (Mass. 1840) (*Pinnel's Case's* rule may be urged in violation of good faith. *Id.*); 1A ARTHUR CORBIN, *supra* note 5, at sect. 183.

20. *Cf.* Williams v. Roffey Bros. & Nicholls (Contractors) Ltd., 1 All Eng. Rep. 512, 527 (1990) (There was a benefit to contractor in carpenter not cutting his losses by breaching.).

21. A well informed bargainer is also less likely to be surprised and need to request a modification, since he or she will make a studied bid and will make fewer errors in judgment about the extent of the performance necessary. Furthermore, the sophisticated bargainer may negotiate successfully for flexible, open-ended language in the original contract to accommodate market shifts, and other possible reasons, for needed maneuverability in a particular type of modern contract.

22. A parallel to the unequal treatment of parties, on the basis of status, in contracts that need adjustments can be found in the way the doctrine of substantial performance has been applied to construction contracts and employment contracts. Contractors were allowed to recover damages on contracts nearly completed under the doctrine of substantial performance in *Cutler v. Close*, but employees, who nearly finished the contract term, were unable to recover in *Cutter v. Powell.* Cutler v. Close, 5 C. & P. 337, 172 Eng. Rep. 1001 (1832) (construction project 7/8 completed); Cutter v. Powell, 6 T.R. 320, 101 Eng. Rep. 573 (1795) (Executor of deceased sailor could not recover wages for deceased who died three weeks before end of three-month voyage.). One can't help finding a bias in favor of entrepreneurs. *See* LAWRENCE FRIEDMAN, CONTRACT LAW IN AMERICA 109–110 (Madison, Wis.: 1965); MORTON HORWITZ, THE TRANSFORMATION OF AMERICAN LAW (1780–1860) 188 (Cambridge, Mass.: 1977) (courts aiding capital investment of building trades).

23. *Contra* RESTATEMENT (SECOND) OF CONTRACTS sect. 148 (Right to make oral rescission may *not* be barred by original contract.). This provides protection to the consumer who enters into a beneficial informal end to a contract.

24. *See* Sanger v. Dun, 47 Wis. 615, 3 N.W. 388, 389 (1879) (failure to read no defense); *cf.* Masterson v. Sine, 68 Cal. 2d 222, 436 P. 2d 561 (1968) (Per Traynor, J.: "[t]he party urging the spoken as against the written work is most often the economic underdog, threatened by severe hardship if the writing is enforced." *Id.* at 564.); *and see* Stewart Macaulay, *Private Legislation and the Duty to Read—Business Run by IBM Machine, The Law of Contracts and Credit Cards,* 19 VAND. L. REV. 1051, 1063–1064 (1966); Henningsen v. Bloomfield Motors, 32 N.J. 358, 161 A. 2d 69,

90–1 (1960) (Fine print disclaimer, probably not read on back of form contract, was not enforced.); Weaver v. American Oil Co., 257 Ind. 458, 276 N.E. 2d 144, 148 (1971) (Objective standard discarded when weaker party didn't know of hardship provision.).

25. U.C.C. sect. 2–209(2) provides that when contract language bars a non-merchant from an oral modification or rescission, it must be signed separately by the non-merchant. *Cp.* RESTATEMENT (SECOND) OF CONTRACTS Section 148 (Protects a consumer, or any party, from losing the right to be discharged by oral agreement of rescission.). The bar on an informal modification may be deemed unconscionable under either U.C.C. sect. 2–302 or RESTATEMENT (SECOND) OF CONTRACTS sect. 208.

26. Restatement (Second) sect. 73 cmt. (c) expressed concern "where an impecunious debtor has paid part of his debt in satisfaction of the whole," and lamely the Commentators hoped that the rules regarding cancellation, discharge and unanticipated circumstances would cause an equitable outcome.

27. The influence of Restatement Section 90 in supporting an alternative ground to consideration for promissory liability is remarkable. Query whether there would be the equivalent ensuing ground swell judicial support to oust the preexisting duty rule. It is true, however, that promissory estoppel had been used almost exclusively for gratuitous promises prior to Section 90, and that there has been a fair amount of movement against the preexisting duty rule in the form of common law and statutory reform. On the other hand, if one searches for caselaw support for a restatement solution of dropping the consideration requirement for all contract modifications, there has only been one common law jurisdiction to date that has done this; at least Restatement Section 90 was bolstered by the widely supported strain of promissory estoppel rulings on gratuitous promises, which provided a foundation for subsequent caselaw growth. It's a close question that goes to the purpose and the possibilities of a restatement of the law.

28. Clayton v. Clark, 74 Miss. 499, 21 So. 565 (1896) (benefit in cash-in-hand and avoiding collection problems); Frye v. Hubbell, 74 N.H. 358, 68 A. 325 (1907) (Debtor's parting with money is detriment and creditor's receipt without needing to enforce is a benefit.); Brown v. Everhard, 52 Wis. 205, 8 N.W. 725 (1881) (Consideration of original contract is imported into modification.).

29. Williams v. Roffey Bros. & Nicholls (Contractors) Ltd., 1 All Eng. Rep. 512, 527 (1990) (Promisor received benefits of avoidance of costs and continuation of performance.).

30. In *Sibree v. Tripp*, Baron Parke rejected the relevancy of adequacy in a modification; he stated: "It may be equal value, but that we cannot enter into: it is sufficient that the parties have so agreed." Sibree v. Tripp, 15 M. & W. 22, 34, 153 Eng. Rep. 745, 750 (1846). Lord Blackburn acknowledged *Sibree's* position but failed to follow up on it. Foakes v. Beer, 9 App. Cas. 605, 621 (1884).

31. Rye v. Phillips, 203 Minn. 567, 282 N.W. 459, 460 (1938). Alabama doesn't require consideration for modification of an *executory* contract. George v. Roberts, 186 Ala. 521, 65 So. 345 (1914); Industrial Development Board of the Town of Section v. Fuqua Ind., Inc., 523 F. 2d 1226, 1241 (1975).

32. Not that much of a risk is taken by a party giving up a portion of a contract right in a modification because the modification only suspends the original contract obligation; and, if it is not satisfied, the party may elect to enforce either the

modification or the original contract terms. *See* RESTATEMENT (SECOND) OF CONTRACTS sect. 281. *Cf.* Browning v. Holloway, 620 S.W. 2d 611, 616 (Tex. App. 1981) (If modification lessens rights and it's unclear whether it's a substituted contract or an accord, it is deemed an accord, thus requiring satisfaction.).

33. *See* Butch Levy Plumbing and Heating, Inc. v. Sallablad, 126 N.W. 2d 380, 385 (Minn. 1964); Winter-Wolff & Co. v. Co-Op Lead & Chem. Co., 261 Minn. 199, 111 N.W. 2d 461, 465 (1961); Cut Price Super Markets v. Kingpin Food, Inc., 98 N.W. 2d 257, 269 (Minn. 1959); Mattfield v. Nester, 32 N.W. 2d 291, 310 (Minn. 1948); Brack v. Brack, 16 N.W. 2d 557, 560 (Minn. 1944); Robert Hillman, *Policing Contract Modifications under the U.C.C.: Good Faith and the Doctrine of Economic Duress*, 64 IA. L. REV. 849, 859–875 (1979).

34. RESTATEMENT (SECOND) OF CONTRACTS sect. 205 (good faith and fair dealing in performance and enforcement of all contracts).

35. Good faith duties during negotiation and bargaining have been required in this century for collective bargaining, for companies clothed with a public interest such as public utilities and insurers, when there has been reliance on representations made during negotiations and in the form of required statutory disclosures to consumers.

36. *See* JOHN BAKER, AN INTRODUCTION TO ENGLISH LEGAL HISTORY 386–387 (London: 3rd ed. 1990) (Canon law concept of a promise made upon good cause goes back to the very origins of doctrine of consideration.). Motive for the promise was another meaning of *causa*.

37. *See* Ronald Coase, *The Nature of the Firm*, 4 ECONOMICA 386, 391–392 (1937); Clyde Summers, *Collective Agreements and the Law of Contracts*, 78 YALE L.J. 525, 528, 534 (1969); Ian Macneil, *Restatement (Second) of Contracts and Presentiation*, 60 VA. L. REV. 589, 595–596 (1974); Walter Pratt, *American Contract Law at the Turn of the Century*, 39 S.C.L. REV. 415, 432–435 (1988).

38. *See* 1 & 2 JAPAN BUSINESS LAW GUIDE sects. 40–320, 40–520, 80–050 (ed. M. Matsushita, CCH: 1991).

39. *See* C.I.S.G. Art. 29(1) ("A contract may be modified or terminated by the mere agreement of the parties."). United Nations Convention on International Sales of Goods (CISG) was enacted by U.S. Congress and became effective on January 1, 1988. It governs sales contracts between American contractors and foreign parties residing in a CISG signatory nation state.

CHAPTER 7

1. There was no *quid pro quo* but rather an earlier benefit to the plaintiff for which he is now promising to pay. *See* H. K. Lücke, *Slade's Case and the Origin of the Common Counts* (pts. 1–3) (Pt. 1), 81 L.Q. REV 422, 434–435 (1965). In the sixteenth century DOCTOR AND STUDENT, the Doctor asked: "But what hold they if a promise be made for a thing past, as I promise thee forty pounds for that thou hast builded me such a house; lieth an action there?" The Student responded: "They suppose nay; but he shall be bound in conscience to perform it after his intent, as is before said." ST. GERMAIN, DOCTOR AND STUDENT, Dial. II, c.24 (1523, Dial. I; 1530, Dial. II), *reprinted in* 91 SELDEN SOC. 231 (hereinafter cited as DOCTOR AND STUDENT). The Student's response was only partially consis-

tent with earlier canon law. *See* ALFRED SIMPSON, A HISTORY OF THE COMMON LAW OF CONTRACT 393–394 (Oxford: 1975).

2. Y. B. Trin. 5 Hen. VII, f.41v, pl. 7 (1490) ("If one sells a thing and afterwards at another place the seller warrants it, this warranty is void, because it was not made *sur le bargain*, and the buyer shall not have an action of deceit."). *See also* Andrew v. Boughey, Dyer, f. 76a, pl. 28 (1552) (warranty of goodness void since made a month after contract entered into, citing 1490 case *supra*).

3. Hunt v. Bate, 3 Dyer 272a, 73 Eng. Rep. 605 (C.P. 1568).

4. Hunt v. Bate, 3 Dyer 272a, 73 Eng. Rep. 605 (C.P. 1568). From a proprietary perspective, it was essentially a gift.

5. *See* H. K. Lücke (pt. 1), *supra* note 1, at 434 (The fear of officious intermeddling may have been the reason for refusing to recognize past consideration.).

6. *See* John Baker, *Origins of the "Doctrine" of Consideration, 1535–1585* in ON THE LAWS AND CUSTOMS OF ENGLAND 344 (Chapel Hill: 1981).

7. Plaintiff would allege that defendant, being indebted (*indebitatus*), undertook (*assumpsit*) to pay. *See Anon.*, Dal. 84 (1572), *reprinted in* JOHN BAKER and STROUD MILSOM, SOURCES OF ENGLISH LEGAL HISTORY (PRIVATE LAW TO 1750) 416 (London: 1986) (Plaintiff lost because he failed to plead the *assumpsit* as subsequent to the debt and therefore the action of debt applied.).

8. *See* STROUD MILSOM, HISTORICAL FOUNDATIONS OF THE COMMON LAW 359 (London: 2d ed. 1981) (The need to show defendant's special request of plaintiff probably comes from reliance element found in trespassory origins of assumpsit.).

9. Slade's Case (a/k/a Slade v. Morley), 4 Co. Rep. 91a, 76 Eng. Rep. 1072 (1602).

10. *See* William Holdsworth, *The Modern History of the Doctrine of Consideration* (pts 1 & 2) (pt. 2), 2 BOSTON U.L.R. 87, 174, 194–195 (1922) (Consideration was a procedural device tied to outmoded forms of action which could've been abandoned once procedure and logic changed.); *contra* 1 ARTHUR CORBIN, CORBIN ON CONTRACTS sect. 111 (St Paul: 1950) (evolving principle of substantive law). *See also* SAMUEL STOLJAR, A HISTORY OF CONTRACT AT COMMON LAW 82–83 (Canberra: 1975) (Once *Slade's Case* dispensed with need for forbearance-assumpsit, the *indebitatus* count could have dropped any reference to consideration.).

11. *See* Willard Barbour, *The History of Contract in Early English Equity* in IV OXFORD STUDIES IN SOCIAL AND LEGAL HISTORY 66, 166 (P. Vinogradoff ed., Oxford: 1914) (Chancery asked whether the promisor made such a promise which in reason and conscience he ought to perform.).

12. *E.g.*, Atkins v. Hill, Cowp. 284 (1775); Trueman v. Fenton, Cowp. 544 (1777); Hawkes v. Saunders, Cowp. 289 (1782). These ideas of Mansfield will be expanded *infra*.

13. *See* John Baker, *New Light on Slade's Case* (pt. 2), 1971 CAMBRIDGE L.J. 213, 218; *see* also H. K. Lücke (pt. 1), *supra* note 1, at 435.

14. Hunt v. Bate, 3 Dyer 272a, 73 Eng. Rep. 605 (C.P. 1568).

15. Hodge v. Vavisour, 3 Bulstr. 222, 1 Rolle Rep. 413 (1617), *reprinted in* BAKER and MILSOM, *supra* note 7, at 504.

16. *Cf.* Alfred Simpson, *Slade's Case in the History of Contract*, 74 L.Q. REV. 381, 391 (1958) (Implied promise and bargain were alleged to have arisen at the same

moment and so consideration wasn't past.). *See* 8 WILLIAM HOLDSWORTH, A HISTORY OF ENGLISH LAW 16 (London: 1926).

17. *Hodge v. Vavisour* (1617), *reprinted in* BAKER and MILSOM, *supra* note 7, at 504. Yet, in this post-*Slade* period, one finds added to the 1617 report of *Hodge v. Vavisour* in 1 Rolle Rep. a query whether the consideration is good because "consideration to forbear for a little while is no good." *Id.* at 505n.

18. Lampleigh v. Braithwait, Hob. 105, 80 Eng. Rep. 255 (1616).

19. Hunt v. Bate, 3 Dyer 272a, 73 Eng. Rep. 605 (1568).

20. Lampleigh v. Braithwait, Hob. 105, 80 Eng. Rep. 255 (1616). Earlier confusion in Docket v. Vogel, Cro. Eliz. 885 (1602) (terms past and executed used as synonyms).

21. Sir John Holt (CJKB 1689–1709) was one of the best common law thinkers to sit on the bench. With the possible exception of Sir Matthew Hale (CBEx 1660–1671, CJKB 1671–1676), Holt was arguably the most astute judicial analyst of the common law since Bracton. Henry de Bracton (Bratton) (d.1268) (JKB 1247–1251 & 1253–1257) is commonly accepted to be the author of DE LEGIBUS ET CONSUETUDINIBUS ANGLIE.

22. Ball v. Hesketh, Comb. 381, 90 Eng. Rep. 541 (1697). *See* Southerton v. Whitlock, 2 Stra. 690, 93 Eng. Rep. 786 (1726) (Ratification of infant's earlier contract held binding.). As a matter of policy, the law will not hold an infant for benefits conferred, but if a promise is made after reaching majority, the coupling of the benefit with the subsequent adult promise was enough, based on a sense of a moral obligation, for Holt to find an enforceable contractual obligation as an exception to consideration construct.

23. Stone v. Wythipol, Cro. Eliz. 126, 78 Eng. Rep. 383 (1589) (Promise to pay for an infant's void obligation is neither a charge to the plaintiff nor a benefit to the defendant.). A promise of a married woman was considered void until the nineteenth century. Loyd v. Lee, 1 Stra. 94, 93 Eng. Rep. 406 (1719).

24. Heyling v. Hastings (a/k/a Hyleing v. Hastings), 1 Ld. Raym. 389, 421, 91 Eng. Rep. 1157, 1179 (1699). A six-year statute of limitations was inaugurated for contract actions on the case in 1623. Stat. 21 Jac. I, c. 16, s.3 (1623).

25. Holt made one other significant reform of the doctrine of consideration. Although he was a supporter of the status quo achieved by Whig commercial interests in 1688, his traditional common law instincts prompted him to apply strict common law contract doctrine to emerging forms of negotiable instruments; but he eventually recognized commercial necessity and ruled "that it was not necessary for the plaintiff to prove, upon what consideration the (promissory) note was given, the defendant having admitted it to have been given upon good consideration by his promise." Meredith v. Chute, 2 Ld. Raym. 759, 760, 92 Eng. Rep. 7 (1702).

26. Lord Mansfield, born William Murray, hailed from Scotland, a civil law jurisdiction. He studied Roman and civil law at Oxford and was influenced by contemporaneous rational ideas of the Enlightenment. Despite his skepticism about the common law, his powerful political standing catapulted him onto the bench.

27. Pillan v. Van Mierop, 3 Burr. 1663, 97 Eng. Rep. 1035 (K.B. 1765).

28. Wilmot, J. remarked negatively about some of the earlier cases on the issue at hand, saying: "Many of the . . . cases are strange and absurd." Pillans v. Van Mierop, 3 Burr. 1663, 1671, 97 Eng. Rep. 1035, 1039 (1765) (Roman, civil law and

the law of nations make moral obligations binding, especially if there is written stipulation, citing Justinian, Grotuis and Puffendorff. *Id.* at 1038.). *See* Meredith v. Chute, 2 Ld. Raym. 759, 760, 92 Eng. Rep. 7 (1702).

29. Pillans v. Van Mierop, 3 Burr. 1663, 1669, 97 Eng. Rep. 1035, 1038 (1765). Statute of Frauds, 29 Car. II, c.3 (1677). Mansfield questioned why consideration should constrict contract after problems of proof were solved by Statute of Frauds and by methodical business practices. *See* THEODORE PLUCKNETT, A CONCISE HISTORY OF THE COMMON LAW 654 (London: 5th ed. 1956); *see also* 8 WILLIAM HOLDSWORTH, A HISTORY OF ENGLISH LAW 47 (London: 1926). Statute of Frauds bestowed upon an unsealed writing a constitutive nature, which was further enhanced during the next generation by parol evidence rule's emergence, but consideration was still required to form such contracts. *See* 9 JOHN WIGMORE, EVIDENCE IN TRIALS AT COMMON LAW 89–91 (Boston: rev. ed. 1979, Supp. 1986).

30. *E.g.*, Losh v. Williamson, 7 T.R. 351, 101 Eng. Rep. 1015n. (1775). This case is discussed in CECIL FIFOOT, LORD MANSFIELD 134 (Oxford: 1936)). *Losh* is one case of the period referred to by name. In *Losh*, the king's bench held that consideration was not required for a written promise supported by love and affection: "The court held that, the instrument being in writing and attested by witnesses, the objection of *nudum pactum* did not lie." *Id.* In Mansfield's trial level proceedings in *Rann v. Hughes*, reported by Brown, it was said that *Pillans v. Van Mierop* provided "that no consideration was necessary when the promise was reduced into writing. That opinion has since been recognized in [the King's Bench], and several judgments founded upon it." Rann v. Hughes, 4 Brown 27, 31, 2 Eng. Rep. 18, 21 (1778).

31. Rann v. Hughes, 4 Brown 27, 2 Eng. Rep. 18; 7 T.R. 350, 101 Eng. Rep. 1014n. (H. L. 1778) (Brown's report has pleadings and trial arguments and T.R. has House of Lords's judicial opinion.). The House of Lords case was a review of the exchequer chamber reversal of a Mansfield ruling, in which he had relied on *Pillans*. The ruling in *Rann* was based on the writing issue alone; the usage of merchants argument was left dangling. The end result of the House of Lords' decision was that the administratrix was not liable on the promise because her past consideration defense prevailed.

32. Lord Skynner said that the Statute of Frauds was merely negative to protect certain debtors and not to charge them with new liabilities. Rann v. Hughes, 7 T.R. 350, 101 Eng. Rep. 1014n. (H.L. 1778). The Statute of Frauds (1677) was passed in order to protect debtors from unscrupulous plaintiffs who could influence the uncontrolled trial by jury system of the day. However, a century later, juries were better controlled due to procedural innovations like modern rules of evidence. By the 1760s, Mansfield saw a more effective form of trial by jury, which he had contributed to controlling; he had confidence in jury's ability to render rational verdicts on moral obligations.

33. The report of the trial in *Rann v. Hughes* stated that, as an alternative to the view that a written promise did not need consideration, consideration could also be found in executrix being liable to show plaintiff what assets she had and how she applied them. Rann v. Hughes, 4 Brown 27, 31, 2 Eng. Rep. 18, 21 (1778) (Inference here that executrix had sufficient estate assets from her promise to pay.).

34. Trueman v. Fenton, 2 Cowp. 544, 98 Eng. Rep. 1232 (1777) (waiver given after filing).

35. Heyling v. Hastings, 1 Ld. Raym. 389, 421, 91 Eng. Rep. 1157, 1179 (1699).

36. Trueman v. Fenton, 2 Cowp. 544, 548, 98 Eng. Rep. 1232, 1234 (1777) (Mansfield thought debtor guilty of fraud or gross dishonesty to buy large quantity of linen from the plaintiff "on the eve of bankruptcy.").

37. Goodright ex dim. Elizabeth Carter v. Straphan, 1 Cowp. 201, 98 Eng. Rep. 1043 (1774).

38. Heyling v. Hastings, 1 Ld. Raym. 389, 421, 91 Eng. Rep. 1157, 1179 (1699).

39. Goodright ex dim. Elizabeth Carter v. Straphan, 1 Cowp. 201, 98 Eng. Rep. 1043, 1044 (1774) (Mansfield said that to allow the widow to hide behind the void nature of the mortgage, that she and her family benefited from, would be "against every principle of natural justice and equity." *Id.*).

40. Loyd v. Lee, 1 Stra. 94, 93 Eng. Rep. 406 (1719) (A widow's later ratification, "where originally there is no cause of action, is no consideration to raise an assumpsit."). One view of why a married woman could not own property separate from her husband was that a chose-in-action could not be owned by a married woman. *See* 3 HOLDSWORTH, *supra* note 29, at 528; *contra* SIMPSON, *supra* note 1, at 545. Another suggestion was that she didn't have her individual will but depended on the will of her husband. *Id.* at 546–547.

41. Atkins v. Hill, 1 Cowp. 284, 98 Eng. Rep. 1088 (1775). Mansfield rejected the jurisdictional objection that estate matters were for the ecclesiastical courts alone because chancery had concurrent jurisdiction and thus he claimed that common law courts were entitled to jurisdiction.

42. The executor's promise was viewed to be based on past consideration since the executor was holding estate funds he later promised to pay as a legacy; it was unclear whether the executor could be forced in law or equity to pay out the legacy. This is the presumption Mansfield makes in *Atkins v. Hill, Rann v. Hughes* and *Hawkes v. Saunders.* However, Buller, J., in Hawkes v. Saunders, 1 Cowp. 289, 291, 98 Eng. Rep. 1091, 1092 (1782), thought the common law would enforce the executor's obligation; if so, it converted the executor's promise into one based on a preexisting obligation rather than a moral obligation. *Also see* Stat. 11 Geo. IV and 1 Will. IV, c. 40 (1830). Until this 1830 statute, if there was no named residuary legatee in a will, the executor could retain the balance after paying all debts; thus the executor had an interest in promising individually to resolve estate bequests and debts so that he or she could take over ownership in the remaining estate assets.

43. Atkins v. Hill, 1 Cowp. 284, 288–289, 98 Eng. Rep. 1088, 1090–1091 (1775) (Mansfield added: "[t]he promise is grounded upon a reasonable and conscientious consideration." *Id.*)

44. Another difference was that an executor's obligation to pay the legacy was presumed to be unenforceable without the promise of the executor. *But cf.* Hawkes v. Saunders, 1 Cowp. 289, 291, 98 Eng. Rep. 1091, 1092 (1782) (Buller thought executor's obligation was enforceable at common law.).

45. Hawkes v. Saunders, 1 Cowp. 289, 98 Eng. Rep. 1091 (1782). *See* James Oldham, *Reinterpretation of 18th-Century English Contract Theory: The View from Lord Mansfield's Trial Notes,* 76 GEO. L.J. 1949, 1962 (1988) for a 1772 case found in

Mansfield's trial notes, which was similar to *Atkins v. Hill* and *Hawkes v. Saunders* in that the executor had assets.

46. Hawkes v. Saunders, 1 Cowp. 289, 290, 98 Eng. Rep. 1091 (1782).

47. Hawkes v. Saunders, 1 Cowp. 289, 290, 98 Eng. Rep. 1091 (1782). The one element present in the earlier precedents, which Mansfield either assumed as a given or neglected to include in these summary statements, was the receipt of a past benefit by the promisor.

48. Hawkes v. Saunders, 1 Cowp. 289, 290, 98 Eng. Rep. 1091 (1782).

49. Atkins v. Hill, 1 Cowp. 284, 98 Eng. Rep. 1088 (1775). Buller was attorney for the plaintiff in *Atkins*. In both *Atkins* and *Hawkes*, Buller invoked the equitable statement in Stone v. Withipool, Latch 21, 82 Eng. Rep. 254 (1589): "It is an usual allegation for a rule, that every thing which is a ground for equity, is a sufficient consideration." Only the untranslated French language report of Latch of *Stone* (of at least six reports of this case) has this statement, which was *not* the rule at common law.

50. Buller said: "[t]he loss to plaintiff is, that the effects which are liable to the payment of the legacy have not been so applied. . . . The benefit to the defendant is, that she has received those effects." Hawkes v. Saunders, 1 Cowp. 289, 294, 98 Eng. Rep. 1091, 1093 (1782).

51. Hawkes v. Saunders, 1 Cowp. 289, 293, 98 Eng. Rep. 1091, 1093 (1782); Reech v. Kennegal, 1 Ves. Sen. 123, 125–126, 27 Eng. Rep. 932, 933 (1748) (Hardwicke decreed executor bound, to extent of estate assets, to promise made to testator during his lifetime to pay a legacy not in will.).

52. Mansfield practiced law before the gifted Chancellor Hardwicke prior to his successful parliamentary career. Mansfield did much to bring chancery practices and precedents into the common law when there was a gap or he disagreed with precedent. His parliamentary experience accentuated his civilian instinct to think legislatively and to dwell on policy.

53. Mansfield also employed the morality principle for other benefits received in the absence of a promise in his pioneering quasi-contract decision Moses v. Macferlan, 2 Burr. 1005, 97 Eng. Rep. 676 (1760). *See* Oldham, *supra* note 45, at 1962–1963 (Moral obligation and quasi-contract were congenial parts of Mansfield's overall philosophy of moral transactional behavior.).

54. Although the Statute of Frauds didn't authorize enforcement of a written contract without consideration, it did make certain categories of contracts constitutive since they could not be enforced thereafter without a writing. *See* WIGMORE, *supra* note 29 at 90–91. The greater respect thereafter accorded unsealed written contracts soon generated the parol evidence rule. *See Id.* at 89–91 (Since juries could not look beyond sealed deeds, judges held that these constitutive writings under the Statute could not be controverted by extrinsic evidence; this treatment soon spread to all writings.). Mansfield and his fellow justices tried to elevate an unsealed writing to the level of consideration-free sealed contracts, just as chancery practices sometimes did. *See* Earl of Feversham v. Watson, 2 Freeman 35, 22 Eng. Rep. 1042 (1677).

55. *See* Meredith v. Chute, 2 Ld. Raym. 759, 760, 92 Eng. Rep. 7 (1702) (Holt read in law merchant when he said "that it was not necessary for the plaintiff to prove, upon what consideration the [promissory note] was given, the defendant having admitted it to have been given upon good consideration by his promise.").

56. *See* promissory restitution and pure restitution precedents in Chapter 9. Un-

der the modern ground of restitution, an obligation may be found implied-in-law to pay for some of these benefits received. Although Mansfield contributed to the development of liability for unjust enrichment, it was not a mature enough doctrine to provide authority for relief here.

57. Style v. Smith (1587), *cited in* Marsh and Rainford's Case, 2 Leon. 111, 74 Eng. Rep. 400, 401 (1588).

58. Marsh and Rainford's Case, 2 Leon. 111, 74 Eng. Rep. 400, 401 (1588).

59. *Id.*

60. Scott v. Nelson, Esp. N.P. 945 (1763) in Reporters' Note to Wennall v. Adney, 3 Bos. & Pul. 248, 127 Eng. Rep. 137, 138n. (1802).

61. *Anon.*, 2 Show. 184, 89 Eng. Rep. 879 (1682) (Action was on natural father's promise.).

62. Y.B. 21 Hen. VII, f. 41, pl. 66 (1506), *reprinted in* CECIL FIFOOT, HISTORY AND SOURCES OF THE COMMON LAW: TORT AND CONTRACT 353 (London: 1949) (Fyneux, C. J. K. B., stated in a speech at Gray's Inn that the action of case could be brought for nonfeasance rather than suing in chancery.). *See* JOHN BAKER, *Introduction* to THE REPORTS OF SIR JOHN SPELMAN, 94 SELDEN SOC. 41 (J. Baker ed. London: 1977) (Fyneux viewed his role as similar to a chancellor's, observing that half of his office involved the exercise of discretion.); *and see* J. Barton, *Early History of Consideration*, 85 LAW Q. REV. 372, 377 (1969) (Fyneux's advice may have come from his concern that chancery would take precedence over the commercial law field.). Borrowing was probably inevitable since common law judges were frequently asked to cross the aisle in Westminster Hall to assist chancellors with difficult cases, and common lawyers practiced in chancery. *Id.*

63. *See* Barbour, *supra* note 11 at 66, 156–157, 164.

64. *See* FIFOOT, *supra* note 62 at 302; Barbour, *supra* note 11, at 99 (relief given from procedural technicalities and for waging "agens faithe and good conscience"). Equity's cancellation of the penalty on a sealed bond likewise exhibited chancery granting relief from the harshness of common law contract. *See* Henderson, *Relief From Bonds in the English Chancery: Mid-Sixteenth Century*, 18 AM. J. LEG. HIST. 298, 299–306 (1974).

65. *See* Barbour, *supra* note 11, at 161–66. Chancery emphasized the promise as an indispensable part of the case. *Id.* at 164.

66. *Id.* at 163–68 (The breach of a promise was a moral wrong. *Id.* at 166.). Church court practice of providing relief under *fidei laesio* for promisor's breach of faith influenced recovery in chancery. *Id.* at 163–64. Barbour thought *fidei laesio* notions entered the common law indirectly via chancery. *Id.* at 158, 163–64. A later revisionist view proposed a common law reception directly from the church courts. *See* R. Helmholz, *Assumpsit and Fidei Laesio*, 91 LAW Q. REV. 406, 420–22, 426–31 (1975) (Pointed to pleading phraseology similarities and the statistical evidence of decline of *fidei laesio* and the rise of assumpsit during anti-clerical Reformation of first half of sixteenth century. *Id.* at 418–21, 426–28.).

67. In 1530, St. Germain had the doctor of the civil law say that if a promise were made to pay after a house was built for the promisor that he was bound in conscience and under church law, and also if a man promised his father a gown to keep him warm that he was bound under church doctrine. DOCTOR AND STUDENT, *supra* note 1, at 229–230. *See* PLUCKNETT, *supra* note 29, at 649–52;

Barbour, *supra* note 11, at 105–06, 132–35. *But cf.* Barton, *supra* note 62, at 380–81 (Promises to make gifts and on past services weren't enforced.).

68. Reech v. Kennegal, 1 Ves. Sen. 123, 27 Eng. Rep. 932 (Ch. 1748). Later, Mansfield would twice refuse the offer of appointment as Chancellor.

69. Reech v. Kennegal, 1 Ves. Sen. 123, 124–25, 27 Eng. Rep. 932, 933 (Ch. 1748). The testator's reliance on the executor's representation by not amending his will is similar to the reliance factor in equitable estoppel used by modern courts in refusing the Statute of Frauds defense once the promisor misrepresented that the Statute of Frauds wouldn't be raised as a defense. *See* Seymour v. Oelrichs, 156 Cal. 782, 106 P. 88 (1909); RESTATEMENT OF CONTRACTS sect. 178, cmt. f (1932). In chancery, when a party relied on a promise, there was said to be a moral duty to fulfill that promise. *See* Barbour, *supra* note 11, at 166. At common law, assumpsit may have included a reliance-based tort adaptation of *fidei laesio. See* Helmholz, *supra* note 66, at 418–21. And, if the church courts influenced the use of reliance, common law courts might have viewed the issue with *causa* in mind. *See* MILSOM, *supra* note 8, at 357.

CHAPTER 8

1. Eastwood v. Kenyon, 11 Ad. & El. 438, 450, 113 Eng. Rep. 482, 486 (1840). Denman criticized the consent-based arguments in Lee v. Muggeridge, 5 Taunt. 36, 128 Eng. Rep. 599, 602 (1813), raised by the plaintiff's eminent counsel, who said that Lord Mansfield thought *nudum pactum* too strict and if parties "make their own agreements on deliberation, and if they did so think fit to make them, that they must be subject to them."

2. Denman thought *Barnes v. Hedley* and *Cooper v. Martin* were, in the main, consistent with the precedents but he could not abide *Lee v. Muggeridge.* (He also bemoaned the fact that none of these three opinions discussed the Reporters' Note to *Wennall v. Adney.*) The real reason for Denman's virulent opposition to *Lee v. Muggeridge* may have been because of its broad equitable rationale, rather than its outcome on the facts, since *Lee* is less of an extension of the facts in prior decisions than the other two cases. There was an actual Mansfield precedent (*Goodright*) on all fours with the facts in *Lee.* Furthermore, the widow's ratification of her void contract in *Lee,* made while under coverture, was less of an extension of Holt's precedent of an adult's ratification of a voidable contract than the enforcement of an illegal usurious contract in *Barnes.* And, as to *Cooper,* the adult stepchild was held to his promise, even though he made no original promise. *See* Eastwood v. Kenyon, 11 Ad. & El. 438, 448–451, 113 Eng. Rep. 482, 486–487 (1840); Barnes v. Hedley, 2 Taunt. 183, 127 Eng. Rep. 1047 (1809); Cooper v. Martin, 4 East. 77, 102 Eng. Rep. 759 (1803); Lee v. Muggeridge, 5 Taunt. 36, 128 Eng. Rep. 599 (1813); Goodright ex dim. Elizabeth Carter v. Straphan, 1 Cowp. 201, 98 Eng. Rep. 1043 (1774); *cf.* REPORTERS' NOTE to Wennall v. Adney, 3 Bos. & Pul. 247, 253, 127 Eng. Rep. 137, 139–140 (1802) (Cases inconsistent with logic and facts of Holt's precedents and *Hunt v. Bate* were explained away by saying that perhaps those courts had inferred that plaintiff made a request of defendant before defendant acted.).

3. Lampleigh v. Braithwait, Hob. 105, 80 Eng. Rep. 255 (1616) (Executed or executory consideration is good but past consideration isn't.). If the plaintiff's act is stimulated by a request of the defendant and the defendant makes an assumpsit,

the promise is binding. Hunt v. Bate, 3 Dyer 272a, 73 Eng. Rep. 605 (1568). *Cf.* Eastwood v. Kenyon, 11 Ad. & El. 438, 449, 113 Eng. Rep. 482, 486 (1840) (Request was implied in *Cooper v. Martin* and request was made by defendant in *Lee v. Muggeridge,* though it was invalid because promisor was then a married woman under coverture.).

4. *E.g.,* Heyling v. Hastings, 1 Ld. Raym. 389, 91 Eng. Rep. 1157 (1699) (Holt's statute of limitations waiver decision); Trueman v. Fenton, 2 Cowp. 544, 98 Eng. Rep. 1232 (1777) (Mansfield's bankruptcy waiver decision).

5. Ball v. Hesketh, Cowp. 381, 90 Eng. Rep. 541 (1697) (Holt's adult ratification decision).

6. Mansfield retired in 1788 after 32 years as Chief Justice of the King's Bench.

7. *See* BARRY NICHOLAS, THE FRENCH LAW OF CONTRACT 144–146 (2d ed. Oxford: 1992). *Cause* is not required in German law. *Id.* at 118; NORBERT HORN, HEIN KÖTZ & HANS LESER, GERMAN PRIVATE AND COMMERCIAL LAW 74 (1982 tr. Tony Weir) (Formation of contract requires declaration of will or intention.).

8. But good *cause* is lacking if it's later discovered that the child is not the father's or that the employee retired to go to work for a competitor. *See* NICHOLAS, *supra* note 7, at 146–148, 123–125 (The only type of gift-promise requiring a formal civilian notarization in France is for a transfer of property, called a *donation. Id.* at 146.). Under German law, any promise of a gift, or a duty inspired only by conscience, must be notarized. *See* JOHN DAWSON, GIFTS AND PROMISES 162–164 (New Haven: 1980).

9. The passage of the Reform Act of 1832 was the watershed event dividing the periods. *See* Robert Stevens, *Basic Concepts and Current Differences in English and American Law,* 6 J. LEG. HIST. 336, 338–339 (1985) (English judges were more adventuresome than American federalists during first quarter of the nineteenth century. *Id.* Jeffersonians leaned toward codification in preference to exercise of regal prerogative. *Id.*).

10. Cooper v. Martin, 4 East. 77, 102 Eng. Rep. 759, 761 (1803). Ellenborough's predecessor as Chief Justice of King's Bench was Lord Kenyon; Kenyon (CJKB 1788–1802) tried to contain Mansfield's civilian ideas, but support for moral obligation was resuscitated with Ellenborough's appointment in 1802. Lord Ellenborough (Edward Law) (CJKB 1802–1818) was aware of both continental and common law ideas, having been educated at Cambridge and at Lincoln's Inn. The French Revolution had tempered Ellenborough's political views but not his support for Enlightenment ideas.

11. Cooper v. Martin, 4 East. 77, 102 Eng. Rep. 759, 761 (1803). *See* New York's approach in Chapter 10.

12. Hawkes v. Saunders, 1 Cowp. 289, 290, 98 Eng. Rep. 1091 (1782).

13. Denman, C.J. did, however, say: "[a]ction would have lain against the defendant whilst an infant, inasmuch as it was for necessaries furnished at his request in regard to which the law raised an implied promise." Eastwood v. Kenyon, 11 Ad. & El. 438, 449, 113 Eng. Rep. 482, 486 (1840).

14. Denman was not actually opposed to the holding in *Cooper v. Martin* but he thought the analysis of consideration was incomplete in failing to discuss the related law, including the Reporters' Note to *Wennall v. Adney.* Eastwood v. Kenyon, 11 Ad. & El. 438, 448, 113 Eng. Rep. 482, 486 (1840).

15. *E.g.*, JOHN POWELL, ESSAY UPON THE LAW OF CONTRACTS AND AGREEMENTS (London: 1790); ROBERT POTHIER, A TREATISE ON THE LAW OF OBLIGATIONS (W. Evans ed. tr. London: 1806) (first published in France in 1761–64); HUGO GROTIUS, DE JURE BELLI AC PACIS LIBRI TRES (1625) (tr. F. Kelsey, Washington: 1964). *See* Alfred Simpson, *Innovation in Nineteenth Century Contract Law*, 91 L.Q. REV. 247 (1975).

16. Barnes v. Hedley, 2 Taunt. 183, 127 Eng. Rep. 1047 (1809).

17. Barnes v. Hedley, 2 Taunt. 183, 127 Eng. Rep. 1047, 1049 (1809).

18. Barnes v. Hedley, 2 Taunt. 183, 127 Eng. Rep. 1047, 1051 (1809). Another defense potentially available was that the corrected, non-usurious promise was a modification agreement barred by the preexisting duty rule.

19. Lee v. Muggeridge, 5 Taunt. 36, 128 Eng. Rep. 599 (1813).

20. Goodright ex dim. Elizabeth Carter v. Straphan, 1 Cowp. 201, 98 Eng. Rep. 1043 (1774); Lee v. Muggeridge, 5 Taunt. 36, 128 Eng. Rep. 599, 602 (1813). In *Lee*, the funds went to the promisor's son-in-law rather than to the promisor.

21. However, Denman rationalized Holt's precedent in saying the moral obligation principle should apply to voidable promises, like an infant's, but not to a void promise, like a married woman's. Eastwood v. Kenyon, 11 Ad. & El. 438, 113 Eng. Rep. 482, 485 (1840).

22. *See* Atkins v. Hill, 1 Cowp. 284, 98 Eng. Rep. 1088 (1775); Hawkes v. Saunders, 1 Cowp. 289, 98 Eng. Rep. 1091 (1782).

23. Eastwood v. Kenyon, 11 Ad. & El. 438, 448, 113 Eng. Rep. 482, 486 (1840). Denman also claimed that in 1831 Lord Tenterden had in effect dissented from the moral obligation principle, but in fact all that Tenterden said was that the principle was subject to boundaries. Tenterden stated: "I must also observe, that the doctrine that a moral obligation is a sufficient consideration for a subsequent promise, is one which should be received with some limitations." Littlefield v. Shee, 2 B. & Ad. 809, 811, 109 Eng. Rep. 1343, 1344 (1831); Eastwood v. Kenyon, 11 Ad. & El. 438, 450, 113 Eng. Rep. 482, 486 (1840) (Tenterden's statement "in truth, amounts to a dissent from the authority of *Lee v. Muggeridge*, where the doctrine is wholly unqualified." *Id.*). Denman tried to find a basis for justifying *Lee v. Muggeridge* within the bargain construct by pointing out that there was an actual request of the plaintiff by the married women, though he admitted it wasn't binding during coverture. *Id.* at 449, 486.

24. Lee v. Muggeridge, 5 Taunt. 36, 128 Eng. Rep. 599, 603 (1813).

25. Lee v. Muggeridge, 5 Taunt. 36, 128 Eng. Rep. 599, 603 (1813). Gibbs, J. said, "[w]henever there is a moral obligation to pay a debt, or perform a duty, a promise to perform that duty, or pay that debt, will be supported by the previous moral obligation." *Id.* Heath, J. was so enthusiastic about the principle being applied that he stated something historically incorrect: "The notion that a promise may be supported by a moral obligation is not modern; in Charles the Second's time it was said, if there be an iota of equity, it is enough consideration for the promise." *Id.* Heath's claim is perhaps a reference to Pemberton, C.J.'s ruling in *Anon.*, 2 Show. 184, 89 Eng. Rep. 879 (1682), which bound a father to perform his promise to pay plaintiff for maintenance earlier provided to his bastard child.

26. Eastwood v. Kenyon, 11 Ad. & El. 438, 450, 113 Eng. Rep. 482, 486 (1840). In the Note to *Wennall v. Adney*, the Reporters Bosanquet and Puller tried to bring seemingly deviating cases back into the "request and promise" paradigm by the

rationalization that a request could be inferred in cases of a father promising to repay plaintiff for costs of his son's funeral and of a father promising to pay a physician for medicine given to his son. REPORTERS' NOTE to Wennall v. Adney, 3 Bos. & Pul. 248, 250n., 253n., 127 Eng. Rep. 137, 138n., 140n. (1802).

27. Eastwood v. Kenyon, 11 Ad. & El. 438, 448, 113 Eng. Rep. 482, 486 (1840).

28. Lee v. Muggeridge, 5 Taunt. 36, 128 Eng. Rep. 599, 603 (1813).

29. *See* REPORTERS' NOTE to Wennall v. Adney, 3 Bos. & Pul. 248, 127 Eng. Rep. 137, 138n. (1802) ("[f]or in each instance the party bound by the promise had received a benefit previous to the promise." *Id.*); Lee v. Muggeridge, 57 Taunt. 36, 128 Eng. Rep. 599, 603 (1813).

30. The cosmopolitan Lord Mansfield translated doctrine from equity, canon law, Roman law, civilian law, the law merchant and the law of nations into common law principles. He didn't observe the past practice of common law judges refraining from taking a case if it overlapped the jurisdiction of a parallel court; much of the equitable principles, which he brought into the common law, were applied on similar facts in courts of conscience. *See, e.g.*, Hawkes v. Saunders, 1 Cowp. 289, 98 Eng. Rep. 1091 (1782) (equitable and ecclesiastical practices). In the quasi-contract area, Mansfield even intruded upon the jurisdiction of a local court of conscience. *See* Moses v. Macferlan, 2 Burr. 1005, 97 Eng. Rep. 676, 678 (1760).

31. *E.g.*, Watson v. Turner, 2 East. 507, 102 Eng. Rep. 463 (1766); Goodright ex dim. Elizabeth Carter v. Straphan, 1 Cowp. 201, 98 Eng. Rep. 1043 (1774); Wennall v. Adney, 3 Bos. & Pul. 248, 127 Eng. Rep. 137, 141 (1802) (Defendant not liable because he didn't promise.).

32. Atkins v. Banwell, 2 East. 505, 102 Eng. Rep. 462 (1802) (Ellenborough distinguished Watson v. Turner, 2 East. 507, 102 Eng. Rep. 463 (1766), where there had been a subsequent express promise.); *accord* Wennall v. Adney, 3 Bos. & Pul. 248, 127 Eng. Rep. 137, 141 (1802); Eastwood v. Kenyon, 11 Ad. & El. 438, 448–451, 113 Eng. Rep. 482, 486–487 (1840). *See* Lon Fuller, *Consideration and Form*, 41 COLUM. L. REV. 799, 822 (1941) (Courts will not order enforcement in the absence of a promise, but once there's a benefit coupled with a subsequent promise, this may tilt the scales for enforcement if court has conviction that promisor ought to pay.).

33. Moses v. Macferlan, 2 Burr. 1005, 97 Eng. Rep. 676 (1760) ("[t]he gist of this kind of action is, that the defendant, upon the circumstances of the case, is obliged by the ties of natural justice and equity to refund the money." *Id.* at 681.).

34. Moses v. Macferlan, 2 Burr. 1005, 97 Eng. Rep. 676, 680 (1760).

35. As Mansfield reformed the common law of obligations by borrowing ideas from courts of conscience, there was inevitable friction and overlap with the jurisdiction of other courts. In some instances, the jurisdiction (but not the principle) was actually later returned to the competing court from whence Mansfield grasped it. The most frequent source of equitable ideas and practices for Mansfield and later judges emanated from chancery, *e.g.*, Hawkes v. Saunders, 1 Cowp. 289, 290, 293, 98 Eng. Rep. 1091, 1092, 1093 (1782); Moses v. Macferlan, 2 Burr. 1005, 1009, 97 Eng. Rep. 676, 678 (1760); Barnes v. Hedley, 2 Taunt. 183, 127 Eng. Rep. 1047, 1049 (1809); Lee v. Muggeridge, 5 Taunt. 36, 128 Eng. Rep. 599, 603 (1813). In some cases, a moral obligation was enforced at common law in lieu of a right otherwise invocable in chancery. *See* Cooper v. Martin, 4 East. 77, 102 Eng. Rep. 759, 761 (1803) (Stepfather could've applied to chancery earlier for access

to stepchild's inheritance fund for child's maintenance.). Mansfield intruded upon chancery jurisdiction, formerly ecclesiastical jurisdiction, in enforcing an executor's moral duty to pay a legacy once there was a promise in *Atkins v. Hill* and *Hawkes v. Saunders*, but in 1794, Kenyon, C. J. curtailed the jurisdictional confusion by returning such estate issues to chancery. Atkins v. Hill, 1 Cowp. 284, 98 Eng. Rep. 1088 (1775); Hawkes v. Saunders, 1 Cowp. 289, 98 Eng. Rep. 1091 (1782); Deeks v. Strutt, 5 T.R. 690, 101 Eng. Rep. 384, 385 (1794) (Kenyon declared: "The whole of this admirable system, which has been founded in a Court of Equity, will fall to the ground, if a Court of Law can enforce the payment of a legacy." *Id.*). And again in 1797, Lord Kenyon reined in Mansfield's practice of usurping decrees of local courts of conscience, as Mansfield had done in Moses v. Macferlan, 2 Burr. 1005, 97 Eng. Rep. 676, 678 (1760). Marriot v. Hampton, 7 T.R. 269, 101 Eng. Rep. 969 (1797) ("After a recovery by process of law there must be an end of litigation, otherwise there would be no security for any person." *Id.*).

36. For early English cases enforcing fathers' promises on similar facts, *see* Scott v. Nelson, Esp. N.P. 945 (1763) (per Mansfield) in Reporters' Note to Wennall v. Adney, 3 Bos. & Pul. 248, 250n., 127 Eng. Rep. 137, 138n. (1802); *Anon.*, 2 Show. 184, 89 Eng. Rep. 879 (1682); Style v. Smith (1587) cited in Marsh and Rainford's Case, 2 Leon. 111, 74 Eng. Rep. 400, 401 (1587). For an early influential American case refusing recovery in this type of case, *see* Mills v. Wyman, 20 Mass. (3 Pick.) 207 (1825). A gift requires an acceptance, but many moral obligation circumstances involve a benefit passing indirectly, unbeknownst to the defendant at the time, as for emergency medical expenses to a relation or a ward of the defendant. When the plaintiff passes the benefit indirectly or otherwise unbeknownst to the defendant, it's only after the fact that the defendant is aware of what he perceives to be a benefit to himself, and only then does he have a chance to either right the imbalance by promising reimbursement or do nothing if he feels no moral obligation. In these cases of indirect benefit to the defendant, the plaintiff was not an officious volunteer because the defendant's relation needed treatment and the defendant wasn't available. The defendant was doing what an honest man ought to do and would not have perceived a moral obligation and subsequently promised restitution if the plaintiff were an intermeddler. *And cf.* Fuller, *supra* note 32, at 821–822. (The lack of great deliberation should not matter so much since he's promising to do what he should've done without the promise.). These early precedents notwithstanding, a majority of jurisdictions today would not enforce the father's promise under the moral obligation principle because the benefit did not involve direct assistance for the father himself.

37. In 1815, a couple cohabiting illicitly, but who were on the verge of separating, entered into an agreement whereby the man would pay an annuity to her, in the event they separated. The court enforced the man's promise to pay for the past injury done to her by the illicit liaison, without any reference to moral obligation or consideration. It seemed an early version of palimony as the court drew an analogy to an agreement for a gratuitous transfer to a wife now a widow. Other consideration was possibly present, though not discussed by the court, in that, when a policy objection to such an agreement was raised, the court responded that the agreement was to induce separation rather than continued illicit cohabitation and further that the annuity was contingent upon her remaining single thereafter. Gibson v. Dickie, 3 M. & S. 463, 105 Eng. Rep. 684 (1815). *But cf.*

Binnington v. Wallis, 4 B. & Ald. 650, 106 Eng. Rep. 1074 (1821) (Agreement not binding because plaintiff failed to plead defendant seduced her. Past illicit cohabitation alone and ceasing to cohabit in the future is not a good consideration.). The *Gibson* declaration didn't allege seduction.

38. Cooper v. Martin, 4 East. 77, 102 Eng. Rep. 759 (1803); Barnes v. Hedley, 2 Taunt. 183, 127 Eng. Rep. 1047 (1809); Lee v. Muggeridge, 5 Taunt. 36, 128 Eng. Rep. 599 (1813).

39. Wing v. Mill, 1 B. & Ald. 104, 106 Eng. Rep. 39 (1817).

40. *Id.* at 40. Bayley, J. added: "[t]he promise made after his death is founded on a legal as well as a moral consideration. . . ." *Id.*

41. Watson v. Turner, Bull. N. P. 129, 2 East. 507, 102 Eng. Rep. 463 (1767).

42. Wells v. Horton, Executor of Blisset, 2 Car. & P. 383, 172 Eng. Rep. 173 (1826).

43. Wells v. Horton, Executor of Blisset, 2 Car. & P. 383, 386, 172 Eng. Rep. 173, 175 (1826). Best denied defenses based on the six-year statute of limitations and the Statute of Frauds on grounds other than waiver. The oral promise was also intended to induce forbearance from suit. Note that Serjeant-at-law Bosanquet, co-author of REPORTERS' NOTE to *Wennall v. Adney*, was an attorney for the plaintiff arguing that the promise was binding.

44. Nicole v. Allen, 3 Car. & P. 36, 172 Eng. Rep. 312 (1827).

45. Nicole v. Allen, 3 Car. & P. 36, 37, 172 Eng. Rep. 312 (1827). *Cf.* WILLIAM SELWYN, NISI PRIUS 56 (London: 6th ed. 1824) (When a person has a moral obligation and another satisfies it without his prior request, his subsequent promise is enforceable.).

46. Nicole v. Allen, 3 Car. & P. 36, 37, 172 Eng. Rep. 312 (1827). Tenterden's incredibly careless opinion is perhaps attributable to the fact that it was a trial level decision.

47. On *negotiorum gestio,* see BARRY NICHOLAS, AN INTRODUCTION TO ROMAN LAW 227–229 (Oxford: 1962). Had there been a subsequent promise, there were precedents allowing recovery for past benefits passing to an infant child rather than to the promising defendant-parent, *e.g.*, Smith v. Style, 2 Leon. 111, 74 Eng. Rep. 401 (1587); *Anon.*, 2 Show. 184, 89 Eng. Rep. 879 (1682); Scott v. Nelson, Esp. N. P. 945 (1763) in REPORTERS' NOTE to Wennall v. Adney, 3 Bos. & Pul. 248, 250n., 127 Eng. Rep. 137, 138n. (1802).

48. Mortimore v. Wright, 6 M. & W. 482, 151 Eng. Rep. 502 (1840).

49. Mortimore v. Wright, 6 M. & W. 482, 486–487, 151 Eng. Rep. 502, 504 (1840). Parke, B. said, "[b]ut the mere moral obligation to do so cannot impose upon him any legal obligation . . . and whatever may be the moral obligations of parties, juries must not be allowed to make them contract without legal evidence." *Id.* at 488/504. Parke said the father had no legal obligation except under an ignored Elizabethan statute. *Id.*

50. Burgeoning commerce and industry demanded predictability. Runaway juries drastically compromised that goal. The jury control devices, of jury instructions, rules of evidence and nonsuit, which were used in *Mortimore v. Wright,* matured during the prior century, partially with Mansfield's aid. Despite the existence of these techniques, it was too often the case that jury instructions gave juries excessive leeway or that courts would not order a new trial or nonsuit when a jury went against the evidence or the law. The exchequer court was active during

the 1840s and 1850s in bringing trial by jury under tighter judicial control. Several of the justices sitting in *Mortimore v. Wright* also sat in that court's development of limitations on juries' awarding remote contract damages in Hadley v. Baxendale, 9 Exch. 341, 156 Eng. Rep. 145 (1854).

51. Wells v. Horton, Executor of Blisset, 2 Car. & P. 388, 172 Eng. Rep. 173 (1826); Nicole v. Allen, 3 Car. & P. 36, 172 Eng. Rep. 312 (1827); Cooper v. Martin, 4 East. 77, 102 Eng. Rep. 759 (1803).

52. Mansfield's dictum under the parallel restitutionary action for quasi-contract expressed the need for restraint: "I am a great friend to the action . . . and therefore I'm not for stretching, lest I should endanger it." Weston v. Downes, 1 Doug. 23, 24, 99 Eng. Rep. 19 (1778).

53. Mills v. Wyman, 20 Mass. (3 Pick.) 207 (1825).

54. Mills v. Wyman, 20 Mass. (3 Pick.) 207, 209–210 (1825) (Society has left a promise like the father's to the "tribunal of [one's] conscience."). And there was no direct benefit to promisor.

55. American decisions followed Holt's and Mansfield's waiver and ratification cases, *e.g.*, Little v. Blunt, 26 Mass. (9 Pick.) 488 (1830) (statute of limitations); Edwards v. Nelson, 51 Mich. 121 (1833) (bankruptcy); Cheshire v. Barrett, 15 S.C. 24 (1825) (infancy).

56. Scott v. Nelson, Esp. N.P. 945 (1763) in Reporters' Note to Wennall v. Adney, 3 Bos. & Pul. 248, 250n., 127 Eng. Rep. 137, 138n. (1802).

57. *Anon.*, 2 Show. 184, 89 Eng. Rep. 879 (1682).

58. Style v. Smith (1587) in Marsh and Rainford's Case, 2 Leon. 111, 74 Eng. Rep. 400, 401 (1588).

59. *See* Stevens, *supra* note 9, at 338–339; Waterman, *Thomas Jefferson and Blackstone's Commentaries*, 27 ILL. L. REV. 629, 642–646 (1933) (Jefferson was opposed to what he saw as Mansfield's discretionary equity.). Nevertheless Jefferson supported natural law solutions obtained by trial by jury and legislation.

60. Lord Tenterden's Act, 9 Geo. IV, c. 14, sect. 1 (1828), now replaced by Stat. 2 & 3 Geo. VI, c. 21, s.24 (1939). Lord Tenterden was Chief Justice of King's Bench and alluded to the need for limitations on the moral obligation principle. Littlefield v. Shee, 2 B. & Ad. 809, 109 Eng. Rep. 1343, 1344 (1831). Ironically, he had gone too far the other way in 1827 in granting restitutionary relief not available even today. Nicole v. Allen, 3 Car. & P. 36, 172 Eng. Rep. 312 (1827).

61. *See* RESTATEMENT OF CONTRACTS sect. 86, cmt. a. (1932). *Cf.* Fuller, *supra* note 32, at 821 (The need for formality and evidentiary security diminishes when promise is backed by moral obligation to do what promisor ought to have done without the promise.).

62. Eastwood v. Kenyon, 11 Ad. & El. 438, 113 Eng. Rep. 482 (1840).

63. In *Eastwood v. Kenyon*, a guardian advanced funds for the benefit of a minor ward, and in adulthood the former minor made a promise to repay the guardian. Denman, C. J. held the promise lacked consideration. In 1825 the Massachusetts court found no consideration to support the father's promise to pay for services rendered to his ill adult son. Mills v. Wyman, 20 Mass. (3 Pick.) 207 (1825). The plaintiff in *Mills* received no direct benefit himself and thus had a heavier burden in convincing the court of an enforceable moral obligation than the plaintiff in *Eastwood.*

64. REPORTERS' NOTE to Wennall v. Adney, 3 Bos. & Pul. 247, 127 Eng. Rep. 137 (1802) (Physician treated injured servant of master, without master's re-

quest. Court held for master because duty must come from contract. It would otherwise be a great burden on masters if they were generally liable.).

65. REPORTERS' NOTE to Wennall v. Adney, 3 Bos. & Pul. 247, 250, 127 Eng. Rep. 137, 138n. (1802); *see* Eastwood v. Kenyon, 11 Ad. & El. 438, 450, 113 Eng. Rep. 482, 486 (1840). This 1802 Reporters' Note performed a function later provided by law review articles in synthesizing and analyzing the law.

66. REPORTERS' NOTE to Wennall v. Adney, 3 Bos. & Pul. 247, 250, 127 Eng. Rep. 137, 140n. (1802); Eastwood v. Kenyon, 11 Ad. & El. 438, 447, 113 Eng. Rep. 482, 485 (1840). *Accord* Earle v. Oliver, 2 Exch. 71, 90, 154 Eng. Rep. 410, 418 (1848) (per Baron Parke).

67. REPORTERS' NOTE to Wennall v. Adney, 3 Bos. & Pul. 247, 250n., 127 Eng. Rep. 137, 140n. (1802).

68. Ball v. Hesketh, Comb. 381, 90 Eng. Rep. 541 (1697). Denman seemed willing to accept Holt's adult ratification precedent but was opposed to Mansfield's precedent of a widow's ratification of contract made while married. Eastwood v. Kenyon, 11 Ad. & El. 438, 113 Eng. Rep. 482, 485 (1840).

69. Goodright ex dim. Elizabeth Carter v. Straphan, 1 Cowp. 201, 98 Eng. Rep. 1043 (1774).

70. Scott v. Nelson, Esp. N.P. (1763) in Reporters' Note to Wennall v. Adney, 3 Bos. & Pul. 248, 250n., 127 Eng. Rep. 137, 138n. (1802).

71. Atkins v. Hill, 1 Cowp. 284, 98 Eng. Rep. 1088 (1775); Hawkes v. Saunders, 1 Cowp. 289, 98 Eng. Rep. 1091 (1782).

72. Hunt v. Bate, 3 Dyer 272a, 73 Eng. Rep. 605 (1568).

73. Eastwood v. Kenyon, 11 Ad. & El. 438, 452, 113 Eng. Rep. 482, 487 (1840) (Otherwise, Denman said suits and "voluntary undertakings would be multiplied, to the prejudice of real creditors." *Id.*). The plaintiff in *Eastwood* had been the guardian of an infant girl and had taken out an individual promissory note to fund her care. In adulthood, while still single, she promised to satisfy the note. She later married, and her husband promised to satisfy the note. Denman denied recovery in an action brought by the plaintiff on the husband's promise. (If action had been against the woman on her promise when single, Cooper v. Martin, 4 East. 77, 102 Eng. Rep. 759 (1803) supported recovery.). As to the action against the husband, it's true that the husband made no prior enforceable promise that was now barred by positive law and the benefit was not directly for the husband himself, but there were analogous precedents favorable to the plaintiff where recovery was allowed on a father's subsequent promise to pay for the indirect benefit of food or care given to a child. *See* Scott v. Nelson, Esp. N.P. 945 (1763) in Reporters' Note to Wennall v. Adney, 3 Bos. & Pul. 248, 250n., 127 Eng. Rep. 137, 138n. (1802); *Anon.*, 2 Show. 184, 89 Eng. Rep. 879 (1693); Style v. Smith (1587) in Marsh and Rainford's Case, 2 Leon. 111, 74 Eng. Rep. 400, 401 (1587). *Cf.* Drake v. Bell, 55 NYS 945, 947 (1899).

74. *See* William Holdsworth, *The New Rules of Pleading in the Hilary Term, 1834*, 1 CAMBRIDGE L.J. 259, 273–274 (1923). Since the seventeenth century, common debts were covered by *indebitatus assumpsit* and the by common counts, and there was rarely a discussion of whether consideration was present. It was typically assumed present if the facts would've fit under the old action of debt, but the 1834 Hilary Rules partially stripped away the mask of the common counts.

75. *See* PATRICK ATIYAH and ROBERT SUMMERS, FORM AND SUBSTANCE IN ANGLO-AMERICAN LAW 242 (Oxford: 1987).

76. *Cf.* JAMES HURST, LAW AND CONDITIONS OF FREEDOM IN THE NINETEENTH CENTURY UNITED STATES 10–11 (Madison: 1956); KARL LLEWELLYN, THE COMMON LAW TRADITION: DECIDING APPEALS 36–37 (Boston: 1960); MORTON HORWITZ, THE TRANSFORMATION OF AMERICAN LAW, (1780–1860), 16–30, 140–159 (Cambridge, Mass.: 1977).

77. William Blackstone's COMMENTARIES ON THE LAWS OF ENGLAND were published in 4 volumes between 1765 and 1769. (Blackstone's opus was generated by his Oxford lectures delivered in 1753 and published in syllabus form in 1756. These lectures, intended to give an overview of the system to mostly non-law students, could not very well be given as catalog listings of abridged cases. The flow of the lectures required discussion of general principles drawn from the jumbled caselaw.) John Powell wrote the first English book devoted to contract law in 1790. JOHN POWELL, *supra* note 15. Subsequent influential early contract writings in England and the U.S. included: J. CHITTY, A PRACTICAL TREATISE ON THE LAW OF CONTRACTS, NOT UNDER SEAL (London: 1826); Theron Metcalf, *Law of Contracts*, 20–23 AMERICAN JURIST (1838–1841); WILLIAM STORY, A TREATISE ON THE LAW OF CONTRACTS, NOT UNDER SEAL (Boston: 1844).

78. *See* Simpson, *supra* note 15, at 277–278; Michael Hoeflich, *Savigny and His Anglo-Saxon Disciples*, 37 AM. J. COMP. LAW 17, 19–20 (1989); *and see* 1 FREDERICK MAITLAND, COLLECTED PAPERS 489 (Cambridge: Fisher ed. 1911) ("When great work has been done, some fertilizing germs have wafted from abroad."). The rational, organizing ideas of the Enlightenment, promoted by Mansfield, contributed to this process.

79. Roscorla v. Thomas, 3 Q.B. 234, 114 Eng. Rep. 496 (1842) (Past consideration rule barred warranty subsequent to sales agreement.).

80. Roscorla v. Thomas, 3 Q.B. 234, 237, 114 Eng. Rep. 496, 498 (1842).

81. Earle v. Oliver, 2 Exch. 71, 89–90, 154 Eng. Rep. 410, 418 (1848).

82. Flight v. Reed, 1 H. & C. 703, 158 Eng. Rep. 1067, 1072 (1863) (ratification of a void usurious contract after usury statute repealed).

83. Barnes v. Hedley, 2 Taunt. 183, 127 Eng. Rep. 1047 (1809). Denman had found *Barnes* to be consistent with the interpretation of the moral obligation principle given in Bosanquet and Puller's Note. Eastwood v. Kenyon, 11 Ad. & El. 438, 449, 113 Eng. Rep. 482, 486 (1840).

84. In 1854, a woman, who had cohabited with the defendant outside of wedlock for five years, tried to enforce his promise of maintenance made at their separation. In this early attempt to collect palimony, the woman tried to extend moral obligation from its use to support promises to pay for past benefits received to a moral obligation to support a promise of maintenance made on account of the injury done to her. (The seduction gave the woman no cause of action against the defendant.). Wightman, J. cited the Note to *Wennall v. Adney* and said: "[a] precedent moral obligation, not capable of creating an original cause of action, will not support an express promise." Beaumont v. Reeve, 8 Q.B. 483, 488, 115 Eng. Rep. 958, 959 (1854). *See also* Gibson v. Dickie, 3 M.&S. 463, 105 Eng. Rep. 684 (1815) (woman recovered); Binnington v. Wallis, 4 B. & Ald. 650, 106 Eng. Rep. 1074 (1821) (woman failed to recover).

85. Jakeman v. Cook, 4 Ex. D. 26, 30–31 (1878) (Interpretation of 1869 Bankruptcy Statute found to bar waiver unless new consideration given.); Limitations Act, s.29 (7) (1980); *but cf.* (English) Bill of Exchange Act, s.27 (1)(b) (1882)

(Antecedent debt is good consideration for a bill of exchange.). Waiver of bankruptcy in the United States was subjected to restrictions unrelated to consideration, for the benefit of debtors, under the 1978 Bankruptcy Code. 11 U.S.C. sect. 524 (c) & (d). The number of remaining English exceptions to the past consideration rule is further diminished because an executor's personal obligation to distribute legacies is inapplicable today.

86. Other reasons given for the English moral obligation principle freezing include the continued availability of the seal to make a deliberate promise binding without consideration and the fact that the failure of English law to fuse chancery's independent trust jurisdiction with the common law in the nineteenth century caused resistance to common law extensions of Mansfield's unjust enrichment notions under constructive trust.

87. *See* ATIYAH and SUMMERS, *supra* note 75, at 241–43. While the common law of contract in the United States today recognizes vibrant forms of the moral obligation principle, good faith duties, unconscionability, economic duress, promissory estoppel and restitution, modern English common law contains, at best, feeble versions of these ameliorating doctrines. Since English judges have also been less solicitous of consumers, Parliament felt obliged to pass a consumer protection statute that is more far reaching than equivalent American legislation. *See* (British) Unfair Contract Terms Act, c.50 (1977). American jurisdictions supportive of expansion of the moral obligation principle during the first half of the nineteenth century included New York, Pennsylvania, Maryland and South Carolina.

88. *Cf.* Stroud Milsom, *A Pageant in Modern Dress*, 84 YALE L.J. 1585, 1587–1588 (1975) (The difference between the two countries' view of promissory estoppel is partially attributable to the scant experimentation possible in the single jurisdiction existing for England and Wales.).

89. *See* JOHN DAWSON, UNJUST ENRICHMENT 25–26 (Boston: 1951); ATIYAH and SUMMERS, *supra* note 75, at 116, 128–132, 240–244. *Cf.* H. MENCKEN, THE AMERICAN LANGUAGE 98–99 (R. McDavid 1 vol. ed. New York: 1963) (American life has been dynamic in contrast to stable English social order with its greater respect for custom and the static nature of society.). The fact that law and equity were not fully fused in England has probably had some adverse impact on judicial reform. Since trust law has remained with equity, it is perhaps understandable that English common law judges don't provide restitutionary constructive trust relief for benefits covered in American moral obligation cases, since the possibility exists of equitable relief for benefits not otherwise recoverable at common law.

90. *See* ATIYAH and SUMMERS, *supra* note 75, at 88–90, 222–223, 229, 240–241, 408–409. The English distrust of trial by jury resulted in its removal from civil actions (except libel) and has contributed to less equitable results. *See Id.* at 38. Whereas the enforcement of sealed promises allowed for enforcement of promises based on moral obligations, the absence of recognition of the seal in most American jurisdictions made it all the more important to develop means of enforcing such promises within the confines of the doctrine of consideration.

91. *E.g.*, Massachusetts Constitution of 1780, Part II, ch. 6, art. 6, cited in WILLIAM NELSON, AMERICANIZATION OF THE COMMON LAW 8 (Cambridge, Mass.: 1975). This was construed to include English common law and colonial modifications made. Sackett v. Sackett, 8 Pick. 309, 316 (Mass. 1829). In 1813,

Tilghman, C. J. said that Pennsylvania common law was "composed partly of the Common Law of England and partly of our own usages." Poor v. Greene, 5 Binney (Pa.) 554 (1813).

92. Heyling v. Hastings, 1 Ld. Raym. 389, 421, 91 Eng. Rep. 1157, 1179 (1699); Ball v. Hesketh, Comb. 381, 90 Eng. Rep. 541 (1697).

93. Atkins v. Hill, 1 Cowp. 284, 98 Eng. Rep. 1088 (1775).

94. Goodright ex dim. Elizabeth Carter v. Straphan, 1 Cowp. 201, 98 Eng. Rep. 1043 (1774).

95. Scott v. Nelson, Esp. N.P. 945, (1763) in Reporters' Note to Wennall v. Adney, 3 Bos. & Pul. 248, 250n., 127 Eng. Rep. 137, 138n. (1802); *accord Anon.*, 2 Show. 184, 89 Eng. Rep. 879 (1682).

96. Pillans v. Van Mierop, 3 Burr. 1663, 1669, 97 Eng. Rep. 1035, 1038 (1765).

97. Rann v. Hughes, 7 T.R. 350, 101 Eng. Rep. 1014n. (H.L. 1778). Since Mansfield's 1774 trial level decision in *Hughes v. Rann* supported the moral obligation principle, a Pennsylvania court cited Mansfield's 1774 trial decision as precedent but refused to cite that case's reversal in 1778 by the House of Lords because a Pennsylvania statute barred citing English precedent dated after July 4, 1776. Clark v. Herring, 5 Bin. (Pa.) 33, 38 (1812) (per Tilghman, C. J.).

98. *E.g.*, Wentz v. Dehaven, 1 Serg. & R. (40 Pa.) 311, 317 (1815). (No consideration necessary for written forgiveness of a debt.).

99. *See* Whitehall v. Wilson, 3 Pen. & W. (Pa.) 405, 24 Am. Dec. 326, 328–329 (1832) (The House of Lords "settled the law," in *Rann v. Hughes*, that an unsealed writing required consideration. *Id.* at 329.); *accord* Cook v. Bradley, 7 Conn. 57, 18 Am. Dec. 79, 82 (1828). The early republican Anglophobia had receded, and English decisions were now more readily cited.

100. Atkins v. Hill, 1 Cowp. 284, 288–289, 98 Eng. Rep. 1088, 1090–1091 (1775); Hawkes v. Saunders, 1 Cowp. 289, 293, 98 Eng. Rep. 1091, 1093 (1782).

101. *E.g.*, State, Use of Stevenson, v. Reigart, 1 Gill. 1, 39 Am. Dec. 628, 633–634 (Md. 1843); Ferguson v. Harris, 17 S.E. 782, 786 (S.C. 1893); McMorris v. Herndon, 18 S.C.L. (2 Bail.) 56 (1830); Hurst v. Mutual Reserve Fund Life Ins. Ass'n, 78 Md. 59, 26 A. 956, 958 (1893); Elliott v. Turner, 4 Md. 476 (1853); Early v. Mahon, 9 Johns. (N.Y.) 47, 10 Am. Dec. 204, 205 (1821); *but cf.* Linz v. Schuck, 67 A. 286, 288 (Md. 1907) (*Eastwood v. Kenyon* overruled *Hawkes v. Saunders.*).

102. *E.g.*, Little v. Blunt, 26 Mass. (9 Pick.) 488 (1830); Tebo v. Robinson, 100 N.Y. 27, 2 N.E. 383 (1885).

103. *E.g.*, Edwards v. Nelson, 51 Mich. 121 (1883); Herrington v. Davitt, 220 N.Y. 162, 115 N.E. 476 (1917). *Cf.* Shephard & Co. v. Rhodes, 7 R.I. 470 (1863) (When, short of bankruptcy, a creditor releases a debtor and the debtor later waives the release, the waiver is unenforceable.).

104. *See* Cheshire v. Barrett, 15 S.C. 24, 17 Am. Dec. 735 (1825) ("A moral obligation is sufficient consideration to support the new understanding."). Judicial explanations were given for enforcing such promises. *See* Stebbins v. Crawford County, 92 Pa. 289 (1879) ("Express promises founded on preexisting equitable obligations . . . remove an impediment erected . . . to protect the debtors from being compelled to pay."); Anderson v. Best, 176 Pa. 498, 35 A. 194 (1896) (The distinction between considerations formerly good, but now barred by statute, and those barred by statute in the first instance, is not substantial.).

105. Boles v. Merrill, 53 N.E. 894 (Mass. 1899) (Administrator ratified incom-

petent's obligation.). Implied waivers often found based on conduct of party. *See* Boles v. Merrill, 173 Mass. 491, 53 N.E. 894 (1899) (misrepresentation defense waived); Forman v. Smith, 102 W. Va. 539, 135 S.E. 653 (1926) (Statute of Frauds defense waived); Anderson v. Best, 176 Pa. 498, 35A. 194 (1896) (Statute of Frauds); Muir v. Kane, 55 Wash. 131, 104 Pac. 153 (1909) (Despite statutory requirement that contract with broker be in writing, the recitation of the sales commission in the subsequent written sales contract constituted an enforceable subsequent promise to pay the commission.); Gallon v. Lloyd-Thomas Co., 264 F. 2d 821, 826 (1959) (duress defense waived and contract ratified). *See also* RESTATEMENT OF CONTRACTS sect. 89 (1932) ("Promise to Perform a Voidable Duty").

106. Eastwood v. Kenyon, 11 Ad. & El. 438, 448, 113 Eng. Rep. 482, 486 (1840).

107. REPORTERS' NOTE to Wennall v. Adney, 3 Bos. & Pul. 248, 250n., 127 Eng. Rep. 137, 138n. (1802).

108. Treatise writers have a penchant for organizing caselaw into formal black letter principles. They tended to ignore the myriad of equitable exceptions in order to formulate the claimed general American principle that moral obligation covered only waivers and ratifications of earlier, now ineffective, legal obligations. The role of the treatise writer since Blackstone has been to draw general principles from the scattered caselaw, in contrast to the earlier abridgers who annotated separate cases. *See, e.g.*, 1 THEOPHILUS PARSONS, THE LAW OF CONTRACTS 358–361 (Boston: 2d ed. 1855) (A moral obligation is a good consideration if the original obligation was enforceable at law. *Id.* at 360. Abstract of *Eastwood v. Kenyon* supplied as note to Parsons' text. *Id.* at 358n.–359n.); CHRISTOPHER LANGDELL, SUMMARY OF THE LAW OF CONTRACTS 89–100 (2d ed. Boston: 1880) (Waivers and ratifications of voidable contracts are the extent of moral obligation's applicability.). Williston's edition of Parsons' treatise in 1893 claimed that the cases of late "settle the question definitively" that, quoting Baron Parke, "a mere moral consideration *is nothing*," outside of the waivers and ratification precedents. 1 THEOPHILUS PARSONS, THE LAW OF CONTRACTS 445 (8th ed. Williston 1893). In his urge to promote predictable, general principles for business planning, Williston chose to ignore the case-by-case exceptional outcomes found in the scattered moral obligation decisions.

109. Mills v. Wyman, 20 Mass. (3 Pick.) 207 (1825). Many nineteenth century decisions opposed extension of moral obligation. *See, e.g.*, Loomis v. Newhall, 15 Pick. (32 Mass.) 159 (1833) (Promise to pay plaintiff for board provided promisor's adult son since no previous request.); Cook v. Bradley, 7 Conn. 57 (1828) (Son not liable on promise to pay for indigent parent's receipt of necessaries.); Allen v. Bryson, 67 Ia. 591, 596 (1885) (Moral obligation alone is no consideration.); Smith v. Tripp, 14 R.I. 112 (1883) (Moral obligation isn't consideration.); Johnson v. Johnson, 10 N.C. 556 (3 Hawks) (1824); Martin's Estate, 131 Pa. 638, 18A. 987 (1890); Rask v. Norman, 169 N.W. 704 (1918 Minn.) (Promise of business associate, at promisee's deathbed, to care for family was based on goodwill, but no pecuniary benefit and so unenforceable.); Kenan v. Holloway, 16 Ala. 53, 50 Am. Dec. 162 (1849); Nightingale v. Barney, 4 G. Greene 106 (Ia. 1853) (A moral obligation won't support a note.); Shugart v. Shugart, 111 Tenn. 179, 76 S.W. 821 (1903) (Daughter had moral obligation herself to provide services for mother that father later promised to pay for.); Wigmore v. Keizer, 6 Ind. 252 (1855) (Promise

to support bastard unenforceable.); Vetten v. Wallace, 39 Ill. App. 390 (1891) (Promise to support bastard unenforceable.).

110. *E.g.*, Kilbourn v. Bradley, 3 Day 356, 3 Am. Dec. 273 (Conn. 1809); Ehle v. Judson, 24 Wend. 97 (N.Y. 1840); Geer v. Archer, 2 Barb. 424 (N.Y. 1848); McElven v. Sloan, 56 Ga. 208 (1876) (Dictum that under Georgia statute, son would be liable for necessaries provided aged parent.); Edwards v. Nelson, 51 Mich. 121 (1883) (bankruptcy discharge); Hemphill v. McClemans, 24 Pa. 367 (1855); Landis v. Royer, 59 Pa. 95 (1868); Stebbins v. Crawford County, 92 Pa. 289 (1879) (Promises founded on preexisting equitable obligation of infant or woman under coverture are enforceable.); Sterbergh v. Provoost, 13 Barb. 365 (N.Y. 1851); State, Use of Stevenson, v. Reigart, 1 Gill. 1, 39 Am. Dec. 628 (Md. 1843) (If enforceable at equity, that's enough.); Ingersoll v. Martin, 58 Md. 67 (1882) (Past obligation can be enforceable at law or equity.); Anderson v. Best, 176 Pa. 498, 35A. 194 (1896) (Distinction between formerly good consideration, now barred by statute, and those barred by a statute in first instance is not great.); Barley v. City of Philadelphia, 31A. 925 (1895); Leonard v. Duffin, 94 Pa. 218 (1880) (Promise after coverture enforceable against third party promisor.); Ferguson v. Harris, 17 S.E. 782 (S.C. 1893) (Woman under coverture bound for benefit received.); McMorris v. Herndon, 18 S.C.L. (2 Bail.) 56 (1830); Hurst v. Mutual Reserve Fund Life Ins. Ass'n., 78 Md. 59, 26A. 956 (1893); Elliott v. Turner, 4 Md. 476 (1853) (Promise of grandfather to pay maintenance to grandchild was enforceable.); Wentz v. Dehaven, 1 Serg. & R. (40 Pa.) 311 (1815) (followed Mansfield); Andover Turnpike Corp. v. Gould, 6 Mass. 40, 4 Am. Dec. 80 (1809) (Dictum that "moral obligation is sufficient to support an action on an express promise."); Shenk v. Mingle, 13 Serg. & R. (Pa.) 29 (1825); Barthe v. LaCroix, 29 La. Ann. 326, 29 Am. Rep. 330 (1877) (Promissory note to employee for past services at low wages was binding.); Worth v. Daniel, 57 S.E. 898 (1907 Ga.) (Sense of duty child feels toward aged parent was good consideration for mutual promises amongst children to support mother.); Trayer v. Setzer, 72 Neb. 845, 101 N.W. 989 (1904) (Father of bastard under moral obligation to support even without statute.); Bunn v. Winthrop, 1 Johns. Ch. 329 (N.Y. 1815) (Dictum that natural obligation of father was to provide for bastard.); Wyant v. Lesher, 23 Pa. 338 (1854) (Moral obligation found enough for past illicit cohabitation promise.); Scott v. Carruth, 9 Yerg. 418 (Tenn. 1836) (Moral obligation to support guardian's promise to ward to make up for not doing a better job.); Drake v. Bell, 26 Misc. 237, 55 N.Y. Supp. 945 (1899) (Landowner bound on promise to pay for improvement plaintiff mistakenly did on his property.). *Cf.* PETER KARSTEN, HEART VERSUS HEAD: JUDGE-MADE LAW IN NINETEENTH-CENTURY AMERICA 3–6 (Chapel Hill: 1997) (While nineteenth century New England jurisdictions conform to English precedent, other American jurisdictions developed neighborly principles favoring disadvantaged plaintiffs over creditors and entrepreneurs.).

111. *E.g.*, 1 THEOPHILUS PARSONS, THE LAW OF CONTRACTS 360 (Boston: 2d ed. 1855) CHRISTOPHER LANGDELL, A SELECTION OF CASES ON THE LAW OF CONTRACTS 370 (Boston: 1871); CHRISTOPHER LANGDELL, A SUMMARY OF THE LAW OF CONTRACTS 94 (2d ed. Boston: 1880); 1 THEOPHILUS PARSONS, THE LAW OF CONTRACTS 446 (Boston: 8th ed. Williston 1893).

112. The American position today does not bind a promisor if the benefit was

not "previously received by the promisor." RESTATEMENT (SECOND) OF CONTRACTS sect. 86 (1) (1981).

113. 1 THEOPHILUS PARSONS, THE LAW OF CONTRACTS 360n. (Boston: 2d ed. 1855).

114. CHRISTOPHER LANGDELL, A SELECTION OF CASES ON THE LAW OF CONTRACTS 370 (Boston: 1871). Actually, a decade later, Langdell made a modernistic remark about *Mills v. Wyman* when he suggested that if the son had been a minor and a member of the father's household, then the decision on the father's promise would've been different (A majority of jurisdictions might not go that far, even today, because the father was not directly benefited.). *See* CHRISTOPHER LANGDELL, A SUMMARY OF THE LAW OF CONTRACTS 94 (2d ed. Boston: 1880).

115. 1 THEOPHILUS PARSONS, THE LAW OF CONTRACTS 446n. (Boston: 8th ed. Williston 1893).

116. *Id.* at 445n.

117. 1 THEOPHILUS PARSONS, THE LAW OF CONTRACTS 445 (Boston: 8th ed. Williston 1893); 1 THEOPHILUS PARSONS, THE LAW OF CONTRACTS 358 (Boston: 2d ed. 1855); Jennings v. Brown, 9 M. & W. 496, 501, 152 Eng. Rep. 210, 212 (1842) (Parke found consideration for promise made by putative father to pay mother for maintenance of bastard in exchange for her taking care of child.). Parke's statement that moral consideration was "nothing" was a comment regarding *Binnington v. Wallis,* which he participated in over twenty years before as an attorney for a defendant who had agreed to pay his former mistress for the harm to her reputation and future. The case turned for the defendant on the failure of the complaint to allege that he seduced her; the *per curiam* rationale stated: "It is not averred, that the defendant was the seducer, and there is no authority to shew that past consideration alone, or the ceasing to cohabit in the future, is a good consideration for a promise of this nature." Binnington v. Wallis, 4 B. & Ald. 650, 652, 106 Eng. Rep. 1074, 1075 (1821) (Attorney Parke had argued: "It is not stated that the plaintiff was seduced. There is not even a moral obligation to provide for a woman for past cohabitation." *Id.* at 651/1075.).

CHAPTER 9

1. REPORTERS' NOTE to Wennall v. Adney, 3 Bos. & Pul. 248, 250n., 127 Eng. Rep. 137, 138n., 140n. (1802).

2. Eastwood v. Kenyon, 11 Ad. & El. 438, 452, 113 Eng. Rep. 482, 487 (1840).

3. Hunt v. Bate, 3 Dyer 272a, 73 Eng. Rep. 605 (1568).

4. *Id.*

5. Style v. Smith, 2 Leon. 111, 74 Eng. Rep. 401 (1587). The emphasis on the physician being a friend was probably intended to show lack of officiousness and to stimulate notions of love and affection, which had supposedly been purged from the doctrine of consideration during the prior generation because the prior affection made it past consideration. *See* Sharington v. Strotton, Plow. 298, 302, 75 Eng. Rep. 454, 460 (1564–1566). *Cf.* Marsh and Rainford's Case, 2 Leon. 111, 74 Eng. Rep. 400 (1588) (Father liable to son-in-law on promise to pay money on account of his daughter's prior marriage to the plaintiff. The court said "the natural affection of his daughter is a sufficient matter of consideration." *Id.* at 401.). Robert

Brooke (CJCP 1554–58) wrote in his FEOFFMENT AL USES, pl. 54 (d. 1558) that many thought a covenant good for a past consideration. Simpson speculated that Brooke may have been referring to covenants in consideration of past marriages. *See* ALFRED SIMPSON, A HISTORY OF THE COMMON LAW OF CONTRACT 453–454 (Oxford: 1975). The categories of moral obligation promises enforced by common law courts prior to the nineteenth century included: (a) waivers of statute of limitations and of bankruptcy; (b) ratification of voidable obligations; (c) ratification of void obligations, as due to usury and coverture; (d) care or benefit provided a child; (e) burial of spouse or child; and (f) other duties enforceable in equity, e.g., executor's promise to pay legacy, promises to pay for a past wrong and promise to pay for benefit received.

6. *Anon.*, 2 Show. 184, 89 Eng. Rep. 879 (1682).

7. Scott v. Nelson, Esp. N.P. 945 (1763) *in* 3 Bos. & Pul. 248, 250n., 127 Eng. Rep. 137, 138n. (1802).

8. Best and Jolly's Case, 1 Sid. 38, 82 Eng. Rep. 955 (1660).

9. Best and Jolly's Case, 1 Sid. 38, 82 Eng. Rep. 955 (1660). Promissory estoppel would be available today.

10. Church v. Church, 3 Dyer 272b, 73 Eng. Rep. 608 (1656). Earlier in Besfich and Coggil's Case, Palm. 559, 81 Eng. Rep. 1219 (1628), the judges were split on whether a father was liable on a promise to repay the plaintiff for burying his son in Spain. Dodderidge, J. supported recovery, and it appears the plaintiff won.

11. Jenkins v. Tucker, 1 H. Bl. 90, 126 Eng. Rep. 55 (1788).

12. Jenkins v. Tucker, 1 H. Bl. 90, 93, 126 Eng. Rep. 55,57 (1788) (Gould, J. said: "[i]mplies a promise to pay it.").

13. Atkins v. Hill, 1 Cowp. 284, 98 Eng. Rep. 1088 (1755); Hawkes v. Saunders, 1 Cowp. 289, 98 Eng. Rep. 1091 (1782).

14. Goodright ex dim. Elizabeth Carter v. Straphan, 1 Cowp. 201, 98 Eng. Rep. 1043 (1774).

15. REPORTERS' NOTE to Wennall v. Adney, 3 Bos. & Pul. 248, 250n., 253n., 127 Eng. Rep. 137, 138n., 140n. (1802) ("Indeed if any of the cases could be sustained on the principle that a father is, by the mere force of moral obligation, bound to pay what has been advanced for his son, because he has subsequently promised to pay it; by the same rule the son should be liable for the debts of the father upon a similar promise." *Id.*).

16. *Id.* at 138n.-139n. (Statement made with reference to *Anon.*, 2 Show. 184, 89 Eng. Rep. 879 (1682).).

17. REPORTERS' NOTE to Wennall v. Adney, 3 Bos. & Pul. 248, 127 Eng. Rep. 137, 138n., 140n. (1802). (Statement made with reference to *Church v. Church* (1656).). In reference to the split judicial opinions on a promise to repay the funeral expenses incurred in burying the defendant's son in Besfich and Coggill's Case, Palm. 559, 81 Eng. Rep. 1219 (1628), the reporters said "[i]t would seem" that the position of the justices opposed to recovery "[w]as the better opinion" because it was not the father's obligation unless the money was "[p]aid by the Plaintiff at the request of the Defendant unto his son." REPORTERS' NOTE to Wennall v. Adney, 3 Bos. & Pul. 248, 250n., 253n., 127 Eng. Rep. 137, 138n., 140n. (1802).

18. *Cf.* SIMPSON, *supra* note 5, at 325.

19. It has been suggested that if the necessaries must be provided in an emer-

gency circumstance, the requirements of both the prior request and the subsequent promise should be dispensed with. *See* Samuel Stoljar, *No Obituary for Wennall v. Adney,* 11 J. LEG. HIST. 250, 262–263 (1990) (The promise in *Style v. Smith* might be grounded in natural affection or moral obligation. *Id.* at 262.).

20. Lee v. Muggeridge, 5 Taunt. 36, 128 Eng. Rep. 599 (1813).

21. Barnes v. Hedley, 2 Taunt. 183, 127 Eng. Rep. 1047 (1809).

22. Eastwood v. Kenyon, 11 Ad. & El. 438, 448, 113 Eng. Rep. 482, 486 (1840).

23. Flight v. Reed, 1 H. & C. 703, 158 Eng. Rep. 1067 (1863). The *Flight* facts varied in that between the time of usurious bill of exchange and subsequent promise, the Statute of Usury was repealed. The subsequent promise was a renewal of the original bill of exchange.

24. Flight v. Reed, 1 H. & C. 703, 158 Eng. Rep. 1067, 1072 (1863). Equity enforced the non-usurious portion of the contract. In addition to the waiver precedents, the usury case was similar to an adult's ratification of a contact made during infancy in that the infant's contracts were deemed void prior to Holt's time on the bench. Pollock's focus on the benefit received by the defendant has a modern ring to it, as will be developed during the remainder of this volume.

25. CHRISTOPHER LANGDELL, A SUMMARY OF THE LAW OF CONTRACTS 96 (2d ed. Boston: 1880).

26. Kilbourn v. Bradley, 3 Day 356, 3 Am. Dec. 273 (Conn. 1809).

27. Ironically, only the defendant cited *Barnes v. Hedley.* (Rapid transatlantic access to case is impressive.)

28. Kilbourn v. Bradley, 3 Day 356, 3 Am. Dec. 273, 274 (Conn. 1809).

29. Early v. Mahon, 19 Johns. (N.Y.) 147, 10 Am. Dec. 204, 205 (1821).

30. Early v. Mahon, 19 Johns. (N.Y.) 147, 10 Am. Dec. 204, 205 (1821). (The court distinguished usury (*malum prohibitum*) from a crime (*malum in se*). *Id.*).

31. Early v. Mahon, 19 Johns. (N.Y.) 147, 10 Am. Dec. 204, 206 (1821).

32. *See* 17 A.L.R. 1299, 1352 (1922). *And see* RESTATEMENT (SECOND) OF CONTRACTS sect. 86 cmt. h (1981) (When second promise makes it non-usurious, it's enforceable.).

33. If a debtor came into equity for relief from a usurious contract, he must do what was right by repaying the loan at the lawful interest rate, whether or not he made a subsequent promise. *See* Rogers v. Rathburn, 1 Johns. Ch. 367 (N.Y. 1806).

34. *E.g.*, Gwinn v. Simes, 61 Mo. 335 (1875) (Moral obligation to repay is sufficient consideration for promise to repay loan made in violation of Sunday law.).

35. *E.g.*, Bates v. Watson, 1 Sneed 376 (Tenn. 1853) (wager); Ludlow v. Hardy, 38 Mich. 690 (1870) (sale of liquor in violation of liquor law); Puckett v. Alexander, 102 N.C. 95, 8 S.E. 767 (1889) (contract for medical service from one not licensed).

36. CHRISTOPHER LANGDELL, *supra* note 25, at 96.

37. Goodright ex dim. Elizabeth Carter v. Straphan, 1 Cowp. 201, 98 Eng. Rep. 1043, 1044 (1774).

38. *See* Cook v. Bradley, 7 Conn. 57, 18 Am. Dec. 79, 85 (1828) (Dictum cited *Lee v. Muggeridge* and said that a married woman's subsequent promise was "founded on a moral obligation" and the subsequent promise "will bind her." *Id.*); Hatchell v. Odom, 19 N.C. (2 Dev. & B.) 302 (1836) (Dictum that such a promise enforced "not merely because there was a former moral obligation, but because there was a former moral obligation which would have had legal efficacy,

but for temporary cause removed before the new promise was made."); Wilson v. Burr, 25 Wend. (N.Y.) 386 (1841) (Dictum).

39. Hemphill v. McClimans, 24 Pa. 367, 371 (1855) ("The law may say what it will about void and voidable contracts, but there is no code of ethics which says that the duty of not abusing the confidence of one who has honestly served you, is a void obligation upon the conscience." *Id.* at 371–372.); *accord* Shenk v. Mingle, 13 Serg. & R. (Pa.) 29 (1825). *See* Kelly v. Eby, 141 Pa. 176, 21A. 512 (1891) (Moral duty was sufficient consideration to mental incompetency.); Young's Estate, 234 Pa. 287, 83A. 201 (1912).

40. Wilson v. Burr, 25 Wend. (N.Y.) 386 (1841) (Court said divorcee would've owed her attorney's fee for her divorce if she had promised to pay subsequent to her divorce, since then the three ingredients of a bargain would've been present: request (in form of original unenforceable promise), service to her benefit and subsequent promise.).

41. Eastwood v. Kenyon, 11 Ad. & El. 438, 449, 113 Eng. Rep. 482, 486 (1840). *And see* Cook v. Bradley, 7 Conn. 57, 18 Am. Dec. 79, 85 (1828) (In *Lee v. Muggeridge*, the subsequent "promise was founded on the advancement of money at her request.").

42. Kent v. Rand, 64 N.H. 45, 5A. 760 (1886).

43. Loyd v. Lee, 1 Str. 94, 93 Eng. Rep. 406 (1719) (Her subsequent promise unsupported by consideration since, unlike infant, her promise during marriage was void.); REPORTERS' NOTE to Wennall v. Adney, 3 Bos. & Pul. 248, 250n., 127 Eng. Rep. 137, 138n. (1802); Eastwood v. Kenyon, 11 Ad. & El. 438, 113 Eng. Rep. 482 (1840); Mills v. Wyman, 20 Mass. (3 Pick.) 207 (1825).

44. Kent v. Rand, 64 N.H. 45, 5A. 760, 763 (1886) (Cited with approval the Note to *Wennall v. Adney* and *Mills v. Wyman.*).

45. *See* 1 SAMUEL WILLISTON, A TREATISE ON THE LAW OF CONTRACTS sect. 156 (2d ed. W. Jaeger, New York: 1957); 1A ARTHUR CORBIN, CORBIN ON CONTRACTS sect. 237 (St. Paul: 1950). By the mid-nineteenth century, English law observed the same dichotomy.

46. *See* Vance v. Wells, 8 Ala. 399 (1845); Viser v. Bertrand, 14 Ark. 267 (1853) (A promise to pay her lawyer for representing her in divorce was chargeable against her separate estate.); Craft v. Rolland, 37 Conn. 491 (1870). An ingenious South Carolina decision used this rule to bind a married woman on her subsequent promise when both the prior request and the subsequent promise were made *during* her marriage. Ferguson v. Harris, 17 S.E. 782 (S.C. 1893) ("Moral obligation resting upon the defendant to pay for the lumber used in the construction of her house constituted a sufficient consideration for her express promise to pay for the same.").

47. *See* 1A CORBIN, *supra* note 45, at sect. 237; 1 WILLISTON, *supra* note 45, at sect. 156 (Since married women still can't enter into certain types of contracts today, the effect of new promise after discoverture still arises.). *See* SIMPSON, *supra* note 5, at 546–547 (At common law, her will depended upon the will of her husband.).

48. *E.g.*, Idaho Code sect. 32–904 (1947) (She can't be surety. Disability removed when for her benefit.); Ill. Rev. Stat. ch. 68, sects. 6, 8 (1955) (no personal services contracts with husband); West Va. Code sect. 4738 (1955) (Contract with husband must be in writing.).

CHAPTER 10

1. *See* REPORTERS' NOTE to Wennall v. Adney, 3 Bos. & Pul. 247, 251–253n., 127 Eng. Rep. 137, 139–140n. (1802).

2. *See* RESTATEMENT (SECOND) OF CONTRACTS sect. 86.

3. REPORTER'S NOTE to Osborne v. Rogers, 1 Wms. Saund. 264n., 85 Eng. Rep. 318, 319n. (1680) (1798).

4. *Id.*

5. Hayes v. Warren, 2 Str. 933, 93 Eng. Rep. 950 (1731).

6. The plaintiff had failed to plead a prior request. The *per curiam* decision suggested that there might have been latitude to infer a request by the defendant had there been a jury verdict based on a full hearing of the surrounding circumstances, but since such circumstances were not aired in the default judgment proceeding, the pleading defect could not be overcome.

7. Cooper v. Martin, 4 East. 77, 83, 102 Eng. Rep. 759, 761 (1803).

8. Southerton v. Whitlock, 2 Str. 690, 93 Eng. Rep. 786 (1726).

9. Ball v. Hesketh, Comb. 381, 90 Eng. Rep. 541 (1697). Whereas the minor had made a voidable promise in the first instance in *Ball v. Hesketh*, in *Southerton v. Whitlock* non-necessaries were delivered to the infant without a promise by the infant to pay for them in the first instance. *And see* Doty v. Wilson, 14 Johns. (N.Y.) 378, 382 (1817) (No promise or actual request prior to benefit being provided, but court found implied previous request and declared that "a subsequent ratification is equivalent to an original command.").

10. James Kent was Justice of New York Supreme Court 1798–1804, Chief Justice 1804–1814 and Chancellor 1814–1823. He did much to bring equity into the law.

11. Livingston v. Rogers, 1 Cai. (N.Y.) 583 (1804). Implied request language in this decision appears dictum since the ruling concerned whether mutual promises were concurrent.

12. Livingston v. Rogers, 1 Cai. (N.Y.) 583, 585 (1804).

13. Pillans v. Van Mierop, 3 Burr. 1663, 1672, 97 Eng. Rep. 1035, 1039 (1765) (extensive citations to Roman law and law of nations). *See* Church v. Church, 3 Dyer 272b, 73 Eng. Rep. 608 (1656) (burying a son); Style v. Smith, 2 Leon. 111, 74 Eng. Rep. 400, 401 (1587) (curing a son). Wilmot's verbiage was strikingly similar to the reporter and losing plaintiff's attorney, Strange, in Hayes v. Warren, 2 Str. 933, 93 Eng. Rep. 950 (1731), a decision which Wilmot found "absurd." Strange urged "common sense" over entertaining the trivial pleading objection of failure to plead a previous request by pointing out that on the same day that the plaintiff performed the defendant subsequently promised to pay. Strange had also cited *Style v. Smith.* Kent preferred citing *pre*-republican English cases.

14. REPORTER'S NOTE to Osborne v. Rogers, 1 Wms. Saund. 264n., 85 Eng. Rep. 318n. (1680) (1798); Livingston v. Rogers, 1 Cai. (N.Y.) 583, 585 (1804).

15. Livingston v. Rogers, 1 Cai. (N.Y.) 583, 586 (1804).

16. Comstock v. Smith, 7 Johns. (N.Y.) 87 (1810).

17. Although the 1810 *Comstock v. Smith* court said the defendant's subsequent promise to pay for land the plaintiff had earlier conveyed to him might well be a good case for implying a request, the failure of the plaintiff to plead that the plaintiff had conveyed good title constituted a failure to aver that the defendant

had received a material benefit. . . . This quibble raises the question of whether the court had much confidence in the new rule without very clear facts supporting the common sense solution of enforceability.

18. Comstock v. Smith, 7 Johns. (N.Y.) 87, 88 (1810).

19. REPORTER'S NOTE to Comstock v. Smith, 7 Johns. (N.Y.) 87, 88n. (1810).

20. *E.g.*, Doty v. Wilson, 14 Johns. (N.Y.) 378, 382 (1817). This decision employed the language "subsequent ratification" in referring to the subsequent promise in order to vaguely keep the case under the mantle of Holt's precedents. Many of these early New York–implied request cases are common sense solutions to overcome technical slip-ups in pleading the intricacies under the ancient forms of action.

21. Hicks v. Burhans, 10 Johns. (N.Y.) 243 (1813). No prior legal obligation existed here.

22. Hicks v. Burhans, 10 Johns. (N.Y.) 243, 244 (1813) (cited solely *Livingston v. Rogers* as authority). (Once notion introduced from English source, as did *Livingston,* later U.S. courts tended to cite solely the instigating American precedent.) The question was then raised in later cases whether the receipt of a material benefit could raise a *promise* as well as an implied request. Turner v. Patridge, 3 Pen. & Watts (Pa.) 172 (1831) rejected the proposition, as most courts have. There were, however, a few aberrational cases which suggested that a promise could either be inferred or was unnecessary. *See* Hatch v. Purcell, 21 N.H. 544 (1850); Nicole v. Allen, 3 Car. & P. 36, 172 Eng. Rep. 312 (1827).

23. Edwards v. Davis, 16 Johns. (N.Y.) 281 (1819).

24. Edwards v. Davis, 16 Johns. (N.Y.) 281, 286 (1819). Many of the early cases speak of a "pecuniary benefit." By the twentieth century, the materiality of the benefit included non-financial benefits, such as one's life being saved at such a great risk that the rescuer became permanently disabled. *See* Webb v. McGowin, 27 Ala. App. 82, 168 So. 196 (1935).

25. REPORTER'S NOTE to Osborne v. Rogers, 1 Wms. Saund. 264n., 85 Eng. Rep. 318, 319n. (1680) (1798).

26. *See* Style v. Smith, 2 Leon. 111, 74 Eng. Rep. 400 (1587); *Anon.*, 2 Show. 184, 89 Eng. Rep. 879 (1682).

27. REPORTER'S NOTE to Edwards v. Davis, 16 Johns. (N.Y.) 281, 283n. (1819). Reporter Johnson criticized *Comstock v. Smith* as too broad, and beyond the caselaw, in suggesting that a beneficial consideration might be inferred from a mere moral obligation.

28. *See, e.g.*, Church v. Church, 3 Dyer 272b, 73 Eng. Rep. 608 (1656); Style v. Smith, 2 Leon. 111, 74 Eng. Rep. 400, 401 (1587); *Anon.*, 2 Show. 184, 89 Eng. Rep. 879 (1682); Scott v. Nelson, Esp. N.P. 945, 3 Bos. & Pul. 248, 250n., 127 Eng. Rep. 137, 138n. (1763).

29. REPORTER'S NOTE to Edwards v. Davis, 16 Johns. (N.Y.) 281, 283n. (1819); REPORTERS' NOTE to Wennall v. Adney, 3 Bos. & Pul. 247, 250n., 127 Eng. Rep. 137, 138n. (1802).

30. *See* RESTATEMENT (SECOND) OF CONTRACTS sect. 86(1).

31. Church v. Church, 3 Dyer 272b, 73 Eng. Rep. 608 (1656).

32. Hayes v. Warren, 2 Str. 933, 93 Eng. Rep. 950 (1731).

33. REPORTERS' NOTE to Wennall v. Adney, 3 Bos. & Pul. 247, 250n., 253n., 127 Eng. Rep. 137, 138n., 140n. (1802).

34. Style v. Smith, 2 Leon. 111, 74 Eng. Rep. 400, 401 (1587).

35. *Id. Cp.* Webb v. McGowin, 27 Ala. App. 82, 168 So. 196 (1935) (Subsequent promise carries with it the "presumption that a previous request for services was made.").

36. *E.g.*, Glass v. Beach, 5 Vt. Rep. 172 (1833) (lifted Kent's verbiage from his COMMENTARIES); Bevan v. Tomlinson, 25 Ind. 253 (1865); Jilson v. Gilbert, 26 Wis. 637 (1870).

37. *See* Mills v. Wyman, 20 Mass. (3 Pick.) 207 (1825). *And see* 1 THEOPHILUS PARSONS, THE LAW OF CONTRACTS 360 (Boston: 2d ed. 1855); CHRISTOPHER LANGDELL, A SELECTION OF CASES ON THE LAW OF CONTRACTS 370 (Boston: 1871).

38. JAMES KENT, COMMENTARIES ON AMERICAN LAW 465 (Boston: 4th ed. 1840) (Cited his own New York decisions in *Livingston v. Rogers, Comstock v. Smith* and *Hicks v. Burhans.*).

39. THERON METCALF, PRINCIPLES OF THE LAW OF CONTRACTS 200 (New York: 1867) (This treatise was drawn from articles Metcalf published in the AMERICAN JURIST between 1838 and 1841.). By 1867, he sat on Massachusetts court. Metcalf cited Sjt. Williams' Note, wherein Williams stated that a request may be implied, "but it is still necessary to aver in the declaration, that it was money paid and laid out for me at my *special instance and request*, and my subsequent conduct will be evidence of it." *See* REPORTER'S NOTE to Osborne v. Rogers, 1 Wms. Saund. 264n., 85 Eng. Rep. 318, 319n. (1680) (1798).

40. Hunt v. Bate, 3 Dyer 272a, 73 Eng. Rep. 605 (1568).

41. *E.g.*, Rex v. Lyme Regis, 1 Doug. 135, 99 Eng. Rep. 89 (1779) (clerical error in mandamus amended by Mansfield); Trueman v. Fenton, 2 Cowp. 544, 98 Eng. Rep. 1232 (1777) (defective pleading overlooked by Mansfield to get to merits of case); *see* James Oldham, *Reinterpretation of 18th-Century Contract Theory: The View from Lord Mansfield's Trial Notes*, 76 GEO. L.J. 1949, 1961, 1982 (1988) (Mansfield's trial notes show intent was prominent.); *see also* CECIL FIFOOT, LORD MANSFIELD 135 (Oxford: 1936); Hamburger, *The Development of the Nineteenth Century Consensus Theory of Contract* 7 LAW & HIST. REV. 241, 246–217 (1989).

42. *See* J. Dillon, *Bentham's Influence on the Reforms of the Nineteenth Century* in 1 SELECT ESSAYS IN ANGLO-AMERICAN LEGAL HISTORY 492, 492–500 (Boston: 1907); William Holdsworth, *Bentham's Place in English Legal History*, 28 CALIF. L. REV. 568, 584–585 (1940).

43. New York's Field Code of Civil Procedure, passed in 1848, abolished the forms of action, simplified pleading rules and fused law and equity. England followed suit in 1852 and 1854 with the passage of the Common Law Procedure Acts and the Judicature Acts of 1873 and 1875. 27 states followed New York's lead in reforming civil procedure by the 1870s. *See* Hepburn, *The Historical Development of Code Pleading in America and England* in 2 SELECT ESSAYS IN ANGLO-AMERICAN LEGAL HISTORY 643, 655–680 (Boston: 1907). Serious attention to pleading reform in England began with the formation of a parliamentary commission in 1830, resulting in a defective, partial revision known as the 1834 Judicial Rules of Hilary, a revision which inhibited the development of the moral obligation principle by the 1840s. *See* William Holdsworth, *The New Rules of Pleading of Hilary Term, 1834*, 1 CAMBRIDGE L. J. 261, 261–272 (1923); Eastwood v. Kenyon, 11 Ad. & E. 438, 113 Eng. Rep. 482 (1840); CECIL FIFOOT, LORD MANSFIELD 232–241 (Oxford: 1936).

44. *Cf.* S.F.C. Milsom, *Law and Fact in Legal Development*, 17 U. TORONTO L.J. 1, 14–15 (1967).

45. *Cf.* CECIL FIFOOT, HISTORY AND SOURCES OF THE COMMON LAW: TORT AND CONTRACT 370–371 (London: 1949); JOHN BAKER, AN INTRODUCTION TO ENGLISH LEGAL HISTORY 80–81, 378–402 (London: 3rd ed. 1990).

46. American and English translations of Pothier's influential French contract work, which enunciated the consensual theory, were widely available and cited by the early nineteenth century. *See* R. POTHIER, A TREATISE ON THE LAW OF OBLIGATIONS (Orleans 1761–1764) (tr. F. Martin, ed. Martin & Ogden, Newbern, N.C.: 1802; and W. Evans. ed., London: 1806). Carolinian attraction to civilian ideas caused Pothier to be translated earlier there than in London.

47. *Cf.* CECIL FIFOOT, LORD MANSFIELD 136–137 (Oxford: 1936).

48. Chancery gave contract relief when "reason and conscience" demanded it. *See* Barbour, *supra* note 11, at 156–157 (P. Vinogradoff ed. 1914). Chancery's approach was more effective than the common law because chancery took a purely contractual view in emphasizing the defendant's promise. It was not burdened by assumpsit's origins in tort logic nor by the consideration test or the attendant historical procedural quirks at law. *Id.* at 161–166. The clerical chancellors often followed canon law procedures. *Id.* at 163–168. Chancellors applied the notion that a promise ought to be enforced if a good reason or *causa* existed. *Id.* at 105–106; 132–135; THEODORE PLUCKNETT, A CONCISE HISTORY OF THE COMMON LAW 649–652 (London: 5th ed. 1956).

49. REPORTER'S NOTE to Osborne v. Rogers, 1 Wms. Saund. 264n., 85 Eng. Rep. 318, 319n. (1680) (1798).

50. Doty v. Wilson, 14 Johns. (N.Y.) 378, 382 (1817) (Defendant promised to pay deputy-sheriff for judgment amount rendered against deputy on account of wrongfully allowing defendant's release from debtor prison, to the detriment of a creditor who obtained judgment against deputy.); REPORTER'S NOTE to Osborne v. Rogers, 1 Wms. Saund. 264n. 85 Eng. Rep. 318, 319n. (1680) (1798). Dictum in Comstock v. Smith, 7 Johns. (N.Y.) 87, 88 (1810) came very close to characterizing the previous request as a mere fiction that need not be pleaded: "[a] beneficial consideration and a request due necessarily implied from the moral obligation under which the party was placed."

51. McMorris v. Herndon, 18 S.C.L. (2 Bail.) 56 (1830) (cited Sjt. Williams' Note and *Hawkes v. Saunders*. In *McMorris*, a defendant-heir promised to pay executor for paying from the executor's individual assets estate debts which had benefited the defendant.). Early S.C. courts were mavericks in their look more to equity and civil law.

52. *E.g.*, Nixon v. Jenkins, 1 Hilt. (N.Y.) 318 (1857).

53. Boothe v. Fitzpatrick, 36 Vt. 681, 683 (1864) (Defendant promised to pay plaintiff for caring for his stray bull.).

54. *E.g.*, Ferguson v. Harris, 17 S.E. 782, 786 (1893); Edson v. Poppe, 24 S.D. 466, 124 N.W. 441 (1910) (cited *Boothe v. Fitzpatrick* and *Doty v. Wilson*); Webb v. McGowin, 27 Ala. App. 82, 168 So. 196 (1935) (cited *Boothe v. Fitzpatrick*).

55. *See* JOHN BAKER, AN INTRODUCTION TO ENGLISH LEGAL HISTORY 231–232 (London: 3rd ed. 1990).

56. Bentley v. Morse, 14 Johns. (N.Y.) 468 (1817).

57. Bentley v. Morse, 14 Johns. (N.Y.) 468, 468–469 (1817).

58. Hawkes v. Saunders, 1 Cowp. 289, 98 Eng. Rep. 1091 (1782).

59. REPORTER'S NOTE to Bentley v. Morse, 14 Johns. (N.Y.) 468, 468n. (1817).

60. REPORTER'S NOTE to Edwards v. Davis, 16 Johns. (N.Y.) 281, 283n. (1819).

61. REPORTERS' NOTE to Wennall v. Adney, 3 Bos. & Pul. 247, 253n. 127 Eng. Rep. 137, 140n. (1802).

62. Seymour v. Town of Marlboro, 40 Vt. 171 (1868).

63. Seymour v. Town of Marlboro, 40 Vt. 171, 179 (1868). The plaintiff's lawyer suggested the alternative justifications of there being the equivalent of a previous request *or* the defendant's receipt of a benefit. *Id.* at 176. The opinion in this case did not actually verbalize the existence of a moral obligation.

64. Drake v. Bell, 26 Misc. 237, 55 N.Y.S. 945 (1899).

65. Mills v. Wyman, 20 Mass. (3 Pick.) 207 (1825).

66. Drake v. Bell, 26 Misc. 237, 55 N.Y.S. 945, 946 (1899); *accord* Boothe v. Fitzpatrick, 36 Vt. 681, 684 (1864).

67. Drake v. Bell, 26 Misc. 237, 55 N.Y.S. 945, 946 (1899). Gaynor made early reputation as muckraker.

68. Eastwood v. Kenyon, 11 Ad. & El. 438, 113 Eng. Rep. 482 (1840).

69. *See* Drake v. Bell, 26 Misc. 237, 55 N.Y.S. 945, 946 (1899) ("If the rule so plainly stated by Lord Mansfield, that a moral obligation was of itself sufficient consideration for a subsequent promise, had been followed, the sole question in each case would be whether there was a moral obligation to support." *Id.* The court went on to say that the present case would thus be resolved in favor of the plaintiff because of the promisor's prior receipt of a benefit. Id.).

70. Drake v. Bell, 26 Misc. 237, 55 N.Y.S. 945, 947 (1899).

71. Eastwood v. Kenyon, 11 Ad. & El. 438, 450, 113 Eng. Rep. 482, 486 (1840).

72. Ferguson v. Harris, 17 S.E. 782, 786 (S.C. 1893); *accord* Muir v. Kane, 55 Wash. 131, 104 P. 153, 156 (1909).

73. REPORTERS' NOTE to Wennall v. Adney, 3 Bos. & Pul. 247, 250n., 127 Eng. Rep. 137, 139n. (1802); Drake v. Bell, 26 Misc. 237, 55 N.Y.S. 945, 946–947 (1899).

74. REPORTER'S NOTE to Edwards v. Davis, 16 Johns. (N.Y.) 281, 285n. (1819).

75. Mills v. Wyman, 20 Mass. (3 Pick.) 207, 212 (1825).

76. Drake v. Bell, 26 Misc. 237, 55 N.Y.S. 945, 946–947 (1899); REPORTERS' NOTE to Wennall v. Adney, 3 Bos. & Pul. 247, 250n., 253n., 127 Eng. Rep., 137, 138n., 140n. (1802).

77. *E.g.*, Boothe v. Fitzpatrick, 36 Vt. 681, 683 (1864); Park Falls State Bank v. Fordyce, 628, 238 N.W. 516, 518 (1931) (also true for promise of purchase in violation of Sunday closing laws).

78. Drake v. Bell, 26 Misc. 237, 55 N.Y.S. 945, 947 (1899).

79. *Id.*

80. *Id.* at 945, 947.

81. For annotated discussion of late nineteenth and early twentieth century cases, *see* Note, *Moral Obligation as a Consideration for an Executory Promise*, 17 A.L.R. 1299, 1317–76 (1922).

82. RESTATEMENT OF CONTRACTS sects. 86–89 (1932).

83. *See* 1 THEOPHILUS PARSONS, THE LAW OF CONTRACTS 445n., 446n. (Boston: Williston 8th ed. 1893).

84. *See* J. E. Keefe, Jr., *Moral Obligation as Consideration for Contract—Modern Trend,* 8 A.L.R. 2d 787–803 (1949) (details supportive caselaw developments from 1920s through 1940s).

CHAPTER 11

1. *See* 1 SAMUEL WILLISTON, A TREATISE ON THE LAW OF CONTRACTS sect. 142 (2d ed. W. Jaeger. New York: 1947).

2. RESTATEMENT (SECOND) OF CONTRACTS sect. 86(1) (1981).

3. *Cf.* Lon Fuller, *Consideration and Form,* 41 COLUM. L. REV. 799, 821 (1941); 1A ARTHUR CORBIN, CORBIN ON CONTRACTS sects. 230–234 (St. Paul: 1950).

4. Park Falls State Bank v. Fordyce, 206 Wis. 628, 238 N.W. 516 (1931); In re Hatten's Estate, 233 Wis. 199, 288 N.W. 278 (1939); In re Gerke's Estate, 271 Wis. 297, 73 N.W. 2d 506 (1955).

5. Muir v. Kane, 55 Wash. 131, 104 P. 153 (1909); Old American Life Ins. Co. v. Biggers, 172 F. 2d 495 (10th Cir. 1949).

6. *E.g.,* Greeves v. McAllister, 2 Bin. (Pa.) 591 (1809); Clark v. Herring, 5 Bin. (Pa.) 33 (1812); Park Falls State Bank v. Fordyce, 206 Wis. 628, 238 N.W. 516 (1931); In re Hatten's Estate, 233 Wis. 199, 288 N.W. 278 (1939); In re Gerke's Estate, 271 Wis. 297, 73 N.W. 2d 506 (1955); Marnon v. Vaughan Motor Co., 194 P. 2d 922 (Ore. 1948); Kaiser v. Fadem, 280 P. 2d 728, 731 (Okla. 1955).

7. Marnon v. Vaughan Motor Co., 194 P. 2d 992, 1009 (Ore. 1948); Kaiser v. Fadem, 280 P. 2d 728, 731 (Okla. 1955).

8. An early draft of Section 86, containing the same basic thrust, appeared as Section 89A of Tentative Draft No. 2 in 1965.

9. Muir v. Kane, 55 Wash. 131, 104 P. 153 (1909); Coulter v. Howard, 262 P. 751 (Cal. 1927); Old American Life Ins. Co. v. Biggers, 172 F. 2d 495 (1949).

10. Muir v. Kane, 55 Wash. 131, 104 P. 153 (1909).

11. Muir v. Kane, 55 Wash. 131, 104 P. 153, 155 (1909). No precedents were in fact cited in which a moral obligation alone supported a subsequent promise.

12. Muir v. Kane, 55 Wash. 131, 104 P. 153, 154 (1909); Coulter v. Howard, 262 P. 751, 753 (1927).

13. *But cf.* Elbinger v. Capitol and Teutonia Co., 208 Wis. 163, 242 N.W. 568 (1932) (Consideration was found for subsequent written promise, which cured a writing deficiency in the original agreement, in the moral obligation to pay for benefit received.). The examples of courts paying little or no heed to the question of consideration, because of judicial preoccupation with required written formality found in *Muir v. Kane* and *Coulter v. Howard,* has also had its influence in the parallel prior obligations field of contract modifications governed by the preexisting duty rule, as discussed in Chapter 3. Wisconsin courts proclaimed that fresh consideration was not required for a subsequent contract modification agreement that fulfilled statutory writing requirements. The authority Wisconsin cited for this proposition was an 1839 English case which made no mention of consideration in solving a Statute of Frauds question. Brown v. Everhard, 8 N.W. 725 (Wis. 1881); Wisconsin Sulphite Fibre Co. v. Jeffries Lumber Co., 111 N.W. 237 (Wis. 1906);

Stead v. Dawber, 113 Eng. Rep. 22, 26 (1839). The Wisconsin approach is reminiscent of Mansfield's disingenuous suggestion in 1765 that a past consideration problem does not exist at common law if the subsequent promise complies with the Statute of Frauds. Pillans v. Van Mierop, 3 Burr. 1663, 1669, 97 Eng. Rep. 1035, 1038 (1765).

14. Old American Life Ins. Co. v. Biggers, 172 F. 2d 495 (1949).

15. Old American Life Ins. Co. v. Biggers, 172 F. 2d 495, 499 (1949). The precedents cited in support of this statement were cases that supplied the alternative theories of moral obligation and consideration.

16. 15 Okla. Stat. Ann. sect. 107 (1940). Other states also attempted to make promises on moral obligations enforceable. *See* N.Y. General Obligations Act, sect. 5–1105 (1970) (written promise required); Cal. Civil Code, 1872, sect. 1606; Georgia Code Anno. sect. 20–303 (1960).

17. *E.g.*, Drake v. Bell, 26 Misc. 237, 55 N.Y.S. 945, 947 (1899); Park Falls State Bank v. Fordyce, 206 Wis. 628, 238 N.W. 516, 519 (1931); In re Hatten's Estate, 233 Wis. 199, 288 N.W. 278 (1939); In re Gerke's Estate, 271 Wis. 297, 73 N.W. 2d 506 (1955). The benefit received constituted evidence of the transaction and operated to replace form functions performed by consideration.

18. Park Falls State Bank v. Fordyce, 206 Wis. 628, 238 N.W. 516, 518 (1931).

19. REPORTERS' NOTE to Wennall v. Adney, 3 Bos. & Pul. 247, 250n., 127 Eng. Rep. 137, 138n. (1802). Seven years later a Pennsylvania court placed similar emphasis on the benefit received, notwithstanding the plaintiff's lawyer's admission that the *Wennall* Note put the moral obligation principle in doubt. Greeves v. McAllister, 2 Bin. (Pa.) 591, 593 (1809) (The court "[l]ooked no further than to the benefit conferred by the plaintiff, and to the morality and honesty of the promise on the part of the defendant." *Id.*). Even the pedantic English common law judge Parke emphasized the importance of the benefit received in an opinion penned eight years after *Eastwood v. Kenyon*: "The principle of the rule laid down by Lord Mansfield is, that where the consideration was originally beneficial to the party promising, yet if he be protected from liability by some provision of the statute or common law, meant for his advantage, he may renounce the benefit of that law; and if he promises to pay the debt, which is only what an honest man ought to do, he is then bound by the law to perform it." Earle v. Oliver, 2 Exch. 71, 90, 154 Eng. Rep. 410, 418 (1848).

20. *E.g.*, Old American Life Ins. Co. v. Biggers, 172 F. 2d 495, 499 (1949) (The plaintiff resuscitated a nearly moribund insurance company through monetary contributions.); *accord* Kaiser v. Fadem, 280 P. 2d 728 (Okla. 1955) (Plaintiff found a factory for defendant to purchase, and defendant subsequently promised to pay a commission.).

21. In re Hatten's Estate, 233 Wis. 199, 288 N.W. 278 (1939).

22. In re Schoenkerman's Estate, 236 Wis. 311, 294 N.W. 810 (1940).

23. Sutch's Estate, 201 Pa. 305, 50 A. 943 (1902); *accord* In re Pohl's Estate, 136 Pa. Super. 91, 7 A. 2d 14 (1939) (son's investment services for benefit of mother).

24. In re Hatten's Estate, 233 Wis. 199, 288 N.W. 278, 286–287 (1939).

25. Jensen v. Anderson, 24 Utah 2d 191, 468 P. 2d 316 (1970). The inference can perhaps be drawn that the society enjoyed by the bachelor was the motive and outweighed the benefit his work provided.

26. REPORTERS' NOTE to Wennall v. Adney, 3 Bos. & Pul. 247, 250n., 253n., 127 Eng. Rep. 137, 138n., 140n. (1802).

27. *E.g.*, Early v. Mahon, 19 Johns. (N.Y.) 147, 10 Am. Dec. 204, 206 (1821) (void usurious contract resuscitated); Hemphill v. McClimans, 24 Pa. 367 (1855) (Divorced woman's ratification of a promise made during coverture enforced.). In England, a promise ratifying a contract made during coverture was enforced in *Lee v. Muggeridge*, but this precedent was later rejected in *Eastwood v. Kenyon.* Lee v. Muggeridge, 5 Taunt. 36, 128 Eng. Rep. 599 (1813); Eastwood v. Kenyon, 11 Ad. & El. 438, 450, 113 Eng. Rep. 482, 486 (1840).

28. *E.g.*, Park Falls State Bank v. Fordyce, 206 Wis. 628, 238 N.W. 516, 518 (1931); *see also* Elbinger v. Capitol & Teutonis Co., 208 Wis. 163, 242 N.W. 568 (1932); In re Estate of Gerke, 271 Wis. 297, 73 N.W. 2d 506, 508 (1955).

29. In re Estate of Gerke, 271 Wis. 297, 73 N.W. 2d 506, 508 (1955). *Accord* Muir v. Kane, 55 Wash. 131, 104 P. 153, 154 (1909); Coulter v. Howard, 262 P. 751, 753 (Cal. 1927).

30. Muir v. Kane, 55 Wash. 131, 104 P. 153, 154 (1909). *Accord* Coulter v. Howard, 262 P. 751, 753 (Cal. 1927) (no moral turpitude in not having a writing).

31. Hawkes v. Saunders, 1 Cowp. 289, 290, 98 Eng. Rep. 1091 (1782). *See also* Atkins v. Hill, 1 Cowp. 284, 288–289, 98 Eng. Rep. 1088, 1090–1091 (1775).

32. Greeves v. McAllister, 2 Bin. (Pa.) 591, 593 (1809) (Citation to *Cooper v. Martin*, a decision consistent with Mansfield's ideas.). Pennsylvania legal and cultural traditions reflected a heightened sense of equity and morality from its founding as a colony on through the early republican period. *See* Jacob Price, *The Great Quaker Business Families of Eighteenth Century London*, in THE WORLD OF WILLIAM PENN 386 (ed. Richard Dunn and Mary Dunn, Philadelphia: 1986) (A legally discharged bankrupt Quaker was held morally bound to repay the debt to best of his ability.). Pennsylvania was unique in fusing law and equity in colonial period. *See* Wentz v. Dehaven, 1 Serg. & R. (40 Pa.) 311, 315 (1815) (Tilghman, C.J. mdeclared: "But in this Commonwealth, where want of equity, the courts of law have assumed chancery powers.").

33. Clark v. Herring, 5 Bin. (Pa.) 33, 38 (1812) (Cited Mansfield's trial decisions in *Hughes v. Rann* (1774) and *Atkins v. Hill* (1775).). An 1849 Pennsylvania decision stated that a prior benefit received "[c]reates a moral obligation of sufficient potency to sustain an express promise." Cunningham v. Garvin, 10 Barr. (Pa.) 366, 368 (1849). *And see* Nesmith v. Drum, 8 W. & S. (Pa.) 9, 10 (1844) ("[a] moral obligation . . . is a consideration for an express contract.").

34. *See, e.g.*, Park Falls State Bank v. Fordyce, 206 Wis. 628, 238 N.W. 516, 518, 519 (1931); In re Estate of Gerke, 271 Wis. 297, 73 N.W. 2d 506, 508 (1955).

35. Atkins v. Hill, 1 Cowp. 284, 288–289, 98 Eng. Rep. 1088, 1090–1091 (1775).

36. Boothe v. Fitzpatrick, 36 Vt. 681 (1864).

37. Roman and civil law enforce a moral obligation to pay, in the absence of a promise, for a useful act which provided a benefit accepted by the defendant. *See* BARRY NICHOLAS, AN INTRODUCTION TO ROMAN LAW 227–229 (Oxford: 1962).

38. *See* In re Estate of Gerke, 271 Wis. 297, 73 N.W. 2d 506 (1955) (Promisee received value of services instead of the promised entire estate.); *but cf.* In re Hatten's Estate, 233 Wis. 199, 288 N.W. 278 (1939) ($25,000 promise was not disproportionate to benefit valued at $6,000.).

Tables of Cases

Anonymous Cases Cited Chronologically

Named Cases Cited Alphabetically

Table of Statutes

Cases Cited Chronologically

Subject Index

About the Author

KEVIN M. TEEVEN received his Juris Doctorate from the University of Illinois College of Law in 1971 and is a Professor at Bradley University in Peoria, Illinois. His research interests include the legal history of the reform of common law contract in both the United States and Great Britain. He is author of numerous law review articles and *A History of the Anglo-American Common Law of Contract* (Greenwood Press, 1990).

ISBN 0-313-30652-4
90000>
EAN
9 780313 306525
HARDCOVER BAR CODE